New Landscapes of Inequality

**School for Advanced Research
Advanced Seminar Series**

James F. Brooks
General Editor

New Landscapes of Inequality

Contributors

Michelle R. Boyd
Departments of African American Studies and Political Science,
University of Illinois at Chicago

Melissa Checker
Department of Urban Studies, Queens College, City University of New York

Jane L. Collins
Department of Rural Sociology and Women's Studies Program,
University of Wisconsin

Micaela di Leonardo
Department of Anthropology, Northwestern University

Amal Hassan Fadlalla
Department of Women's Studies and Center for Afroamerican and African Studies,
University of Michigan

Roger N. Lancaster
Cultural Studies Program, George Mason University

Nancy MacLean
Department of History, Northwestern University

Gina M. Pérez
Comparative American Studies Program, Oberlin College

Dorothy Roberts
Northwestern University School of Law

Brett Williams
Department of Anthropology, American University

New Landscapes of Inequality

Neoliberalism and the Erosion of Democracy in America

Edited by Jane L. Collins, Micaela di Leonardo,
and Brett Williams

School for Advanced Research Press

Santa Fe

School for Advanced Research Press

Post Office Box 2188
Santa Fe, New Mexico 87504-2188
www.sarpress.sarweb.org

Co-Director and Editor: Catherine Cocks
Manuscript Editor: Kate Whelan
Designer and Production Manager: Cynthia Dyer
Proofreader: Sarah Soliz
Indexer: Bruce Tracy

Library of Congress Cataloging-in-Publication Data:

New landscapes of inequality : neoliberalism and the erosion of democracy in America / edited by Jane Collins, Micaela di Leonardo, and Brett Williams. – 1st ed.
    p. cm. – (School for advanced research advanced seminar series)
  Includes bibliographical references and index.
  ISBN 978-1-934691-01-4 (pa : alk. paper)
  1. United States–Social policy. 2. Welfare state–United States. 3. United States–Race relations–Political aspects. I. Collins, Jane Lou, 1954- II. Di Leonardo, Micaela, 1949- III. Williams, Brett.

HN59.2.N485 2008
320.51–dc22

2007038391

Library of Congress Catalog Card Number 2007038391
International Standard Book Number 978-1-934691-01-4
First edition 2008. Third paperback printing 2022.

Cover illustration by Cynthia Dyer from photographs of Columbus, Ohio, at dusk, © Photodisc, Getty Images and debris and litter-filled yard and shack © Lushpix, Unlisted Images, Inc.

Contents

Figures

Acknowledgments

The editors first thank our fellow advanced seminar participants for their intelligent enthusiasm. Because of their contributions, the New Landscapes of Inequality conference was intellectually fruitful and wonderfully enjoyable. Much gratitude to Leslie Shipman and Carla Tozcano for all their help and care with the complex travel and housing arrangements—and the magnificent meals they provided. Heartfelt thanks to all SAR staff, but especially to past SAR president George Gumerman, who funded Micaela di Leonardo's advanced seminar proposal, current president James Brooks, SAR Press co-director Catherine Cocks, director of scholar programs Nancy Owen Lewis, institutional advancement associate Jean Schaumberg, librarian Laura Holt, research associate Rebecca Allahyari, and copy editor Kate Whelan for many kinds of help and intellectual stimulation. We also thank our anonymous reviewers and, finally, the 2005–2006 SAR residential fellows—especially Caroline Yezer and Jean Langford—for their engagement with our project and for their lively selves.

Preface

A competent observer of the American scene, transported via time machine from the 1960s or early 1970s to the present, would marvel at a range of unanticipated social transformations. After all, the gap between rich and poor had progressively narrowed over the mid-twentieth century, and by the 1960s the legitimacy of democratic governments everywhere depended on their ability to foster social equality. But from the early 1980s on, ruling elites have scaled back or abolished government instruments for redistributing wealth. Wages have declined relative to profits, and economic inequalities have progressively widened. Instead of the Age of Aquarius, history delivered a New Gilded Age.

Similarly, in the 1960s and 1970s, laws and penal codes were submitted to a process of rational revision. Victimless crimes were being progressively decriminalized. The goal of law enforcement was generally conceived in terms of "correction," or rehabilitation. After the 1972 Supreme Court decision ruling the death penalty, as then practiced, "cruel and unusual," capital punishment was suspended—presumably to be abolished at a later date. These and other reforms were grounded in painstaking research by criminologists and sociologists; they were also motivated by the desire for a more just system of justice. Today, virtually nothing remains of these progressive legacies. Successive revisions of the criminal code have mandated ever longer periods of incarceration for ever lesser offenses. State and local governments invest in prisons, not schools. The United States is one of the leading practitioners of judicial murder—quite behind China but not far behind Iran. No doubt, our imaginary time traveler would pause for a long time over the following observation: the United States now ranks first in the world both in the rate of imprisonment and in the absolute number of people imprisoned—with a majority of its internees incarcerated for nonviolent offenses.

Also, our illustrative visitor from another time would likely note substantial changes in the meanings of democracy, although he or she would find these changes difficult to quantify. The 1960s and 1970s were scarcely free of conflict, and many of those conflicts—the war in Vietnam, the violent suppression of Black Power—gave cause for despair. But out of those conflicts and that despair grew a robust, even optimistic, conception of American democracy—a democracy "engaged in change, in a perpetual, peaceful revolution," as Franklin Delano Roosevelt glossed the shape of American history in 1941. By comparison, politics today might seem constricted, unimaginative, and even downright mean-spirited. Philip Jenkins summarizes changes in American cultural temperament dating from the late 1970s and continuing to the present: liberal and libertarian optimism has been replaced by "a more pessimistic, more threatening interpretation of human behavior," by "more sinister visions of the enemies facing Americans and their nation" (Jenkins 2006:11).

The contributors to this volume do not pose as temporally dislocated observers but serve instead as witnesses to history and documenters of its trends. The chapters examine three broad social trends, drawing out and analyzing the connections among them. First, they explore the real workings of neoliberal economics. Back in the late 1970s and early 1980s, advocates of neoliberal reforms asserted that the new economic regime would "get big government off our backs," liberate people's creativity, stimulate innovation, and foster economic growth. Plainly, deregulation and privatization have not worked as their Reagan-era advocates predicted: "A rising tide lifts all boats," poor dinghies as well as rich yachts. Instead, neoliberal economics has stoked what Marx called "primitive accumulation," a process of "accumulation by dispossession" (Harvey 2005). That is, the rich get richer by taking ever bigger bites out of workers' salaries, by revoking customary rights and benefits, and by eviscerating and cannibalizing the public good. Economic disparities in American society are now greater than at any time since the late 1920s. This, the restoration of an unambiguously predatory capitalism, has happened on a national and international scale. Far from becoming economically vibrant, those countries of the global South that—at the insistence of the International Monetary Fund (IMF) and the World Bank—most wholeheartedly adopted policies of deregulation, privatization, and free trade have registered anemic economic growth rates, weathered major fiscal crises, and witnessed new class/ethnic polarizations as foreign competition has gutted local agriculture and industry.

Second, these chapters trace the rise, and examine the contours, of what might best be dubbed "punitive governance." Early on, critics of the neoliberal era noted an apparent irony: as the state got out of the business of regulating the economy, it seemed more and more eager to regulate the personal lives of citizens. This dynamic, with its redefinition of "public good," has carried through to the present day. Instead of resources, disadvantaged people get surveillance, discipline, and punishment. Instead of a second chance, those who run afoul of the law get a permanently stigmatized status. A symbolic order that equates punishment with justice is what sustains punitive governance. It can be summed up with the following aphorism: Instead of a hand up, you get a short, sharp kick down.

Our current zeal for punishment turns on the cultivation of outsized fears: as crime rates have declined, media coverage of crime has actually increased—almost half the airtime of local newscasts now consists of crime reportage. While the news media have profiteered off sensational coverage of the crime beat, right-wing political interests have manipulated it, stoking fear of crime and predation to win elections—and, more enduringly, to reshape the social contract. This new social contract involves ever more "sticks" and ever fewer "carrots." The resulting "culture of fear" most obviously contributes to the ongoing avalanche of incarcerations in America. It also has prepared the way for actions associated with the current wave of terror panics: the preemptive logic of the invasion of Iraq; the indefinite detention of prisoners dubbed "enemy combatants"; the assorted horrors of Abu Ghraib and Guantánamo. No doubt, puritanism has deep roots in American culture. But punitive governance, as this volume traces it, is a truly modern phenomenon: it tethers a neoconservative political orientation, with its emphasis on order, policing, and traditional authority, to economic deregulation and privatization. That is to say, punitiveness is the flip side—the real cultural logic—of neoliberalism. The studies collected here are therefore mindful of the most basic facts: A public defined by its fears cannot pursue its rational interests. A political system that revolves around fear cannot long remain democratic in any meaningful sense. An empire organized around fear is predisposed toward disastrous undertakings.

Third, the research presented in this volume examines new forms of citizenship. That is, our chapters look at how time-honored ideas about citizenship are being transformed or undermined under conditions of economic deregulation and punitive governance; they also examine, from various angles, the neoliberalization of consciousness. For generations,

Americans have looked to government to achieve the goals that participant citizens have decided are important: workers' rights, civil rights, environmental protections, and more equality, not less. Today, citizenship is eroded by policies that take away key rights from people who seek public benefits. Worse yet, unfair treatment in the courts and a rage for "lock 'em up" policies effectively strip a growing number of Americans of their citizenship. Meanwhile, as labor unions and progressive social movements become increasingly peripheral political players, the political process reduces participant citizens to passive consumers: to cast one's vote is tantamount to purchasing one's commodity. Or worse, the political process steers citizens' participation into narrow, corralled venues that reinforce privatization, punitiveness, and emaciated definitions of citizenship. (Myriad post-Carter-era social movements take this form: they underscore security as the dominant paradigm of government and thus foster the expansion of what we used to call a police state.)

These are epochal shifts, fundamental transformations in the social landscape. Although consistent with the logic of a certain kind of capitalism, they were not inevitable: they are the result of a long, involved, and contentious set of social and political struggles. They are also not necessarily permanent. We hope that our studies help those who continue to struggle for a better world—by equipping them with facts and insights. We have nothing to lose and a world to win.

Roger N. Lancaster

New Landscapes of Inequality

1

Introduction

New Global and American Landscapes of Inequality

Micaela di Leonardo

Back in the late twentieth century, in attempting to come to terms with global and national shifts, many of us used the line from Charles Dickens' novel of the French revolution, *A Tale of Two Cities*: "It was the best of times, it was the worst of times."[1] Indeed, the fin de siècle saw the international florescence of a cosmopolitan, multicultural, and tolerant culture—alongside widening gaps between rich and poor. But the events of the post-9/11 years, in particular, have made it increasingly difficult to make arguments for the positive side of the ledger. We cannot avoid noticing the proliferating array of markers of human misery: Endemic warfare continues in the Middle East, Central Asia, and parts of Latin America and Africa—including, most dramatically, the harrowing of Darfur and the redevastation of Lebanon. Post-9/11 American wars of occupation are punctuated by civil war and terror attacks in Madrid, London, and Mumbai. A series of natural disasters of biblical proportions have occurred: tsunami in South and Southeast Asia, hurricanes on the Gulf Coast, earthquake in Pakistan. The global AIDS epidemic continues, and tuberculosis and malaria, as well as other diseases of poverty—and, we might say, of globalization, such as the SARS and avian flu epidemics—are on the increase. Finally, there is a definitive body of scientific evidence for global warming, a process that may be irreversible and could destroy large swathes of habitable global environment.

Behind the headlines of war, famine, and environmental and public health disasters, though, are a series of closely connected but longer-term political-economic processes. These processes are often glossed by the misleadingly general term *globalization*. Even that questionable term is highly polysemous. Some construe it, in a cultural studies vein, to indicate simply the technologically driven, heightened global flows of cultural material over the past few decades (Appadurai 2002; Inda and Rosaldo 2002). Others, in the tradition of neoclassical economics, envision globalization as something like the unfolding of natural law: the necessary freeing of markets, and therefore heightened trade and migration, with the demise of Communism and the triumph of global capitalism (Bhagwati 2004; Friedman 2005). All these phenomena, however, have occurred coincident with another set of processes and ideological shifts—the rise of neoliberal capitalism. For that reason, many critics refer not to "globalization," but to "neoliberal globalization," or simply "neoliberalism."

GLOBAL SHIFT AND NEOLIBERALIZATION

Neoliberalism is a widely used and understood term in Europe, Latin America, and other parts of the world, but still largely confined to scholarly work in the United States. Neoliberal ideology, nevertheless, has had a decades-long developmental process. Beginning perhaps in the 1970s with the Carter administration's domestic budget cutbacks in the post–oil shock "era of limits" (di Leonardo 1998:264–265), it came to real, institutionalized fruition in the Clinton/Blair West and vis-à-vis International Monetary Fund (IMF)/World Bank policies for the global South (Harvey 2005; Went 2000).

We must first trace neoliberalism back to classic nineteenth-century liberalism—which is not consonant with our twentieth- and twenty-first-century notions of liberal-versus-conservative political slants. Nineteenth-century liberalism, as articulated by theorists Adam Smith, James Mill, John Stuart Mill, and many others, was a theory of whole Western economies that asserted that allowing markets to rule without government interference would bring about the best, most efficient social ends. As Adam Smith wrote, echoing religious framings of the Deity's all-benevolent relationship to humans, the "invisible hand" of the market would intervene to produce the best outcomes.

Even across the nineteenth century, many currents of Western theory and practice—from socialisms, to Christian charities, to anti-modernist interpretations—contested liberal political theory's overreliance on market mechanisms. These diverse social actors and groups both called for and created institutions to ameliorate the human misery caused by unchecked capitalist growth: labor unions, settlement houses and other private charities, state supports for the poor. In the early decades of the twentieth century, Western governments, under duress from below and within, instituted state programs guaranteeing public education, sanitation, public health and workplace safety, minimum wages and unemployment insurance, public housing for the poor, and aid to the elderly, disabled, and ill.

As Keynesian economic theory, with its focus on the necessity of state stimulation of the economy and the key importance of mass consumption, strengthened toward mid-century, a state of affairs that scholars label the regulatory regime of "Fordism" took hold. That is, there evolved an implicit compact among large corporations, labor unions, and states: corporations would guarantee living wages and some benefits to most of their workers, who could then afford to buy the consumer durables (such as Ford cars) they were producing. Unions would guarantee labor peace in exchange for relatively high wages and benefits. The state would provide the essential benefits—unemployment insurance, AFDC (Aid to Families with Dependent Children, or welfare)—that would support those workers who fell through the cracks of Fordism, thus guaranteeing general social peace (Braverman 1974; Piven and Cloward 1971).

Fordism, like other regulatory regimes, was always a set of tendencies, not an ironclad set of rules. Just as the majority of 1930s black American workers, in agricultural and domestic service jobs, were excluded from the benefits of Roosevelt's Depression-era New Deal (see MacLean, chapter 2, this volume), the bulk of minority and white women workers—absent, for example, auto workers—failed to benefit as much as white males from the guarantees of Fordism. The legislative and policy gains garnered by the civil rights and feminist movements of the 1960s and 1970s, however, began to integrate those benefits—just as Fordism began to unravel with the rise of neoliberalism.

Neoliberalism, as developed over the second half of the twentieth century, is an intellectual/political stance that presumes that capitalist trade "liberalization"—the end of all state regulations on business, and indeed, the end of all state-run business—will lead inevitably to market growth and, *ceteris paribus*, to optimal social ends:

> Neoliberalism is in the first instance a theory of political economic practices that proposes that human well-being can best be advanced by liberating individual entrepreneurial freedoms and skills within an institutional framework characterized by strong

> private property rights, free markets, and free trade.... State
> interventions in markets...must be kept to a bare minimum
> because, according to the theory, the state cannot possibly pos-
> sess enough information to second-guess market signals (prices)
> and because powerful interest groups will inevitably distort and
> bias state interventions (particularly in democracies) for their
> own benefit. [Harvey 2005:2]

As former prime minister Margaret Thatcher's dour, unconsciously Orwellian acronym slogan TINA proclaims, "there is no alternative." John Gledhill (2005:340) has noted that this stance goes considerably further than that of the classic liberal political theorists: "What makes neoliberalism something that a classical liberal such as Adam Smith would have found as disturbing as Pope John Paul II does is its elision of the distinction between a market *economy* and a market *society*, to the point where the latter seems to engulf life itself."

In the United States, Europe, India, Japan, and other industrialized states, neoliberal policies have mandated the shrinkage and selling off of state-run utilities and services and have withdrawn support for independent labor organizing/unions, thus backpedaling from welfare state (or semi-welfare, in the United States' case) provisions and regulations that ameliorated the naked operations of capital and provided widespread social safety nets. (One of neoliberalism's innate contradictions is its reliance on "unnecessary" states to intervene repeatedly in economies to shore up business—to provide a "good business climate" [Harvey 2005: 117].) In the global South, neoliberal ideology has been implemented through World Bank/IMF "structural adjustment programs," beginning with Chile's experiment under the post-1973 coup dictator Augusto Pinochet. These programs demand that states denationalize industries, end protectionist policies that safeguard native industries, open their markets to international trade, and ruthlessly cut back social programs. In some cases, as in the People's Republic of China (PRC), neoliberal policies have stimulated economic growth, but always at the cost of increasing inequality and heightened poverty populations.

Despite the immense social suffering that has resulted from the implementation of neoliberal ideology, it has gained enormous purchase, worldwide, through its celebration of rapid technological change; through the spectacle of new cornucopias of globally traded goods and individualized consumption—furthering the commodification of identity that Marx first analyzed; through faux-populist rebellions against "useless government bureaucracies"; and, finally, through neoliberalism's novel melding of neo-classical economic theory with an identity politics reading of civil liberties. That is, neoliberal ideology incorporates the notion of various populations' civil, but not economic, rights. Thus, politicians, North and South, can claim to stand for the rights of women, racial and religious minorities, and even homosexuals while blandly observing the growing immiseration that disproportionately affects most of those populations.

RETURN TO IMMISERATION: THE HISTORICAL BARBELL

We might thus envision the past century in the West as having a barbell shape: Anatole France's fin de siècle, in which the state in its infinite majesty forbade both the rich and the poor to sleep under bridges, would constitute one end. The long Keynesian decades of the twentieth century, in which states, responding to Progressive Era ideologies and to working-class and left organizing pressure, established social welfare programs and constrained industries' exploitation of (white, male) labor, would be the shaft in between. The current era of neoliberal capitalism triumphant, with its associated identity politics minus class discourse, as well as its burgeoning wealth and immiseration, would constitute the other end of the bar.

This immiseration, although often ignored by cheerleaders of capital-ism triumphant, is clearly real. Worldwide, we face the disappearance of middle class sectors as extreme wealth and poverty increase rapidly within and across most nation-states (World Resources Institute 1999). In the United States, economist Paul Krugman has written extensively on the heightened inequalities and disappearing middle classes created by post-Fordist deregulation and the shift to regressive taxation in the late twenti-eth century (Krugman 2002). The US Gini Index, the measure of income inequality since 1913, indicates that American incomes seemed to be "depolarizing" from Depression-era inequalities over the middle decades of the twentieth century but then repolarized, "thanks first to the deep recession of the mid-70s, the subsequent inflation, and then the long wave of social spending cuts, union-busting, factory closures, the explosion of Wall Street wealth and power, and all the other familiar features of the neoliberalism of the 1980s and 1990s" (Henwood 2004:4).

In 2004 the US Gini Index reached its highest (most unequal) level since the early 1940s (Henwood 2004:4). A recent Congressional Budget Office study indicates that "income gains have become increasingly concen-trated at the top of the income scale over the past two and a half decades" and that the "income gap widened significantly between 2002 and 2003"

(Shapiro and Friedman 2006). The *New York Times* reported in late 2006 that "the buying power of the minimum wage is at a 50-year low" and that "wages and salaries now make up the lowest share of the nation's gross domestic product...[while] corporate profits have climbed to their highest share since the 1960's" (Greenhouse and Leonhardt 2006).

Much of this new income and wealth inequality may be traced to changed corporate policies: good, unionized jobs are outsourced, leaving laid-off workers to struggle to find lower-paid, often service sector jobs while CEOs are now hyper-rewarded. Over the past thirty years, the average CEO compensation in the top one hundred US corporations has mushroomed from thirty-nine times the average worker's pay to more than a thousand times that average (Krugman 2002). In late 2005 the US Census Bureau reported that "even as the economy grew, incomes stagnated and the poverty rate rose" (Leonhardt 2005). For the first time on record, "American household incomes failed to increase for five straight years" (Leonhardt 2005).

These worsening indices of inequality in the United States are also highly racialized. Since the Reagan presidency—including the two Clinton terms, despite common progressive apprehensions—we have had a stalled civil rights revolution. Two years after the fiftieth anniversary of *Brown v. Board of Education*, racial segregation in American public schools, once on the downturn, is worsening and has been since the late 1980s (Cohen 2004). The capital and muscle the federal government has not put into improving education have gone instead into incarceration—a run-up to about two million people jailed in the United States, disproportionately black and brown, most for nonviolent crimes. Amnesty International reported in 2004 that the United States is one of just four countries responsible for 84 percent of all executions worldwide (Huggler 2004). A series of "innocence projects," especially in Illinois, have exonerated hundreds of those convicted of serious crimes—including many men on death row. A University of Michigan study suggests that there are thousands of wrongfully convicted people in US prisons (Liptak 2004). For those black Americans who manage to avoid incarceration, recent studies, reported in the *Wall Street Journal*, indicate how profoundly the job market is not a level playing field: "The disadvantage carried by a young black man applying for a job as a dishwasher is equivalent to forcing a white man to carry an 18-month prison record on his back" (Wessel 2003).

The American labor market is thus extremely disadvantageous to both male and female residents of color. But even white women, despite a quarter-century of feminist organizing, protest, and legislation, are doing poorly. The famous 59 cents rallying cry—women earning 59 cents for every male dollar—has improved since the 1970s to 78 or 79 cents. But most of the improvement from the 1990s forward is due to men's worsening status rather than to women's higher pay (Fisher 2003; Uchitelle 2004), and women bear the brunt of social program cutbacks—worsening health care, child care, and nursing home access.

Post-9/11, the neoliberal effects on the American economy have been partially masked by two phenomena—the housing bubble and the trade imbalance with the PRC, Japan, and Middle Eastern oil producers. The latter is often remarked (Bajaj 2006), but rarely in terms of what it could portend: that, as Paul Krugman (2006) notes, "the dollar will eventually have to fall 30 percent or more to eliminate the trade deficit." The former was perhaps more important for its masking effect. That is, post-9/11, the Federal Reserve Bank deliberately kept interest rates low to stimulate the economy. Given the stock meltdown of 2000, consumers saw real estate as a relatively safe investment, as well as the opportunities for refinancing their existing mortgages at much lower rates, and the industry heated up accordingly. Rising home prices, compounded by ongoing cheap interest, led to a huge increase in home equity loans. Homeowners withdrew what they saw as new wealth from their homes to spend on consumer items—many of which were produced in the PRC and other low-wage states. Many commentators noted that this process alone propped up the US economy from 2002 forward. But they also noted the potential for a bursting housing bubble, which would leave millions of home owners without collateral with which to repay their increased consumer debt. Indeed, by 2007 the housing market began to slow, subprime lending scandals broke, and the press began to report a wave of home foreclosures (Bajaj 2007b).

Internationally speaking, "the 400 highest income earners in the United States make as much money in a year as the entire population of 20 African nations—more than 300 million people" (Weissman 2003:1). The gulf between the globe's poor and wealthy has been widening very rapidly: "The income gap between the fifth of the world's people living in the richest countries and the fifth in the poorest was 74 to 1 in 1997, up from 60 to 1 in 1990 and 30 to 1 in 1960" (United Nations Development Program 1999:3). Or, if we consider the richest and poorest 10 percent of the world population's income, that gap jumped from 79 to 1 in 1980 to 117 to 1 in 2000 (Weissman 2003:1).

When we consider the enormous effects on global inequality, it is no coincidence that neoliberal globalization "took off" concurrent with the fall of the Soviet sphere and China's capitalist turn. First, during the Cold

War, those states played key ideological and material roles in representing an egalitarian social ideal against which the West, the United States in particular, felt it necessary to compete in order to appear democratic to the nonaligned states. The US State Department's integration of the US military under Truman and the Supreme Court's 1954 ruling against school segregation in *Brown v. Board of Education*, for example, were self-consciously crafted with an eye to their effects on the US profile as a democracy on the global stage (Dudziak 2000; McAlister 2001). The post–Cold War United States has cut foreign aid to a mere slice of its previous largesse. Second, although acting most often for its own realpolitik reasons, the Soviet Union, until its demise, helped to underwrite fledgling anti-colonial movements throughout the global South—the most distinguished of which was the African National Congress of South Africa.

Third and finally, the unraveling of the Soviet sphere and China's capitalist opening provided vast opportunities for expanded capitalist accumulation through the privatization of lands and industries and the "freeing" of hundreds of millions of laborers to work for what the market would bear. The new proletarianization of Chinese workers has created social cleavages that have even been "compared unfavorably with Africa's poorest nations" (Harvey 2005:142). For the female half of that newly capitalized labor force, that freedom has led to an explosion of prostitution, of sex tourism, and especially of sex trafficking in both the PRC and the former Soviet sphere, assimilating them to the status of that industry in the global South. These are clear indices of women's overall lack of political power, their drastically lowered economic status in formerly Communist states, and the globally heightened commodification of sex (Kligman and Limoncelli 2005; Schein 1997). Whatever we may think of the economic problems and lack of civil liberties in the former and failed Communist states, their existence did act as a brake on global capitalist accumulation and its human effects. Globally, it is now the case that we have no ongoing state alternatives to the capitalist mode of production.

ACCUMULATION BY DISPOSSESSION

To analyze more clearly the multifarious processes of the recent past and present that we gloss as globalization, David Harvey, in *The New Imperialism* (2003), reworks Marx's fundamental construct, "primitive accumulation"—the process of forced transformation of modes of production, as in the UK enclosure movement or the European conquest of Latin America, that enabled early capitalist growth. Harvey instead wishes us to envision this process as a longer-term "accumulation by dispossession," endemic to all capitalist growth and of key importance in the recent past and present:

> Primitive accumulation…entails appropriation and co-optation of pre-existing cultural and social achievements as well as confrontation and supersession….The credit system and finance capital…became…major levers of predation, fraud, and thievery…. The strong wave of financialization that set in after 1973 has been every bit as spectacular for its speculative and predatory style. Stock promotions, ponzi schemes, structured asset destruction through inflation, asset-stripping through mergers and acquisitions, and the promotion of levels of debt incumbency that reduce whole populations, even in the advanced capitalist countries, to debt peonage, to say nothing of corporate fraud and dispossession of assets (the raiding of pension funds and their decimation by stock and corporate collapses) by credit and stock manipulations….But above all we have to look at the speculative raiding carried out by hedge funds and other major institutions of finance capital as the cutting edge of accumulation by dispossession in recent times. [Harvey 2003:146–147]

This financialization process took place over the course of the late 1960s to late 1970s in the wake of the collapse of the Bretton Woods system of fixed international exchange rates (Went 2000:57–58):

> [Political decisions to deregulate financial markets] cleared the way for the rapid growth of international financial flows, integration and deregulation of financial markets, and for a stream of derivatives and other financial innovations designed as ways to profit from interest rate variations and exchange rate turbulence, which became much more common after Bretton Woods' collapse. The 1980s were the years of financial revolution. In 1980 futures, swaps and options still barely existed; ten years later there were over seven trillion dollars' worth of these and other financial derivatives in existence around the world. [Went 2000:58]

This process of extreme financialization, which involves rather more than can be described using Arjun Appadurai's (2002) ahistorical and political economy–less notion of "finance-scapes," has fostered recurrent cycles of more tangible accumulation by dispossession: the sell-off of formerly communal businesses, land, and natural resources in the former Soviet sphere and the PRC; the denationalization of industries and commodification of natural resources such as water in the global South; the trend among US corporations (United Airlines, General Motors, IBM) to divest themselves of legal obligations to provide pensions and other benefits to current and former employees—even the stark giveaway of federally financed research products to Big Pharma (Angell 2004; Harvey 2005:57) and the parallel and recurrent gift of bandwidth to telecommunication giants (McChesney 2004).

As Harvey (2005) notes, neoliberalization proceeds precisely *through* uneven geographic development and creates extreme volatility, along with increasing stratifications. These accumulation-by-dispossession cycles have specific effects in shifting national and global spatialities. The most obvious of these are rapidly changing land use patterns that tip and re-tip property away from use-value and toward exchange value. In the United States, we have seen the hyperdevelopment of the coasts; the creation of the Southern and Southwestern Gunbelt (Markusen 1991); the gentrification of inner cities (Logan and Molotch 1987); the touristification of all possible sites as industry continues to move abroad; infilling McMansions in inner suburbs; the rise of gated communities; the use and then rapid abandonment of suburban land for big-box stores; corporate and state abandonment of old industrial centers, small towns, and rural areas (in some cases, replaced by privatized prison corporations); and so on (Low 2003; Sassen 1998, 2001; Zukin 1995). In the global South, we see many of these patterns as well, but also the depeopling of countrysides and vast accumulation of urban-ring squatter settlements as states abandon former regional supports, the enormous expansion of refugee camps on the edges of endemic war zones and natural disaster regions such as South and Southeast Asia tsunami sites, where states have stripped victims of their property rights and given away coastal lands for tourism development (Price 2006).

These shifts in built environment spatiality are innately connected to the shifting patterns of human migration as changes in capital flows and the withdrawal of state supports dictate massive, self-directed labor migration—from North Africa and Eastern Europe to Western Europe, from post-structural-adjustment Mexico, Latin America, and Asia to the United States—or more specific, state-directed labor migrations such as those of Filipino female health workers and caregivers to Italy and the United States (Parreñas 2001) and the forced removal of three hundred thousand–plus New Orleanians in the wake of Hurricane Katrina to multiple sites not of their choosing (M. Davis 2006).

Labor organizers have labeled the process of labor and communities chasing shifting capital "the race to the bottom"—noting the smaller and smaller shares of corporate profit flowing to labor and communities (Ross 1997). Jane Collins (n.d.) has analyzed this process, more technically, as "reverse Fordism," tracing that movement from the Keynesian shaft of the barbell toward the neoliberal end of the bar.

US WAR, OUTSOURCING, AND ACCUMULATION BY DISPOSSESSION

The American state has retreated from its legally mandated obligations to its citizens—disaster relief, health and safety inspection of industrial sites such as mines and of the nation's foodstuffs, adequate provision for its own military. This retreat has been central in US headline news for several years. As President Bush's plummeting poll figures attest, American citizens have not been oblivious to these processes. Nevertheless, technical knowledge of the direct connections between governmental pullbacks and processes of accumulation by dispossession is not necessarily widespread.

For example, information on American failures in Iraq is not hard to come by, but mainstream media have not stressed the direct connection between these failures and the fact that this is the first heavily outsourced war of the modern era. That is, on good neoliberal principles, the American military has subcontracted not only the infrastructural rebuilding of the country but also much of the supply functions for its own soldiers. This is the reason why, beyond former secretary of defense Donald Rumsfeld's desire not to have a "large footprint" on the ground in Iraq, American soldiers have lacked not only the proper equipment—especially body and vehicle armor—and sufficient medical help but also water, toilet paper, and food. Journalist Herbert Docena, in *Asia Times* (2003), documented the corporate logic of Halliburton, Bechtel, and others in Iraq, which has prevented any infrastructure rebuilding, because to do the job logically and quickly, given the sourcing of Iraq's present infrastructure, would demand buying spare parts and technology from multinational sources, not supplying entirely new infrastructure, heavily marked up in price, from its own subsidiaries:

> The US and its contractors are not even trying, for a simple reason: it's not the point. To assume that they are striving, but are merely failing because of factors beyond their control, is to presuppose that there is an earnest effort to succeed. There isn't. If there were, there should have been a coherent plan and process

in which the welfare of the Iraqis—and not of the corporations—
actually comes first. Instead, the Iraqis' need for electricity
comes after Bechtel's need for billion-dollar projects. The Iraqis'
need for decent living wages becomes relevant only after
Halliburton has maximized its profits. Indeed, if there were a
sincere attempt to succeed, the US, as the responsible occupying
power, should have had no qualms giving Iraqis what many
emphatically say they need to finally make things work: the
authority and the resources. "If only the money and the spare
parts were provided," electricity official Jasm said, "we could do a
surgical Khsab....We have been doing this for the past 30 years
without KBR. Give me the money and give me the proper
authority and I'll do it." But the US won't because who knows
what the Iraqis would do? Ask the Russians to repair their power
plants? Actually succeed in reconstructing their country without
the involvement of Bechtel and Halliburton? [Docena 2003]

This is truly a new and brazenly open form of corporate welfare and crony
capitalism.

Outsourcing is one key to the bizarre phenomenon of the inherent
contradictions of a state that is simultaneously neoliberal, neoconservative,
and engaged in ongoing imperial war. The Vietnam War, for example, was
waged largely on the basis of Cold War domino theory, but *this* war was
planned long before its inception, in a post-Soviet climate, for New Rightist
imperial geopolitical advantage and for the superprofits to be reaped for
corporate friends of the White House: from exploitation of Iraqi oil
reserves and from the highly advantageous, no-bid government contracts
for so-called rebuilding awarded to Halliburton, Bechtel, Raytheon,
Boeing, Northrop Gruman, and others (Kwiatowski 2004). That prior
model, of course, has now been extended to the "rebuilding" contracting
on the Gulf Coast post-Katrina, where Halliburton has again benefited and
is again failing to provide its contractual services—in this case, hiring
undocumented Latin American workers for pennies and overcharging
FEMA at every turn for its own profits (M. Davis 2006).

Clearly, both the New Right geopolitical strategy and crony capitalism
violate neoliberal tenets. Neither allows for the "frictionless" workings of
the market. Each is highly wasteful of lives and resources and leads to
unpleasant public-sphere critiques of oligopoly, fraud, and waste. To date,
the Bush White House has responded with threats and a further ratcheting
up of the culture of fear. Harvey speculates that we are seeing, in fact,

a global convergence toward authoritarian rule as "democratic" states attempt to silence their critics:

> Whether or not this portends a more general reconfiguration of governance structures worldwide remains to be seen. It is, however, interesting to note how neoliberalization in authoritarian states such as China and Singapore seems to be converging with the increasing authoritarianism evident in neoliberal states such as the US and Britain. [Harvey 2005:81]

Actually, our American culture of fear in response to terrorist attacks is part of a much broader phenomenon—the contradictory, simultaneous development of a less and less regulated economy and defunded social programs, with a yet more and more regulated private sphere. That is, we are in the midst of a new cycle of moral panic, encompassing notions of widespread terror, sexual, and familial threats (see Lancaster, chapter 3, this volume). As well as spiking levels of arrest and imprisonment, we see heightened state surveillance and discipline, in short, punitive governance. We have come to equate justice with punishment rather than the achievement of equal rights, to accept the social stigmatization of broad swathes of US residents and the curtailment of fundamental rights of citizenship.

PROTEST, ORGANIZING, AND THE UNCERTAIN PRESENT

The instantaneous, transnational communications connections and the volatile movements of capital that are simultaneously the herald and vehicle of global capitalist neoliberalization have both hindered and facilitated global, anti-neoliberal political activism. As Collins notes in *Threads* (2003), for example, the globalization of the apparel industry deterritorialized its labor forces, weakening union and worker strength and ability to plan, protest, or strike through the always present threat of entire factories decamping elsewhere. At the same time, the reemergence of global sweatshops and the sudden impoverishment of towns and regions with capital flight have stimulated union cooperation and amalgamation—as in the founding of UNITE HERE from several previous garment, hotel, and restaurant worker unions—and fostered new organizing energy and international communication and solidarity. As the objects of organizing become ever less palpable, organizers become more transparently visible to one another. Similarly, we have seen the rise of truly global and mutually cooperative anti-racist, feminist, gay, environmental, antiwar, and human rights organizations. Their partial success in the late 1990s, particularly through anti-globalization protest, was reversed by the American conservative putsch in the wake of the 9/11 attacks.

That conservatizing turn in the United States and elsewhere has been enhanced by the neoliberalization of national and global media: state abandonment of media industry regulations, encouraging mergers and acquisitions within and across industries, allowing new conservative dominance and less room for dissent in television, radio, and print news media (McChesney 2004). As mentioned, the attractive technological-fix, commodity-rich, positive-identity-politics face of neoliberalism vitiates much potential opposition.

Nevertheless, much organizing continues on the ground, and we have also seen anti-neoliberal electoral shifts, particularly in "pink tide" Latin America and in Europe.

IN THIS VOLUME

The chapters in this volume range broadly across our new landscapes of inequality, with a primary focus on US realities. They light on a number of key themes and topics and proceed from varying disciplinary perspectives. Although all work from political economy, all also escape what we might label the "Harvey effect." That is, much important political-economic analysis still neglects to attend sufficiently to the profoundly important ways in which race, gender, and other stratification processes are inherently part of capitalist growth processes. This failure has been encouraged in the contemporary neoliberal climate, with its seeming acquiescence in civil and women's rights. In reality, as we have seen, neoliberalism in practice leverages race- and gender-based exploitation in the service of profit.

Our contributors collectively recognize the racial and gender hypocrisy inherent in neoliberal ideology and attend not only to shifting political economy but also to evolving race and gender relations. As a case in point, historian Nancy MacLean (chapter 2) opens our discussion with a pointed critique of David Harvey and other progressive commentators' failure to recognize the southern United States—and therefore profoundly raced—origins of the rise of American neoliberal ideology and practice. "Odd as it may sound," she writes, "nineteenth-century southern planters were America's original neoliberals." She points out that the core of their "very particular interpretation of freedom" was "devotion to private property rights, hostility to a strong federal state for other than military purposes, faith in punitive governance as the key to social order, and enthusiasm for international trade." Anthropologist Roger Lancaster (chapter 3) then demonstrates how punitive governance is rationalized in the American present, focusing on the histories and connections—racial, gendered, sexual, political—among our current popular-cultural moral panics.

Anthropologist Brett Williams (chapter 4) builds on Lancaster's analysis of the contemporary moral-panic dehumanization of others, by documenting the massive rise of individual indebtedness in the United States. She makes clear the connections among gender, race, increased poverty, and stressed working and middle classes, deregulation of the finance industry, and outsourced, punitive, and dehumanizing collection firms. Political scientist Michelle Boyd (chapter 5) explores the trap of neoliberal discourse in her case study of community development in Chicago's historically black Bronzeville district. Boyd links the neoliberal defunding of cities to the "narrative of lost social capital." That is, as urban areas become more dependent on cultural strategies of economic development, black activists tend to shift their focus from political agitation to economic development and are inclined toward "expressions of racial nostalgia" that sanitize the Jim Crow past and the unequal present.

Anthropologist Gina Pérez (chapter 6) adds to this analysis of racial minority investment in neoliberal discourse and picks up the thread of curtailed citizenship rights under neoliberalism. Looking at Latino student involvement in Junior ROTC (Reserve Officer Training Corps) programs in public high schools, Pérez establishes the defunded wasteland in which well-funded military recruitment programs appear to provide desperately needed services and the ways in which Latino youth, longing for respect and convinced that they lack "discipline," see JROTC training as the key to full political and economic citizenship.

Anthropologist Jane Collins (chapter 7) explicitly names this trend toward the curtailment of economic citizenship "the specter of slavery" in her analysis of the ways in which the post-1996 TANF (Temporary Assistance for Needy Families) programs systematically strip poor, largely minority women of their rights to choose their place of employment. Like the burgeoning moral-panic victimization of nonterrorists and nonsexual predators, like the stigmatization and hounding of debtors, poor women who may have held skilled positions are redefined as unskilled, fit only to cut brush on highway medians. Legal scholar Dorothy Roberts (chapter 8) adds to this portrait of the punitive contemporary neoliberal state in her case-study analysis of the impact of child welfare supervision on a poor black neighborhood in Chicago. The narrative of "child savers" disrupting families and placing children in violent and abusive situations is not new, but Roberts discovered that Woodlawn residents demanded greater agency involvement: "As these neighborhoods are stripped of social programs in the government's shift to market solutions for poverty, their residents must increasingly rely on more punitive state institutions to meet their needs."

Anthropologist Melissa Checker's Georgia case study (chapter 9) further advances our understanding of the spatial consequences of American neoliberalism. She documents how preexisting racist structures such as segregated neighborhoods, never sufficiently ameliorated during the all-too-short era of civil rights reform, have become the fulcrum for economic development—in this case, the siting of hazardous waste production and disposal in black and brown neighborhoods. Checker also shows us how determined community activists against environmental racism may, through strategically harnessing neoliberal discourses, be hobbled in their quest for justice.

Anthropologist Micaela di Leonardo's dual case-study piece (chapter 10) investigates the negative entailments of and gaps in the neoliberalization of American consciousness. She notes the ways in which residents of New Haven, Connecticut, across class and color, have shifted their understandings of city space over the decades, ending in focusing on rising home-property values in the post-9/11 housing bubble. In the same era, a politically progressive, nationally syndicated black radio show demonstrates the ongoing racial segregation of American media and the political limits of a commercialized press.

Finally, anthropologist Amal Hassan Fadlalla (chapter 11) investigates the neoliberalization of practice and consciousness in an arena rarely considered—the new, high-profile, celebrity-driven institution of privatized international refugee and disaster aid. Fadlalla focuses on the particular case of Darfur and lays out the historical political-economic background that has been occulted by widespread representations of raped and murdered women, of starving refugee children—by our new, neoliberal, humanitarian consciousness. She also shows how religiously inspired activism concerning Darfur engages with neoliberal and neoconservative ideologies that misrepresent Islam and Middle Eastern politics.

Fadlalla's piece illustrates on the global scale what our other contributors fully investigate on American ground: the ways in which the globalization of newly untrammeled capitalism has exacerbated preexisting inequalities, how the retreat of the (somewhat) benevolent state and the rise of the punitive, imperial state are related, how poorly privatized institutions substitute for responsible state provisioning for its citizens and residents—while ensuring hefty profits for their CEOs and shareholders—how overarching cultural tropes meld neoliberal and neoconservative ideologies, how recurrent moral panics misrepresent class, race, gendered, and sexual realities on the ground. We hope that this volume will be of use to those working to clarify analyses of the unfortunate present and engaged in organizing to alter the future.

Acknowledgments

I thank the other advanced seminar participants—especially Jane Collins—for help in clarifying the arguments in this chapter. As well, several generations of graduate students in my globalization seminar at Northwestern brought skill, dedication, and necessary humor to our mutual project of tracing the rise and entailments of neoliberal globalization.

Notes

1. Some material in this chapter appeared, in a different form, in my "Global Inequality, War, and the American Scene" (in two parts), *North American Dialogue* 7(2 and 3).

2

Southern Dominance in Borrowed Language

The Regional Origins
of American Neoliberalism

Nancy MacLean

More than a hundred years ago, a new regional alliance led to a civil war that ended slavery in the United States. The "new math" undermined the planter class's previous national power as North plus West proved a combination hard to beat. This chapter sketches out the broad lines of an analogous process of regional shifts in our own time, albeit one less propitious for humanity than its antebellum predecessor, for this one is eviscerating a welfare state long assumed in the North and in Europe to be synonymous with modernity. Paying attention to the new regional equation can help explain the massive shifts in American and global political economy and culture since the 1970s. But that requires going to places many liberal politicians and intellectuals avoid: the so-called fly-over states of the South and West. If we look there, what critics have called "neoliberalism" turns out not to be so new at all in important ways—and not so liberal either.[1]

It is stunning that even the best work on neoliberalism evinces no recognition of its regional origins in the United States. In David Harvey's state-of-the-art treatment, *A Brief History of Neoliberalism* (2005:4), he promises readers "the political-economic story of where neoliberalization came from and how it has proliferated so comprehensively on the world stage." The book offers a synthesis of developments since the 1970s that contains many important insights, yet its origins story fails to uncover the source of the winds of change that howled so fiercely in the 1970s. Although a geographer by trade, Harvey misses the extent to which place matters in this story. This neglect is surprising because nearly all the best-known American architects of what has come to be called "neoliberalism" were conservatives from the West and South, among them, Barry Goldwater and Ronald Reagan. Nor does it seem coincidental that the Democrats who have most advanced the neoliberal project are Southerners, from Jimmy Carter to Bill Clinton. The reasons go much deeper than individual biography. They are to be found in the economic and political rise of these regions since World War II and in the historic traditions that this rise has allowed their leaders to spread to other parts of the nation (Applebome 1996; Egerton 1974; Sale 1975; Schulman 1991). This, I submit, is the best answer to the question Harvey poses as "the crux of the problem we have to solve": "how and why neoliberalism emerged victorious" as the elite solution to the crisis of capital accumulation in the 1970s (Harvey 2005:13).

Although the western roots of neoliberalism deserve more study, their influence is less surprising and also less challenging to the sunny self-packaging of neoliberalism, with its constant chatter about "choice" and "freedom" (Goldberg 1995; McGirr 2001; White 1991:601–611). I believe that it is more revealing of the coercive drive at the core of this project (Elsner 2004; Sherry 2005) to concentrate on the South's contribution, particularly the states of the former Confederacy, which long maintained the most anti-democratic political system in the country. As the South's conservative elites have amassed power, they have succeeded in imposing more and more of their historic model of political economy on the nation as a whole, indeed, on the wider world. "If the southern border of the United States had run along the Mason-Dixon line rather than the Rio Grande," one observer notes, "then American history in the last decades of the old millennium would have been quite different" (Lind 2005:253; Stepan 1985).[2] But we still face the puzzle of how exactly those southern traditions came to shape this history. I argue that the main medium of transmission for the change has been the modern American conservative movement. The sheer power the mainstream right has built attracts much scrutiny today, but the role of place in its rise deserves more attention.

From its official launching in 1955 with the founding of the *National Review*, the modern American conservative movement has revered the South, in particular, as a model of the good society, the just state, and "traditional" culture. By its spokespersons' estimation, no region has better embodied the right's ideals (MacLean 2006:44–51). Defending the South's devotion to the "principle of exclusion" and an "aristocratic" social order, the leading conservative intellectual Richard Weaver equated the "heavy assault" on "the regime of the South," as he put it, "by Liberalism" in the 1950s with what he saw as the self-destruction of the larger society by the same forces (Weaver 1959:587–589). Writing for the *National Review* in 1958, Anthony Harrigan summed up the movement's views when he praised this region of "essential conservatism" for what he called its "built-in power brake" (Harrigan 1958:225–227). None of the right's founders and few of its key movement builders over the years have seen a contradiction between their core catechism of capitalist freedom and the South's traditions, and there are some intriguing reasons for the perceived affinity.

Odd as it may sound, nineteenth-century southern planters were America's original neoliberals. True, they trafficked in human beings and disdained civil liberties. But today's so-called neoliberals (and we have to remember that this is a term few of them embrace), although more accepting than their predecessors of formal equal opportunity for all, can hardly be described as concerned about fair treatment of workers or respectful of human rights. Their practice demonstrates that what matters most to them is a very particular interpretation of freedom, which they take from nineteenth-century defenders of slavery such as John C. Calhoun. Its core is devotion to private property rights, hostility to a strong federal state for other than military purposes, faith in punitive governance as the key to social order, and enthusiasm for international trade. These are not new goals. Their centrality to southern political tradition helps explain how the Young Americans for Freedom could have chosen Strom Thurmond for a Freedom Award in 1962 and why Ronald Reagan, the first Republican to sweep the entire South and West, employed the word *freedom* more frequently than any other president in US history (Foner 1998:315, 321). Trent Lott in his prime went so far as to assert that Reagan-era GOP goals "from tax policy to foreign policy, from individual rights to neighborhood security" were "all things Jefferson Davis and his people believed in" (Lott 1984:44–45). I would not conflate the two so crudely, but some kinship is undeniable.

The South's white elite both before and after the Civil War wanted low labor costs, a weak state as far as the public welfare was concerned, and, above all, open foreign markets in which to peddle its commodities. Southern leaders vehemently rejected the labor protections, quality public education, infrastructure investments, rehabilitative justice, and active federal government sought by some Northerners, moved by economic changes and social movements like those that led European nations toward social democracy. No better tutors could be found than conservative southern elites for what David Harvey depicts as the core project of neoliberalism: the reassertion of class power in its rawest form so as to reduce everything to a commodity, especially labor, in the quest to free capital of social obligation and political constraint (Harvey 2005:11, 19, 76, 165). The mounting power of conservative Southerners and Westerners, in turn, is not only deepening class and racial inequality nationwide but also widening the breach between the United States and the rest of the industrialized world on social policy matters from abortion to lesbian and gay rights and the teaching of evolution (Adam 2003:262–265). It is time we paid closer attention to the spatial sources of all this.

To get at the regionally based, conservative roots of neoliberalism, however, one must first remove mental barriers to seeing clearly what has happened and why. One barrier comes from the important observation, articulated often in the heyday of Black Power, that racism is not a southern problem but a national problem, perpetuated by national institutions. This is true, and no one said it better than Malcolm X. "America is Mississippi," he said, challenging the liberal portrayal of the South as an anomaly. "There's no such thing as the South—it's America. If one room in your house is dirty, you've got a dirty house....And the mistake that you and I make is letting these *Northern* crackers shift the weight to the Southern crackers" (X and Breitman 1966:108–109). Arguments like his helped draw attention to northern complicity in southern practices. They also helped explain the virulent racism of whites north of the Mason-Dixon line who bitterly fought fair housing, equal employment, and educational equity from the 1940s forward even in supposedly cosmopolitan liberal cities like New York (Biondi 2003; Hirsch 1983; Sugrue 1996).

But that once radical intervention has since ossified into a moralistic dismissal among activists, and some scholars, of the proposition that different regions had varied political economies and cultures that might actually matter in determining national outcomes. Few historians, at least, would deny that the power of racism and xenophobia came from the particular historical circumstances that led elites of the South and West to develop thoroughly racialized class structures. Most scholars now agree that particular labor force and land dynamics of those places proved pivotal in spawning hatreds that then spread far and wide. The plantation South of the former Confederacy thus played the premier role in generating anti-black racism, the ranching Southwest in generating anti-Mexican racism, and the industrializing West Coast in generating anti-Asian racism. For generations after these systems developed, their beneficiaries continued to resist any national policies that might endanger their accumulated advantages (see, for example, Bloom 1987; Glenn 2002; Montejano 1987; White 1991). Recognition that racial inequality and bigotry are national problems, then, should not rule out attempts to identify powerful regional sources of resistance to change, rooted not in some geographical essence but in historical processes that unfolded in specific places and times.

Another important obstacle to reckoning with the regional right's influence is the intellectual inheritance of the New Left, which shaped thinking about political economy and class politics among two generations of progressive scholars. The core idea of the New Left analytical synthesis was "corporate liberalism": that the driving force behind twentieth-century reform was far-sighted capitalists and their political and intellectual allies, who sought to rationalize government policy in the service of business interests (Kolko 1963; Weinstein 1968). Scholarship in this tradition yielded important insights, but its presuppositions have not worn well in the age of the Republican right's rise to power. New Left intellectuals were not so much wrong about the fact of corporate power in the United States as they were partial, to the point of gross distortion, about the varieties of corporate power.[3] Showing a regional solipsism akin to the classic *New Yorker* cartoon equating Manhattan with the nation, the New Left analysis simply assumed that Northeastern capital could stand in for the whole. It cannot.

Failing to include the South and the West in their calculations, such thinkers missed the most important development of their time: the regionally anchored rise of the right. Like the Kremlinologists who never anticipated the smashup of the Soviet Union, they looked in the wrong places and thus missed the key variable in the emerging equation of national politics. The New Left scholars, like the consensus scholars against whom they pitted themselves, never took actual conservatism seriously (Ribuffo 1994). In their zeal to expose liberal reform as nothing but conservatism in sophisticated packaging, they missed something far more ominous: the actual right wing gathering strength as they wrote. Obsessed with the simulacrum, they ignored the real McCoy. They took as axiomatic the Port Huron Statement's pronouncement that "the Dixiecrat-GOP coalition is the weakest point in the dominating complex of corporate, military, and political power" (Bloom and Breines 1995:72). Most progressives assumed that the only alternative to America's half-hearted liberalism and semi-welfare state was a participatory social democracy. Few imagined that the South could win in the end. But in important ways it has, and a reckoning with how it did so is overdue. This chapter delineates the broad contours of the regional power shift that put neoliberal ideas in their current commanding position. Without connecting all the dots, it suggests a research agenda that can. But first, let me outline a road not taken, an alternative model of development whose defeat helps explain the ultimate outcome.

There was a time when it seemed that things would go the other way: conservatives would lose power as the South became more like the North in a transformation that would clear the prime obstacle to a European-style welfare state in the United States. A desire to realize that regional recalibration drove the civil rights unionism of the 1930s and 1940s. As a host of historians have recently exposed, southern workers, black and white, organized creatively and extensively in these years, with help from radicals of the left-led Popular Front. Black workers especially posed the democratization of Dixie as the way to guarantee national progress as they turned unions into vehicles for racial, as well as economic, justice. As the North Carolina tobacco worker Ruby Jones put it, it was "like being reconstructed when the union came" (Korstad 2003:7; more generally, Hall 2005). Pulled left by the grassroots activism of the Congress of Industrial Organizations (CIO) in particular, even Franklin Roosevelt by 1937 came to realize that the future hinged on bringing democracy to the South. By then, half of the South's representatives in the Senate constantly voted against his initiatives. This is why he tried, briefly and unsuccessfully, to tear up the crazy-quilt coalition of the Democratic Party and sew together in its stead a modern party system based on coherent class interests and ideology, which necessitated ending the racial dictatorship on which his southern antagonists relied to stay in power. Gearing up for the congressional elections of 1938, FDR told a Georgia audience: "When you come right down to it, there is little difference between the feudal system and the fascist system. If you believe in one, you lean on the other" (Sullivan 1996:62, 104). Roosevelt's gambit failed and his opponents stayed in power, but their rule was growing less secure.

During World War II and especially right after the war, African American activists and their allies internationalized the struggle as they looked to the new United Nations to help bring democracy to the South. With the NAACP in the lead and radicals working the grassroots, they built support for a human rights declaration with teeth. Only a human rights standard, they saw, could produce substantive equality in everyday life, above all, the robust initiatives in employment, housing, education, and health care needed to end the deprivation that hit African Americans hardest but affected all working-class people in some way. Midwesterners such as

Robert Taft also fought the adoption of the human rights standard. But always, the most determined opponents were southern Democrats in Congress such as Strom Thurmond; they understood that human rights standards would threaten Jim Crow, disfranchisement, and the low-wage southern labor system these practices buttressed. Eleanor Roosevelt and the US State Department sought to appease the southern conservatives, who were backed by Republican unilateralists, by watering down the effort. Yet, it gathered momentum in the late forties (Anderson 2003).

The Cold War intervened and in the end undermined the opportunity for realignment. The vision of a transformed South faded in the stark light of anti-communism, which already by 1938 was weakening the forces of reform nationally. Republican successes in the mid-term elections of that year emboldened the right; Texas representative Martin Dies launched the House Committee to Investigate Un-American Activity. As conservative southern Democrats moved into the anti–New Deal coalition, the Dies committee did all it could to undermine the CIO and its civil rights union-ism and roll back the era's reforms (Sullivan 1996:104–105). The same alliance of conservative southern Democrats and pro-business midwestern Republicans produced the Taft-Hartley Act, perhaps the single biggest blow to the project of using labor's power to democratize the South, and one that rolled out the carpet to capital flight from the North to a South that would now be nearly impossible to unionize (Cowie 1999; Lichtenstein 2003:114–118).

Success emboldened the right nowhere more than in the South. After 1948, anti-communism became a veritable civil religion for southern white supremacists. Soon, Mississippi senator James Eastland added his Internal Security Subcommittee to the House's Dies committee, founded by Repre-sentative Martin Dies of Texas. Both were joined by a profusion of state and local anti-red initiatives in the South, of which Mississippi's State Sovereignty Commission is the most notorious. One recent scholar concludes: "The southern red scare was in many ways a byproduct of the region's massive resistance to integration," led by "a conservative white-power elite" from the plantation belt, the area that empowered anti–New Deal senators such as Eastland and Strom Thurmond (Woods 2004:5, 6, 37–38, 42).

By 1953 the red scare had so decimated the NAACP, along with the left and labor, that the congressional conservative bloc of southern Democrats and northern right-wing Republicans was able to defeat the human rights initiative with an ingenious device: the Bricker Amendment. This constitu-tional amendment "would require all treaties and executive agreements first to be ratified by two-thirds of the U.S. Senate, *then* by both houses of

Congress with enabling legislation, and finally, as the proposed amendment mutated, by *all* 48 state legislatures" (Anderson 2003:220). Bizarre as it sounds, the Bricker Amendment won the backing of every GOP senator but three, and eighteen (mostly southern) Democrats. To preserve the president's ability to carry out foreign policy, Dwight Eisenhower jettisoned the Human Rights Covenants and even the Genocide Convention, which had been the main spur to the right's mobilization. The conservative bloc's success created the first open breach between the United States and its European allies, arguably the roots of the split being widened by today's heirs of the Bricker Amendment's backers in their devotion to unilateral American power (Anderson 2003:220–228, 238, 255).

Its control thus preserved, the South's elite managed to use the New Deal and the Second World War and Cold War that followed to augment its power by developing the regional economy without democratizing the polity. New Deal farm programs helped farm owners to rationalize production, not farmworkers to better their life chances. Planters virtually designed the Agricultural Adjustment Administration (AAA) codes, which subsidized nonproduction and thus encouraged the laying off of farm labor. This was the first blow to the old sharecropping system and the isolated southern labor market that had staved off economic development and African American advance in the region. At the same time, New Deal industrial policies, partial though they were, raised factory conditions in the South and narrowed the regional wage differential (Wright 1986). Yet, rather than empower African Americans and other workers, as long anticipated, the industrialization of the region fed the reactionary force Lyndon Johnson once called "the great beast," such that it developed national reach (Clifford 1991:417). "The toppling of Rooseveltian liberalism by Reaganite conservatism," Michael Lind sagely notes, "involved the displacement of one set of elites by another, with a different group of economic, ethnic, and regional constituencies" (Lind 2005:285).

If the New Deal opened the region to change, the Second World War and the Cold War brought it, but on terms shaped by that newly secure, conservative elite. Huge, new military contracts for southern firms, the building of naval shipyards along the coast, and the siting of military bases in the Sunbelt helped transform local economies. This new employment demand, combined with massive out-migration for the factories of the North and West, in turn raised labor costs. As millions of workers left rural areas for better opportunities elsewhere, planters turned to mechanization and drove out more sharecroppers, now treated as surplus, disposable labor whose work could be more cheaply done by mechanical pickers. In the 1950s, machines picked 5 percent of the cotton in the United States; twenty years later, they picked 98 percent. The regional economy was fundamentally transformed (Daniel 1985).

Where the South's local and state governments once worked hard to insulate their labor market from outside influences, now they devoted themselves to boosterism. To attract outside investors, particularly low-wage employers for whom the South held comparative advantage, they promised low taxes, concessions on even those, subsidies for infrastructure, and a "friendly" business climate that included anti-union "right-to-work" laws. Government money augmented the corporate investment flowing southward. In 1952 only 17 percent of federal per capita spending flowed to the South; by 1970 it was almost 50 percent. As the South's growth rates outpaced the North's, the regional wage differential shrank, and a truly national economy emerged in place of the old insulated one. The South's economy was liberalized. The region's politics were not (Cobb 1982, 1984; Wright 1986).

Having accrued power through a "racial dictatorship" back home, Southerners in Congress allied with northern business Republicans to block or eviscerate nearly all attempts to complete the New Deal and remedy its exclusions (MacLean 2000:216–217; Omi and Winant 1986). Although fewer than one in four Americans lived in the South, southern congressmen controlled key congressional committees such as the House Ways and Means and the Senate Finance committees, thanks to the unrivaled seniority they accrued in a one-party region with an artificially shrunken electorate. When Roosevelt became more pro-labor in the so-called second New Deal, the southern elites who had welcomed AAA subsidies turned hostile. "After 1937," notes historian Harvard Sitkoff, "Roosevelt faced a shifting, informal, but highly effective conservative coalition resolved to block, or at least limit severely, all efforts to aid Negroes, labor unions, urban areas, and disadvantaged workers and farmers" (Sitkoff 1978:111). The South's representatives in Washington were at the forefront of resistance to democratization in any form well into the postwar era. The NAACP journal, *The Crisis*, editorialized: "The rest of the country has come to realize that Senators and Congressmen from poll tax states menace the democratic process everywhere because they enjoy a power in Washington which they would not wield if the elections were free" (Sullivan 1996:106). They used that power to defeat multiple attempts at a permanent, federal Fair Employment Practice Committee and to doom national health insurance despite widespread popular support for it (Gordon 2003:172–209; Reed 1991).

By the time progressives again gained enough power to force substantial reform, thanks to the civil rights movement, the terrain had changed such that realignment came on the right's terms, not the left's. The AFL-CIO, the merged national federation of trade unions, under George Meany was a far cry from the militant movement that had pulled the whole nation left in the depression decade. Some pockets of progressivism notwithstanding, the labor movement had lost its broad social vision and allowed its organizing muscle to atrophy from disuse. Its member unions were deeply divided internally from so many years of capitulation to the conservative craft unions, from whence Meany himself came, and to their own white members, whose solidarity was often with their race rather than with the whole working class. In cities around the country, the New Deal coalition began to crack as early as the 1940s along the fault lines present at its creation, when white Democrats resisted pressure from African Americans to share equally in jobs, housing, and schooling (Hirsch 1983; Quadagno 1994; Self 2003; Sugrue 1996).

Moreover, having lacked the power to win universal government programs in areas such as health care and pensions, unions constructed their own private semi-welfare state through collective bargaining agreements that created, as one scholar puts it, "islands of security, with high waters all around" (Klein 2003:257). This system was a product not of labor's choice but of capital's strength. Nevertheless, it proved an Achilles heel for progressive politics because it widened the political split between union members and the unorganized; white union members, especially, came to resent pressure to, in effect, pay twice, once for their own employer-provided benefits and then again in taxes for those, imagined as black, who were not so lucky. Thus paralyzed by its own contradictions, the labor movement proved unable to advance the reform momentum the civil rights movement created. Unions varied, and there were strong civil-rights currents animating, for example, the growing public employee and health care unions. But the AFL-CIO and the Democratic Party, as a whole, proved grossly unequal to the historic opportunity the civil rights movement had created.

The right showed no such hesitation. Lyndon Johnson rued to an aide on the night of his landmark success in steering the Civil Rights Act through passage: "I think we just delivered the South to the Republican Party for my lifetime and yours" (Schulman 1994:76). From the clash over civil rights came future white GOP leaders committed to rolling back reform. The Goldwater–Johnson contest, said the later Mississippi US senator and Senate majority leader Trent Lott, was the first time they "really started thinking, 'Gee, maybe we are Republicans'" (Perlstein 2001;

Schulman 1994:79). As Southerners linked up in the same party with new-style western conservatives and old-school business Republicans of the North, they remade both conservatism and the nation. Never again after 1964 did a Democratic presidential candidate win a majority of the southern white vote or carry the South (Goldberg 1995:223). By 1972 the shift became a surge: for the first time in American history, Republicans won every southern state.

GOP strategists found their prospects enhanced by the way economic growth built the population base, hence the congressional representation, of the Sunbelt, which was now attracting millions of new migrants away from the regions of the country more supportive of progressive public policies. From 1950 to 2000, following the shift of jobs, the proportion of Americans living in the Northeast and Midwest declined (from 29 to 23 percent and from 26 to 19 percent, respectively), whereas that of the South and West grew (from 31 to 36 percent and from 14 to 22 percent). While Democratic strongholds such as New York and Massachusetts lost residents, the states that attracted the most newcomers were GOP dominated, such as Arizona, Colorado, and Nevada and the suburban conurbations of the former Confederacy, with metro Atlanta being the best example (Lassiter 2006; Lind 2005:268–269; also Phillips 1969).

Thriving on their home ground, the elites of what was fast becoming the "Gunbelt," thanks to lucrative military contracts, rendered vital assistance to the nascent conservative movement (Markusen 1991). Beginning in 1948, southern textile corporations, in particular, joined with small manufacturers and with retailers like the Goldwater family of Arizona to organize for anti-union state right-to-work laws. By 1955 they acquired enough momentum to fund the National Right-to-Work Committee (Lichtenstein 2003:138; Perlstein 2001:22–34). This was the year that the Montgomery bus boycott posed its historic challenge to Jim Crow. It was also the year that William F. Buckley Jr., with a $50,000 start-up investment from a Texas oilman, founded the *National Review*, declaring that the new cause "stands athwart history, yelling Stop" (MacLean 2006:44–51; *National Review*, Nov. 19, 1955, p. 5; Perlstein 2001:498). Meanwhile, the South and West supplied a disproportionate share of the early mass base for the conservative movement's rise, with thriving chapters of the John Birch Society and other anti-communist, free-enterprise groups and southern anti-desegregation groups that converted over time into all-purpose conservative organizations (Kruse 2005; McGirr 2001).

One telling sign of the growing weakness of the northern elite was its inability to maintain its once tight grip on the Republican Party. Thanks to the ferment in the South and West, not only the liberal Rockefeller Republicans of the East Coast but even the Taft-led conservative Republicans in the Midwest saw their power eclipsed. The most dramatic demonstration of their decline was the success of the regionally based right in making Barry Goldwater the party's choice for president in 1964. Goldwater's backers found the prevailing acceptance of the New Deal, civil rights, and multilateralism in foreign policy to be anathema. They despised Dwight Eisenhower for conceding the legitimacy of the American welfare state. The first politician to whom they looked for support was Arkansas governor Orval Faubus, newly famous from the Little Rock schools confrontation. They aimed well, because nowhere was Goldwater's message more enthusiastically received than the South, where he baited Lyndon Johnson as a "counterfeit Confederate." Won over to the GOP, Strom Thurmond placed radio ads announcing, "A vote for Barry Goldwater is a vote to end judicial tyranny." John Birch Society activists were blunter: "JOHNSON IS A NIGGER LOVER" read one South Carolina placard. Goldwater attracted his most avid following in the Deep South; in November, he won only six states, five there and the sixth, his home state of Arizona (Goldberg 1995:146, 208; Perlstein 2001:465). In Mississippi, he garnered 87 percent of the white vote. A Goldwater biographer writes: "A power shift had occurred that signaled the rise of a western-southern coalition and the decline of the East in Republican Party politics. The new conservative elite rejected Modern Republicanism's acceptance of New Deal social programs, the activist role of the federal government, and the importance of the black vote" (Goldberg 1995:208; also Perlstein 2001).

Before the right could win nationwide elections, however, its members had to shed their heaviest regional baggage: the overt commitment to white supremacy. To cope in the new environment created by the very civil rights laws they had so vehemently resisted, conservatives learned new ways to protect old privileges and avoid sharing power, sometimes under the tutelage of Northerners determined to slow the pace of racial reform. The lessons took more easily than they might have years before, because the old plantation elites most loyal to white supremacy had been eclipsed in the regional power structure by the business leaders of the New South. Their power came not from cotton sharecropping but from manufacturing, extraction, retailing, and government contracts. The new leaders found it easier to appreciate the virtues of "color-blind" talk and race-neutral public policy. Particularly in the fast multiplying suburbs where moderate-voting residents were repelled by blatant racism but nonetheless determined to preserve their racial privileges, politicians learned that those privileges were best protected now in the race-neutral language of "freedom of association" and earned class advantages. Inequality, they came to argue, came not from discrimination but simply from the operation of market forces and meritocracy. In the North, whites who sought to defend the old order, especially by fighting affirmative action, received tutoring in a new language of color blindness from the neoconservatives who vastly augmented the intellectual firepower of the right in the 1970s and after. Giving up its last bastion of anti-market sentiment, the conservative movement thus emerged from the remodeling of the 1970s ready to champion wholeheartedly the new cause that came to be labeled (by others) neoliberalism. As it assumed near hegemony in national politics and the market became enshrined as the arbiter of fairness, an ironic reversal occurred. Where once racism had eased the way to acceptance of class injustice, now class prerogatives could protect racial injustice from challenge (Kruse 2005; Lassiter 2006; MacLean 2006).

By 1980 the victory of Ronald Reagan, whose first exposure in national politics came from his ringing endorsement of Goldwater, crowned the victory of the rising southern and western conservatives over the older, more liberal Northeastern wing of the GOP (Brennan 1995; Rae 1989). With the regionally anchored right running the party, it would soon be hard to remember that as late as the mid-1970s, much of the Republican Party— including all its black leadership—was more liberal on racial politics than many Democrats or that the party, as a whole, backed the Equal Rights Amendment for women for forty years. Historical memory grew so faulty that observers would come to call the resulting conservative compound "neoliberalism."

This is a highly compressed account of a vast drama that unfolded over decades, one that needs much more study and nuanced analysis. Yet, for all its limitations and oversimplification of complex processes, this backstory provides essential context for making sense of the vast changes in public policy and political culture in the United States over the past three decades. Of course, the rise of the South and West does not alone explain why neoliberalism emerged as the answer to capital's troubles in the 1970s. Other factors contributed a great deal, among them the economic challenge that came from the resurgence of historic competitors in Germany and Japan and the growing popularity of theories in domains from economics to philosophy that legitimated reliance on market forces. There was also the popular disenchantment with government that mounted in the 1960s with Vietnam and grew with Watergate. Since the 1980s the distrust has become self-reinforcing as eviscerated government offers less and less to win popular appreciation. "Through its power over the government it professes to hate, the right has put itself in a position to create a government that is ever more deserving of hatred," Barbara Ehrenreich has astutely observed. "The less government does for us, the easier it is to believe the right's antigovernment propaganda; and the more we believe it, the less likely we are to vote for anyone who might use government to actually improve our lives" (Ehrenreich 1997:11). Offering welfare that impoverishes, schools that extinguish the desire to learn, and starved bureaucracies that descend into chaos during crises rather than provide relief, neoliberal government appears less and less appealing to millions of ordinary Americans in need. So they look elsewhere—especially to the religious bodies that have filled people's needs in the face of the public void (Wuthnow 1990, 1998).

But if the rise of the South and West and the growing influence of their elites in no way explain all of the shape that change has taken, these do suggest new places to look for the origins of some of the distinctive features of the emerging order. This history reminds us, for one, that much of what we are seeing in the reign of neoliberalism is not new. There are Americans with long experience in packaging labor-repressive political economies in the garb of liberty. As the historian James Cobb once quipped, anti-unionism is "the South's most respectable prejudice" (Cobb 1982:259). Wal-Mart's base in Arkansas is thus hardly insignificant. As the political scientist Dorian Warren puts it, "Wal-Mart is a direct descendant of Southern political economy, ideology, and culture," which is why Reverend Jesse Jackson referred to it as a "Confederate Economic Trojan Horse" (Warren 2005: 8–15; see also Moreton 2006).

Determined to hold down wages for their workers and deny them benefits so as to garner a greater share of profits in highly competitive world markets, southern leaders also grew expert in marking the victims of their policies as outsiders undeserving of full citizenship or cultural belonging. Treating the majority as dehumanized instruments for accruing wealth rather than as subject-citizens, they denied public responsibility for social needs such as education and health care. Providing bare minimums, they dragged down national standards by inviting capital flight from more generous states and localities (Cowie 1999). Such a system requires a firm hand to rule effectively, and the South's leaders early on discovered ways to over-represent conservative interests and restrict popular voting power. The poll tax and the grandfather clauses used to suppress black and low-income white turnout are legendary, but just as important was the county unit voting system, which gave rural areas grossly disproportionate power compared with cities of much larger populations. Southern elites also mastered the techniques of punitive governance, from the death penalty to measures forcing the poor to work on terms freer citizens might resist. These included vagrancy laws and municipal ordinances that coerced African Americans into picking cotton on planters' terms, measures that seem eerie anticipations of today's work-or-starve welfare policies. Even signature practices of neoliberalism such as the outsourcing of once public work can be read as updated versions of southern inventions like the convict lease system (Kahn and Minnich 2005; Lichtenstein 1996).

And, of course, there is the legal dimension of conservative strategy: the very rules of national life are being rewritten in ways that would have pleased turn-of-the-century southern elites in all but their commitment to formal racial equality. The rightward turn in the judiciary, much of it initiated by southern- and western-based legal funds and sanctioned by the conservative judges these back, is seeking to enshrine the kind of framework those elites had and then lost after 1937. With the misleading battle cry of "original intent" constitutionalism, they seek to restore a kind of pre–New Deal judiciary protective of property rights, inimical to the idea of shared public responsibility for social problems, and restrictive of the very ability of representative democracy to address inequality in resources and power (Breyer 2005; Sunstein 2005; Wills 1999:57).

As the conflict over immigration reform illustrates, the right has deep fault lines of its own, and the trajectory of change might yet be altered. The regional alliance on which its power rests, for one, is unstable because, as pollster Celinda Lake (Kuttner 2005:13) notes, the West "is far more libertarian than the South." White evangelical Christians, the right's most avid voters, make up only one-third of the West's Christians, compared with two-thirds of the South's. Similarly, serious issues divide the neoconservatives, centered in the Northeast, from the paleo-conservatives, based in the South, and immigration causes friction between business interests and cultural traditionalists (Kuttner 2005:13; see also Murphy 2001). Indeed, the right's deepest vulnerability lies in the curious class coalition undergirding its power. That coalition unites working-class whites with those emptying their pensions, raising their premiums, defunding their schools, and sending them off to multiple tours in disastrous wars (Frank 2004). On the other side, the left has some new sources of strength, among them the energy and internationalist vision that large numbers of immigrant activists are providing to the labor movement. Even with GOP dominance, moreover, some three in ten southern whites still vote Democratic, a proportion that might grow with cultivation (Fine 2006; Lynd and Lynd 2000; Teixiera and Rogers 2001).

But people who are alarmed about the direction of the country should not take comfort in happy tales of what might have happened with different tactics in this or that election. The cause of social justice has lost very significant ground, thanks to the empowerment of the South's conservative elite. This ground will not be won back easily because its cession is, in good part, due to seismic shifts in economic activity, demographic distribution, and ruling class strategies vis-à-vis both major parties. The Democratic Party's disinclination to break up the class coalition of its adversaries with bold initiatives to stem surging inequality flows not from simple, thick-headed refusal to heed its most loyal supporters, but from the shrinking power of labor generally and the growing power of corporate money as elections become ever more expensive to wage (Reed 2005:1–15).

Even cultural ground earlier won by the left has been turned to the right's advantage in stunning jujitsu moves, as the case of civil rights illustrates. It means something that the right has felt compelled to rob the grave of Martin Luther King Jr. and cynically press him into service as a ventriloquist's dummy for an agenda that would have appalled him. At the least, this practice suggests that anti-racist activists' success in changing the culture was more important than the left recognizes. It also indicates the right's self-perceived vulnerability to charges of bias and unfairness. King, after all, once called the neoliberal standard-bearer Barry Goldwater "the most dangerous man in America" (Washington 1986:373). How, then, can the forces that Goldwater galvanized now claim King's mantle? The right's greatest cultural feat may be its success in inducing widespread public amnesia about the true sources of its ideas and policies. Few Americans today have any idea that the seductive promises of neoliberalism came first from business leaders who fought the New Deal and from white supremacists who aimed to defeat the civil rights movement.

One reason the right gets away with its dishonest packaging is the regional solipsism that keeps its adversaries from coming to terms with the southern anchor of neoliberalism. Two British conservative sympathizers have noted that "the dominance of the Southern wing prevents the GOP from presenting itself as a big-tent national party" and warned that "the greatest danger" to the Republican Party today is "the prospect of seeming intolerant" (Micklethwait and Wooldridge 2004:262, 264). It is past time to focus more attention on the deep roots of these vulnerabilities. Scholars of the modern United States need to think more about the spatial dimension of the power shift the right has engineered and to come to terms with how historic processes that played out in the South have affected the nation and, indeed, the world. That those remaking the world in the name of freedom have authoritarian tendencies turns out not to be such a puzzle after all. Their critics ought not to be misled by our own neologism; the prime neoliberals have always been conservatives.

Notes

1. The terms in common usage act to obstruct understanding. Alan Brinkley (1994:415) notes: "Much of American conservatism in the twentieth century has rested on a philosophical foundation not readily distinguishable from the liberal tradition, to which it is, in theory, opposed." Brinkley (1994:417) also notes in passing the "strong regional base" of conservatism, though he emphasizes the West, whereas I point more to the South.

2. For the influence of the "Virginia school" of political economy on the Chilean junta under Pinochet, particularly its strategy of using the market to undermine capacities for political resistance, see Alfred Stepan 1985:322–323.

3. For illustration of the new understanding that attention to such variety can yield, see Hall and Soskice 2001, and for the relation between rural and urban class politics and forms of state power, see Luebbert 1991. For a related critique of the concept of corporate liberalism, see Lichtenstein 2003:106.

3

State of Panic

Roger N. Lancaster

Beware of those in whom the will to punish is strong.

—*Friedrich Nietzsche*, Thus Spake Zarathustra

"It all seemed darkly funny at first." So claims the opening line of a story published in the *Washington Post* (Kunkle 2006), a story I take as illustrative. Eric Haskett, age twenty-eight, arrived early for a dinner date with his girlfriend, Ali Huenger, age twenty. Tired and reluctant to risk falling asleep while waiting for his date at her mother's home, Haskett napped for a few minutes in his car, just a few doors down from the house. This innocent napping in Frederick County, Maryland, was to set in motion a chain reaction involving snoopy neighbors, community vigilantes, the Internet, varied modes of surveillance (some of them plainly unlawful), local police investigators, and no fewer than three FBI agents.

SUBURBAN NERVOUSNESS
According to the *Post* article, the rural-to-suburban neighborhood was already "on edge from reports [it is unclear whose reports] a month earlier about a strange car lurking in the cul-de-sacs." A few days after Haskett's untimely nap, Stefani Shuster, age thirty-nine, took preventative measures: she sent an email message to her neighbors, apprising them of "an older gray box-style car" that had been "hanging out at odd times." Her email moreover reported that the car's license plate number had been given to the police, who traced the car to Haskett—and to an address that was *also*

the home of a registered sex offender, Donald M. Sanders. (Sanders had been sentenced to five years' probation nearly six years earlier for having sex—apparently, given the probationary sentence, without coercion—with a fourteen-year-old male.) The *Post* story demurs as to exactly how Haskett's name and address were obtained using his license plate number, nor does it tell readers whether there was any investigation into this violation of privacy laws, possibly by someone working for the police.

The author's tone is light throughout, but the article does offer a glimpse into the mingling of empirical fact with dark fantasy in modern America. The story also shows how little it takes nowadays to ignite a full-scale state of panic. In Shuster's email message, she speculated, imagining a possible relationship between Haskett and Sanders, then warned her neighbors: "He [Sanders] is most likely living with and borrowing this car from Haskett....Please pass on this e-mail to as many people as you know in this neighborhood."

Word of a possible child molester stalking the streets was quickly spread by multiple email postings (one resident reports receiving the email twenty times) and by impromptu fliers handed out by members of the community at the local elementary school. (In news reports, those who post or distribute such fliers are always referred to as either "citizens" or "members of the community," these conditions apparently being defined in relation to such acts.) Haskett—who was a gainfully employed man with no criminal record, who was not under any criminal investigation, and who had moved into the boarding house about the same time Sanders moved out—found himself under intense suspicion. It is unclear why local law enforcement, much less the FBI, should have launched investigations into Haskett's activities based on the nervous twitchings of a nosy neighbor or even on the ravings of a latter-day electronic mob. "It blew me away that a federal agent was sticking a badge in my face," Haskett said. "*Three* agents, dog—like I'm the ringleader!" After answering questions and assuaging investigators' concerns, Haskett asked how he could clear his name. Logically, he feared losing his job, or worse. Law enforcement officials were not very sanguine about repairing his reputation. "They said the best bet is to leave the area," Haskett reports. (According to the *Post* article, Sanders had left the area earlier precisely because of this sort of communal harassment.)

One might imagine that participants in these collective hysterics would express remorse over the needless panic they had caused or over the intense anxieties they visited upon their hapless victim. After all, Haskett was a member in good standing of the very community whose urge to protect the vulnerable had precipitated such misguided actions. Surely, his utter innocence in the face of a gross misunderstanding would invite empathy. But nothing of the sort surfaces in the *Post* story. In the minds of the vigilant citizens, imagined victimization takes precedence over any real victimization. Shuster insists that her intentions were good and gives the soccer-mom-turned-security-mom defense: "I have a family to protect....My original e-mail was to inform people." Ali Huenger's mother, Scottie C. Burdette, forty-five, is more truculent. Hinting at a contagious theory of sexual predation, she says that her "gut feeling" was that Haskett was not a sexual predator but she thought that he might be hanging around with one. She warns: "Don't [mess] with suburbia, because we will chew you up and spit you out." It is, of course, clear that no one "messed" with suburbia. But what is not clear, from the *Post* story, is why suburbia should be such a fearful, angry place.

DON'T MESS WITH SUBURBIA: A BRIEF HISTORY OF THE PRESENT

Other stories of the post-9/11 period could not be labeled funny, not even darkly so. For this was the period when Americans cemented a process long under way, definitively reinventing their identity as a nation of aggrieved victims. I will try to situate the drama of suburban nervousness by placing it alongside a more prominent storyline in the national narrative, that of "9/11." Out of correspondences between the two, I shall build my case. I have already sketched portions of this argument (Lancaster 2003: 331–334), which draws on a substantial body of queer, critical, and sex-positive feminist scholarship on "moral panics" (Jenkins 1998; Kincaid 1998; Nathan and Snedeker 1995; Rubin 1984; Shevory 2004; Weeks 1981), as well as sociological treatments of "the culture of fear" (Glassner 1999) and political histories of the uses of fear (Robin 2004; Sherry 2005). My analysis also owes considerable debt to Lauren Berlant (1997), who has traced the emergence of an "infantilized" model of citizenship—the notion that the normative model for public policy has become not the deliberative adult but the innocent child (or even "pre-child" fetus)—along with the spread of pernicious "narratives of rescue" as the dominant justification for civic action.

In broad outlines, I sketch below how the cultivation of a perpetual state of panic gives rise to a new mode of citizenship, to a distorted definition of what might count as public good, and to endless calls for more punitive forms of governance. If I am right, then these four elements define an emergent social formation, the institutional nexus on which neoliberal capitalism presently rests. Sex figures prominently in this arrangement—even, I would argue, when sexual content is not manifestly evident. Ongoing since the conservative turn of the 1970s, sex panics provide a basic template for the production of other states of panic. Moreover, the logic of punitive governance has been further advanced by sex panics than by any other means (including ongoing panics around crime, drugs, and even terror). Much of what follows, then, is an argument about sex, and anxiety about it. But in America, stories about sex are never entirely innocent of stories about race, and I shall try to be alert to these connections.

AMERICAN INNOCENCE, LIVE

Consider how American culture metabolized the outrages of September 11, 2001. Live, nonstop news coverage stoked a sense of collective trauma, fanning fear into the hinterlands, far beyond the sites of any logical terror targets. Over and above the monstrous images on screen, voice-over narratives fed a mass-produced sense of threat and catastrophe. Talking heads aired rumors of other attacks under way, then pondered the safety of America's nuclear power plants, water supply, and mass transit systems. As these scenes and narratives played and replayed over subsequent days, by means of a repetition at once morbid and perverse, TV audiences relived the terror, panic, and thrill—the spectacle—of 9/11 (Afflicted Powers 2004).

In the throes of events, the public was enjoined to be vigilant: report suspicious packages, report suspicious activity. A citizen informer was initially praised for reporting the sinister plotting of Muslims in a Georgia diner, but it later turned out that the three medical students had no ties to terror cells and no bombs in their car and had expressed no ill will toward the United States (CNN 2001). Hate crimes against Muslims and Arab Americans, not to mention everyday acts of discourtesy, spiked (Uniform Crime Report, FBI 2001). In Arizona, a disturbed gunman enacted fantasies of vengeance by going on a shooting spree against Muslims, ultimately murdering a Sikh gas station owner he had misidentified as Muslim (Lewin 2001).

Critical commentators have noted how public narratives around this signal date excluded treatment—or even acknowledgment—of the Islamists' political aims, effectively rendering the horrific events of the day as the criminal acts of inscrutable "evildoers" (George W. Bush's favored term for describing the terrorists). Invariably, public narratives rebuffed even friendly suggestions that some measure and proportion be applied in understanding the fiery devastation of 9/11. The suffering of Americans was to be understood as unique, not comparable to the suffering of any others (Smith 2004). Discreet silences further sharpened the picture of an innocent, victimized nation: mostly excluded from the serious public sphere was discussion of the US role in cultivating, organizing, and funding Islamist terror cells during the Soviet occupation of Afghanistan (Johnson 2001, 2004). From within so much forgetfulness and trauma, new rationales for steel and strength were devised. Various pundits took up arms against a sea of troubles by trying on the mantle of empire: not since Rome had one nation possessed so much power, it was suddenly discovered. A chafed, restive, and increasingly dangerous world would benefit from the benevolent exercise of American tutelage, so it was said (Ignatieff 2003; see also Hartung 2003). It was also said that we, citizens of a free, democratic nation, had no choice but to surrender some ill-defined portion of our freedoms in exchange for security.

In rapid tow came the announcement of an open-ended, indeterminate "war on terror," during which the rules of the Geneva Convention would not apply to the treatment of "unlawful enemy combatants" (a specious legal category hastily devised to skirt the procedures of both international conventions and criminal law). The United States invaded and occupied Afghanistan, then launched a preemptive war of occupation against Iraq, whose government was falsely portrayed as possessing weapons of mass destruction and as having conspired with Al Qaeda in the days leading up to 9/11. In the conduct of these wars, long-standing human rights conventions were abrogated. Administrative legal memos attempted to redefine "torture" and authorized the use of certain forms of torture. Meanwhile, as part of a policy of "extraordinary rendition," intelligence operatives were kidnapping foreign citizens for interrogation and extraditing them to secret CIA prisons overseas or to foreign intelligence services in other countries using more extreme forms of torture (ACLU 2006; Mayer 2005).

At home, federal agents rounded up and detained more than 1,200 immigrants, often on the word of neighbors, holding them in solitary confinement for extended periods without charges, and without access to counsel. Under the National Security Exit-Entry Registration System (NSEERS), male immigrants between the ages of sixteen and forty-five from twenty-five Arab, Muslim, and South Asian countries were required to register with the US government once a year. Registrants were photographed, fingerprinted, and interrogated under oath by INS (Immigration and Naturalization Service) officials. No terrorists were located through either of these procedures, but thousands were deported on various immigration law violations (Chisti et al. 2003). Meanwhile, the Patriot Act centralized federal agencies associated with policing and expanded government powers of surveillance. Mysterious "No-Fly" lists were devised. Government prosecutors brought high-profile charges against "terrorists" and "terror cells," sometimes on scant evidence (for example, a defendant was heard to express a vague wish that harm would come to the United States), sometimes on evidence that could only be described as "entrapment" (that is, undercover agents solicited conspiracy to commit criminal acts). In many of these cases, defendants pled guilty to lesser charges rather than risk execution on capital offenses or reclassification as "unlawful combatants." In Detroit, convictions were overturned on appeal because of prosecutorial mistakes and withheld evidence (Hakim 2004).

In this domestic war on terror, sacred rights and ancient privileges of citizenship were upended. Iconic of an increasingly lawless law, José Padilla was effectively stripped of American citizenship to be held indefinitely without trial as an "enemy combatant." Lynne Stewart, the court-appointed attorney for Sheik Abdel Rahman (the blind cleric convicted in the 1993 World Trade Center bombing), and her translator were convicted on charges of aiding and abetting terrorists. (Elaine Cassel [2004] provides a bracing review of these and other cases. See also ACLU 2003, 2006.)[1] In addition to what was then becoming legally allowable under relaxed rules, the Bush administration launched a broad domestic spying program, widely monitoring Americans' email communications, Internet activity, phone calls, phone records, and financial transactions.

In view of the utter failure of the American political system to check these developments, which cut against deeply embedded tenets of democratic governance ("the right to privacy," "innocent until proven guilty," "everyone deserves his day in court," "war as a last resort," "coequal branches of government," "a republic, not an empire"), one is tempted to echo the Frankfurt School's pessimistic wail from an earlier era: some spring embedded deeply inside the workings of American democracy appears to have snapped. But nothing ever "snaps" all at once. Even apparently sudden social transformations are anticipated long in advance—by heaves, groans, and other indicators of stress. Every reaction to the terror attacks drew inspiration from a cultural template that has become so normalized, its operations scarcely attract scrutiny anymore.

PANIC: A USER'S GUIDE

Moral panic can be defined broadly as any mass movement that emerges in response to a false, exaggerated, or ill-defined *moral* threat to society and that proposes to address this threat via punitive measures: tougher enforcement, "zero tolerance," new laws, communal vigilance, violent purges (Cohen 2002; Goode and Ben-Yehuda 1994; Jenkins 1998; Shevory 2004:3–4; Weeks 1981). Witch hunts are classic examples of moral panics in small, tribal, or agrarian communities (Boyer and Nissenbaum 1974). McCarthyism is the obvious example of a moral panic fueled by the mass media and tethered to repressive governance (Griffith 1987). The response to 9/11 provides a modern instance of the same: instead of opening a pointed military drive to capture, eliminate, or contain Al Qaeda operatives (whose "sleeper cells" in America appear to have been exhausted in one day of spectacular violence), the Bush administration launched an open-ended, global war on something vaguely dubbed "terror," exploiting the occasion to draft new laws, to expand police powers, and to engineer new relations between the state and its citizens.

The manner in which moral panics operate—the mechanics of panic, if you will—is the stuff of both archaic and postmodern social forms. Moral panics thus bear some similarity to what anthropologists once dubbed "social revitalization movements." They represent deliberate attempts to reconstruct social relations in the face of some real or perceived threat or some real or perceived condition of moral decline and social disrepair (Wallace 1956). Another item from the anthropological reliquary seems germane: "scapegoating" is implicit in the full spectrum of panic's forms (Frazer 2005; Girard 1986). Either the person designated as the scapegoat is said to embody the moral threat in his or her person (nineteenth-century theories of racial or sexual degeneracy stimulated pseudoscientific social purity movements such as eugenics), or, alternatively, his or her actions are said to constitute the moral threat—usually in pernicious, conspiratorial, or occult ways. (For as long as I can remember, unidentifiable evildoers, sometimes figured as Satanists, supposedly have been spiking Halloween candy with razors or poison. Fear of candy tampering was present at a low level in the 1960s, then grew in the 1970s, and exploded in the 1980s. In recent years, this fantasized non-occurrence has prompted elaborate schemes of parental supervision and the programming of alternative religious events in place of the traditional trick or treat. See Best and Horiuchi 1985; Brunvald 1989:51–54.) A bugbear manufactured to be tracked, hounded, and pummeled, the dreaded scapegoat can also serve as a repository of secret desires, his extravagant evil a projection and condensation of widely distributed feelings or desires (Kincaid 1998:93–95).

Moral panics generate certain well-known forms of political organization. Self-styled leaders of the movement—"moral entrepreneurs"—

convince others that containment, punishment, banishment, or destruction of the person or persons designated as scapegoat will set things right. This is never the case. Moreover, the acute state of fear cultivated by the movement's leaders effaces meaningful distinctions between threats significant and insignificant, real and imaginary. Invariably, moral panics tend to escalate.

What Freudians call "displacement" is a key feature of moral panics: panics often express, in an irrational, spectral, or misguided way, real social anxieties. This is what makes them such useful instruments of class rule. Classical anti-Semitism deflected onto Jews, in an irrational manner, many of the European peasantry's rational anxieties around money, the market, and capitalism. (August Bebel called anti-Semitism "the socialism of fools.") At the turn of the past century, panics around "white slavery" crystallized, in an imaginary manner, the economic decline of the Victorian middle class and white, native-born skilled workers (Bederman 1995:20–22; Diffee 2005). In the 1960s the British press anguished over the socialization of British youth—and the future of a Britain recently divested of empire and great power status—in sensationalist reportage on youth subcultures: the Mods versus the Rockers. (It was Cohen's 1972 study of this phenomenon that coined the term *moral panic*.)

The element of imagination plays a prominent role in panic mongering: the object of panic might be either an imaginary entity (the devil, witches) or a real person or group portrayed in an imaginary manner (diabolized Jews, Negro satyrs, conspiratorial communists, plotting homosexuals). Because fantasy and imagination are given such wide girth in the contemplation of social ills and moral threats (which can be entirely imaginary), panics can gather together into a single movement any number of forms of dread and loathing. McCarthyism is generally remembered as the "red scare," but the homosexual purges associated with it lasted longer and wrecked more lives than did the anti-communist witch hunts (Johnson 2003).

Mass media are essential to the dynamics of modern moral panics—so much so that Thomas Shevory (2004:4) prefers the term *media panic* (see also Altheide 2002). But not all media panics are the same. Fear and confusion propagate faster via radio and TV than by way of mass-produced broadsides or flyers; the Internet is a more efficient means of converting anecdote into evidence than was the Hearst newspaper chain. As means of communication have sped up and expanded, panics, too, have accelerated and intensified. Media conglomerates, institutional actors, and political factions all have a stake in the production and management of certain kinds of fear (Hall et al. 1978). They provoke panic to sell newspapers, to forge "community," to curb social movements posited as counter to the imagined moral community, or to foster various kinds of social discipline. All these factors tend toward the production of panic as the normative condition in contemporary America. Just as mass media create "audiences," media panics tend to forge a certain kind of citizenship and a certain kind of state: when audience-communities become truly alarmed, they demand action, usually repressive action against an "enemy" (Hall et al. 1978). Vox populi, vox poena. As panic has become a defining feature of media culture (Shevory 2004:8), it has also become ever more intricately woven into the basic structure of governance.

Panics, and their residues, are woven into the warp and woof of modern society because they precipitate edicts, statutes, laws, institutions, and other durable forms of social organization. Historians and sociologists have suggested that nineteenth-century race panics—fear of violent slave uprisings, often imagined in lurid sexual terms—contributed to the production of a durable "culture of fear" and suspicion in America (Foner 1971; Glassner 1999:107–128). Certainly, these laid groundwork for a pervasive culture of sexual fear. Stoked again during Reconstruction and reinforced under Jim Crow (Cardyn 2002; Gilmore 1996:esp. 88, 117; Woodward 2002:86–87), the specter of the violent, sexually predatory, black bogeyman recurs in various epochs and haunts the white American psyche to this day. Radical critics of policing have also stressed the role that nineteenth-century moral panics around prostitution and vice played in the definition of "crime" and the development of modern policing (Williams 2003; see also Stansell 1987; Walkowitz 1992). Indeed, owing to the relative weakness of labor unions, socialist parties, or social-democratic modes of organization in the United States, it is difficult to think of any modern American bureaucracy whose origin or development was not expressly prompted in some way by some perceived moral threat. The development of social services is a clear case in point. Historically, sensitivity to moral threats emanating from the lower classes virtually defines American middle-class respectability, and strategies of containment or moral uplift pretty much define liberal progressivism. "Panic," like "morality," is that which ever prods some new disciplinary apparatus, some new definition of social good— some conception of the subject citizen as anything *but* a class subject.

Estelle Freedman's (1987) essay on the emergence of the "sexual psychopath" as a figure in American popular culture and policing aptly illustrates the multilateral relationships among moral panics, the mass media, law enforcement, citizens groups, and established professions. It is worthwhile retracing some of the links she establishes, because these seem paradigmatic of current trends. Fritz Lang's 1931 German film *M*, which cast Peter Lorre as a compulsive child murderer, stoked in America a popular interest in sensational reportage on sex crimes, especially murderous sex crimes against children. By 1937 the *New York Times*—whose writers had been initially reluctant to wade into this swamp—created a hitherto nonexistent index category, "Sex Crimes," to cover the 143 articles it published on the subject that year (Freedman 1987:83). During the 1930s and, again, after World War II, newspapers and magazines broadcast imaginary sex-crime waves. Thus was born the modern sex fiend. Publicity bred action: arrest rates undoubtedly rose—not for the horrendous acts given media fanfare but mostly for assorted sexual offenses of a consensual, nonviolent, or less violent nature (Freedman 1987:84). Despite the skepticism of many psychiatrists, new statutes were passed, and the "sexual psychopath" became the shared province of law enforcement and psychiatry.[2]

Child rape and murder figured prominently in sensational discussions of sex offenses; these events triggered mob attacks and the organization of parent-citizens groups. Because every sex offender was viewed as posing the threat of violence, nonviolent offenders charged with sodomy and exhibitionism could also be incarcerated under sexual psychopath laws (Freedman 1987:92–94, 98). Thus, a connection between homosexuality and child murder was drawn. Various psychiatric professionals, journalists, law enforcement officials, and popular writers explicitly equated homosexuality with sexual psychopathology and violence, either seizing upon isolated incidents or conjuring stereotypes about the seduction of innocents by oversexed perverts. Sensational media stories about child molestation invariably triggered police sweeps of gay bars and cruising grounds. Broad statutes allowed lifetime psychiatric commitment for consensual adult same-sex acts, if the offender's desires were deemed "uncontrollable." "Treatment" for sex offenders included group therapy, drug regimens, electro-shock, and frontal lobotomy (Freedman 1987:99, 103–104).

Eventually, sex panics of the 1940s and 1950s waned, McCarthyism ended, the sexual and due process revolutions of the 1960s began, and, in consummation of long-standing critiques from within psychiatry and psychology, catchall notions of sexual psychopathology were slowly de-emphasized, disaggregated, or (sometimes) retired. By 1968 Michigan, the first state to pass such statutes, struck its psychopath laws and eliminated the legal category "criminal sexual psychopath" (Freedman 1987:95–96, 100). As part of a general revision of social boundaries around "normal" and "abnormal" sex, the slow process of decriminalizing consensual same-sex acts began. Sex, in a word, changed, and so did American culture. Still, sex panics of the mid-twentieth century left lasting residues in American culture, starting with the distillation of a vague and amorphous journalistic category, "sex crime." Moreover, sexual psychopathology laws (some still on the books) partially "de-raced" the predatory bogeyman and gave scientific credence to long-standing ideas about predation and sexual danger. Lastly, mid-century sex panics refined certain institutional mechanisms involving media, citizens, expressible demands, and the state. Sensationalist reportage of statistically uncommon occurrences triggered, as though by Pavlovian response, the formation of vigilant citizens organizations, the demand for police protection, and the writing of laws that fail to discriminate between serious and minor offenses. In decline through the 1960s, these elements were taken up again with a vengeance from the 1970s forward.

FLASH: THE PREDATORY PERVERT LIVES

Although drugs and crime have provided reliable objects of sensational reportage—and reliable means of cathecting white racial animosities—since the close of the 1960s (Dyer 2000; Garland 2001; Parenti 1999; Wright and Herivel 2003), modern moral panics in America have increasingly revolved around sex. Ongoing panics treat abortion, unwed mothers, pornography, homosexuality, and the condition of marriage as the sole institution within which sex might be legitimately practiced. Because these touch on reproduction, alliance, and the socialization of successive generations into heterosexual adulthood, modern sex panics invariably express anxieties about ongoing institutional changes triggered by the new social movements of the 1960s: the sexual revolution, the women's movement, and gay liberation. Because these panics focus on morality, so-called, they have obstructed clear public discussion of the ongoing *economic* shifts that potently underlie the reorganization of what Gramsci (1971:299–300) once dubbed "the institutions connected with sexual life": the decline of the family wage and the increase of part-time work, temporary jobs, and insecure working conditions. The predatory pervert makes his new life in modern America, where, more or less, the mass media and major political parties expressly forbid critical discussions of deregulation, downsizing, outsourcing, and the role these play in fostering personal insecurity, unstable lives, and social breakdown. His madness provides a distorted mirror image of unbridled capitalist predation; his sexuality, a zone of fantasy and projection; his doings, a hieroglyph of the instability of real social relations; and his containment, a sort of hypochondriac obsession.

Sometimes articulated, sometimes implicit, the homophobic element in modern sex panics seems ubiquitous (see Edelman 2004:112–113;

Ohi 2000:195). Indeed, overtly homophobic sex panics inaugurated many of the current conventions for talking about teen sexuality and child sex abuse. By the 1970s, panics around teenage male prostitution evoked earlier sex panics and embodied, in another sort of way, the nascent backlash against gay liberation (Kaye 2003:42–46). Mid-1970s movements to turn back gay rights ordinances in several cities expressly organized under the banner "Save Our Children." From there began a new series of panics around sex and minors, which continues unabated.

The most spectacular of these modern child sex panics—the "Satanic Ritual Abuse" (SRA) scares of the 1980s—have been thoroughly discredited (Nathan and Snedeker 1995). But in history, timing is everything, and these latter-day witch hunts came at a crucial historical moment of cultural retrenchment and political backlash. The decay of New Left social movements played an important part in this setting of the stage. Anti-porn crusades, ongoing since the mid-1970s, had spurred the development of an increasingly puritanical sect of cultural feminism—a variant whose rhetoric bore little resemblance to either the sexual liberationists of the early second wave *or* the anti-violence, rape crisis activists of the early 1970s. By the early 1980s, anti-sex feminists found themselves speaking the same language as (and, in many instances, making common political cause with) evangelical Christians (Vance 1997).

Because Reagan-era sex panics allied antagonistic social movements against a common phantasmic threat, they had important cultural consequences. They buttressed conservative Christian notions of childhood sexual innocence while twining with neo-Victorian feminist accounts of sex as trauma. As Gayle Rubin (1984) rightly prognosticated while SRA fantasies were still raging, the long trajectory of these and other sex panics would leave indelible marks on American professional and legal culture. They spawned entire subfields of pseudoscience—most notably, the psychoanalysis of "repressed" or "recovered" memories, which persists to this day in popular and sometimes legal form. They powerfully contributed to the consolidation of an ever more expansive culture of "child protection," thus extending the purviews of both long-standing official bureaucracies (Child Protection Services) and newer, quasi-official ones ("victims' rights advocates"). These panics have secreted new terminologies, sedimented new ways of speaking and thinking: *pedophile*, a term that had no clinical standing before the 1960s, has become a household word, applied to an ever broader range of desires and predilections. Pick up virtually any pop psychology text—or, for that matter, a large sampling of high feminist academic treatises—and you will likely encounter a certain dark picture of childhood: encircled by sinister forces, menaced by innumerable threats, stalked by shadowy evildoers. Read virtually any issue of any newspaper and you will encounter all the myriad ways innocence can be snatched from the young. It has become every citizen's duty everywhere to be alert to the dangers embodied by strangers.

"Megan's Law Saves Lives" announces the gateway website for public sex offender registries mandated by federal law in 1994. But there is no real evidence that children are any safer in a world of overzealous child protection. There are reasons to think the contrary: penalties or stigmas that blur the difference between degrees of infraction are ineffective and can even serve as perverse incentives. If both kidnapping and murder are capital crimes, then a panicked kidnapper might murder his victim to attempt to avoid detection. Current sex offender laws—including Megan's Law, which prescribes lengthy terms of surveillance and monitoring for even minor and nonviolent offenses—offer a remarkable assemblage of perverse incentives. Said laws moreover intensify the feelings of guilt, shame, stigma, and disgust that seem to be involved in the commission of the most violent offenses.

More broadly, Judith Levine (2003) has convincingly argued that the established culture of child protection—with its fetishization of virginity and its constant battery of alarmist messages equating sex with predation— actually harms children psychologically and socially (see also Irvine 2004). A British study has found that in the United Kingdom, where sex panics rival those of the United States, the irrational fear of strangers has driven children indoors, contributing to a sedentary lifestyle and a fear of the outside environment (Hill 2004). Children, too, have become objects of public wrath in the ever escalating panics around sex. Minors who fail to conform to adult fantasies of sexual innocence may be labeled "SACY" (sexually aggressive children and youth) and can be subjected to many of the same forms of prosecution, supervision, and surveillance prescribed for adult sex offenders.

After thirty years of nonstop sex panics, a culture of primal sexual fear has driven deep roots into American social life. This culture revivifies Victorian motifs of innocence and predation (Kincaid 1998). It also greatly resembles the psychological milieu of the late Weimar cinema (Kracauer 2004), whose dread of the city, fear of strangers, and celebration of the safety of the hearth anticipated the coming of fascism.

NOTES ON SEX AND TERROR

Consider now, by way of an argument that will be first primarily illustrative, then analytical, how mass-mediated panics of one sort (terror) "fit," *en cours*, with panics of another sort (sex). First came extensive mass-media coverage of the September 11 terror attacks. If public portrayals of an immaculate, innocent nation resonated with long-standing cultural motifs, then the organized response likewise drew on a familiar template: in the name of "family" and "victimization," families of the victims of 9/11 organized to press for compensation, to monitor congressional hearings on intelligence failures, to serve as a pressure group in lower Manhattan redevelopment plans, and to press for redress in varied criminal trials having little or nothing to do with 9/11. Assorted actions by various of these groups have sometimes tilted rightward, other times leftward, but have always traded in the dominant cultural logic, which derives a sort of sacral authority from aggrieved victimization.

Then, in short order, came a period of intense reportage on the Catholic Church sex abuse scandals. In this reportage, major crimes (child rape) were conflated with minor ones (fondlings, pinchings, noncoercive sexual relations with near-adults). In the context of ubiquitous media narratives pitting predatory evil against victimized innocence, it seemed natural that journalistic scrutiny synchronized with the conduct of several high-stakes lawsuits by trial attorneys—whose strategy, in no small part, was to leverage negative publicity in order to force large settlements. The form taken by reportage also seemed predictable because it followed on a long-term, gradual redefinition of what might count as "news" in a rapidly deteriorating public sphere. A recurring cast of ready-to-hand "experts" and advocates gave prosecution-friendly media interviews on these cases. Such techniques blurred with reportage around the Scott Peterson and Michael Jackson trials and the Kobe Bryant case. Jackson, in particular, was characterized as a "sexual predator." Although no child pornography was discovered in police raids of Neverland Ranch, objets d'art found there were publicly described as being "consistent" with those that might be found in a pedophile's possession.

It is not just that public presumptions of innocence were suspended in the priest-abuse panics. A willingness to believe any allegation, no matter how improbable, seized the minds of prosecutors, public functionaries, and jurists alike. In this context, deliberate deceptions enter, unqualified, into the public record. The Boston case of Father Paul Shanley is instructive. Citing church records and Shanley's journals, prosecutors falsely claimed—and the press uncritically reported—that Shanley had admitted to past rapes, had received a psychiatric evaluation that concluded, "His pathology is beyond repair," and was a founding member of the North American Man/Boy Love Association. (JoAnn Wypijewski [2004] has been virtually alone in picking through the details of this case, including the prosecution's misrepresentations.) Thus was shaped the image of a pedophile monster. In fact, Shanley's journals recount that he had had a great deal of consensual sex with sexually mature teenagers and young men—some of whom eventually won large sex-abuse settlements from the Church, based on claims that they had had sex with Shanley while they were in their twenties. No doubt, Shanley's relations with teenagers and young men in his professional counsel were inappropriate. But false statements by the prosecution, conveyed in sensational reportage, created a prejudicial environment for Shanley's trial on other, very different charges: the former priest was accused of repeatedly raping a young boy from the age of six over several years in the 1980s. The result of prosecutorial mendacity and media frenzy was what can only be described as a show trial. Shanley was convicted on discredited "recovered memories" testimony—a pseudoscientific relic of the SRA panics—in the absence of any substantiating evidence or testimony (Wypijewski 2004). In fact, testimony by others present suggested that the alleged rapes did not occur.

Tales of predatory victimization bred yet more tales of wanton evil. By the time these sensational trials were winding down, the national mass media were giving extensive airplay to a string of gruesome crimes involving child abduction, rape, and murder, giving the impression that statistically rare occurrences were "epidemic" and that predatory recidivists were wreaking havoc across the heartland. Two unrelated but closely timed kidnapping/sex/murder cases in Florida involving violent repeat offenders drew especially intense national attention (Goodenough 2005; Woodruff 2005). I stress the exceedingly rare nature of such occurrences.

Any given year, hundreds of thousands of children are reported missing. The Center for Missing and Exploited Children often invokes figures in the range of 750,000. The overwhelming majority of these "missing" children are home within twenty-four hours. (Most "missing" minors had lost track of time—or had briefly run away from home.) Child custody disputes account for much of the remainder. Teenage runaways and throwaways account for another substantial sector. Most of the three thousand or so child abductions per year by *non*-family members involve family acquaintances, pose low risk of violence, and are usually quickly resolved. In a nation whose population approaches three hundred million, there are currently around one hundred high-risk stranger abductions of children per year, and of these, about fifty end in murder. You would not know it from news reports or political deliberations, but the incidence for *all* varieties of child disappearance and abduction is down significantly from the 1980s (along with most other forms of violent crime).[3] In real terms, then, a child's risk of being killed by a sexually predatory stranger is comparable to his or her chance of being struck and killed by lightning (1 in 1,000,000 versus 1 in 1,200,000) (STATS 2002; Whittaker 1986:542). In raw numbers, abduction-murder ranks far below more common causes of child death—disease or congenital illness (36,180), motor vehicle accident (7,981), drowning (1,158), accidental suffocation or strangulation (953), fire (606), firearm accident (167) (National MCH Center for Child Death Review n.d.)—including death at the hands of a family member. The US Department of Health and Human Services (2005a, 2005c) reckons roughly 1,500 child fatalities per year resulting from abuse or neglect. Only a tiny percentage of these child deaths (3 percent) is caused by strangers, as opposed to nearly 80 percent caused by one or both parents. And less than 1 percent of all child deaths caused by abuse or neglect involves sexual abuse (National Clearinghouse on Child Abuse and Neglect Information n.d.).

Such unusual events once would have been treated as strictly local stories—a family's personal horror, surely, but neither a nation's collective ordeal nor an instructive morality play. But intense competition among twenty-four-hour news services such as CNN and Fox drew sensationalist stories to the fore, fudging the difference between local and national news stories. And media practices developed around the AMBER (America's Missing: Broadcast Emergency Response) Alert system, established by the 2003 PROTECT Act, dovetailed with this "tabloidization" of the public sphere to further blur the difference between policing, vigilantism, and journalism. When law enforcement officials determine that a minor has been kidnapped, AMBER Alerts interrupt regular TV and radio programming, are broadcast on news reports and electronic highway signs, can be beamed to mobile phones, and may be printed on lottery tickets (Office of Justice Programs n.d.). The net result has been (and remains) a steady drumbeat of news stories on rare but highly inflammatory events: modes of address that incite every citizen to live in a state of watchfulness, preparedness, and panic.

With the same stupefied, magical approach to statistical phenomena that turns a summer statistical blip into a "crime wave," victims' rights advocates have agitated for new laws, and organizations like the National Center for Missing and Exploited Children have worked to capitalize on the resulting confusion. Calls for more policing, more surveillance, more monitoring—for surveillance cameras on every street corner and in every parking lot—reveal most clearly the emergence of a new citizen subject (the victim, potential victim, or victim's advocate), a new mode of political participation (perpetual vigilance as the model for good citizenship), a new form of governance (which can best be described as punitive, because it surrenders freedom, privacy, or rights in the name of risk reduction, but which also deserves the name *paranoid*).

The model evildoer in narratives of child predation is the strange "sexual predator," the violent "repeat offender." But this ignominious figure's ability to conjure fear, rally citizens, and inspire legislation is based not on any significant statistical facts but on the outrage his invocation stirs. According to a US Department of Justice (2003) study that tracked male sex offenders (men convicted of rape or sexual assault, including child molestation and statutory rape) released from prison in 1994, 5.3 percent were rearrested (and 3.5 percent reconvicted) for another sex crime within three years. Advocates for the rights of sex offenders and their families thus point out that recidivism rates are significantly *lower* for convicted sex offenders than for burglars, robbers, larcenists, drug offenders, and so on. Contrary to the prevailing narratives, repeat offenders and/or strangers are responsible for only a very small percentage of new sex crimes, including sex crimes against children (News and Noteworthy 2006). It should be clear that public sex offender registries and other sweeping "get tough" measures serve no real preventative ends; they represent a punitive, theatrical politics.

No doubt, a small number of violent repeat offenders, serial rapists, and child stalkers are included in the burgeoning registries of sex offenders. But a great many of the offenses included in sex offender registries are less violent, even nonviolent; indeed, many would not be classed as sex offenses under European laws, which set significantly lower ages of consent than do American laws. As one anonymous writer ("Pariah" 2006) suggests, the "typical" registered sex offender is a far more vernacular figure than the official narrative suggests: the kindly uncle who only once fondled a niece during a lapse in judgment, the geeky young gay man who sought sex and companionship with a teenage minor, the lonely female schoolteacher who foolishly fell in love with one of her students. Among the swelling ranks of convicted and registered sex offenders are, doubtless, many innocent persons, falsely accused, tried in the press, then wrongfully convicted by incensed judges and juries. A study of exonerations of defendants convicted of serious crimes suggests that inflammatory charges, such as murder or cross-racial rape, raise the risk of wrongful convictions (Gross et al. 2005:2–3; Liptak 2004); the risk to those wrongfully accused of child abuse would seem especially high.

"No passion so effectually robs the mind of all its powers of acting and reasoning as terror," wrote Edmund Burke (1990:53). Still, there are uses for terror, as Burke well knew. The rhetorical flourishes of the moral entre-preneurs who both produce and capitalize on the prevailing state of panic are revealing. In Florida, where a minor's abduction from a parking lot was caught on videotape, a state legislator appeared before cameras to cry "No more!" in a weeping rage so fearsome, one would have thought that her own child had been snatched from her breast and brutally put to death. The case at hand was an especially heinous act; the proposed legislation, however, applied broadly to a host of minor or nonviolent sex offenses. So goes the associative logic of panic.

Oprah Winfrey—whose career was importantly shaped in the 1980s when she floated several different claims of her own experiences with childhood sexual abuse (Siegel 2006)—staged much the same perfor-mance on her syndicated TV talk show, launching a national "Child Predator Watch List" and offering $100,000 rewards for information lead-ing to the capture of various fugitives and nonregistrants (men who refused to register as sex offenders under Megan's Law). "The children of this nation...are being stolen, raped, tortured, and killed by sexual preda-tors who are walking right into your homes. How many times does it have to happen? How many children have to be sacrificed? What price are we as a society willing to continue to pay before we rise up and take to the streets and say: Enough. Enough. Enough!"

Winfrey's pitch, delivered personally on her website, bears examina-tion because it trades in so many tropes that have come to substitute for politics in a badly deteriorated public sphere: the ritual enactment of out-rage, the vow to undertake a quasi-religious crusade, the evocation of secre-tive, conspiratorial evildoers who plot against a long-suffering common folk. It is also worth noting that Winfrey's nation of beleaguered innocents, violated in their own homes, bears striking resemblance to lynch mob incitements of the Jim Crow era, which invariably depicted white women and children being menaced in their very homes by black rapists. As though to exorcise ghosts of the "black beast," Winfrey's website featured a multiracial cast of mug shots. Despite the alarmist rhetoric, the sex crimes with which the men were charged varied considerably in terms of harm or intensity. Some were, indeed, accused of having raped children, others of having noncoercive sex with teenage minors, others of inappropriately touching minors of various ages. Some were not actually wanted by author-ities for having committed any offense *other* than failing to register as sex offenders (Winfrey 2005).

Winfrey's was only one of many such expansive cries from the period. Prosecutor-turned-journalist Nancy Grace kept such narratives going nightly on CNN. NBC's *Nightline* marketed "To Catch a Predator," a pseudo-news event aired during sweeps week. In this recurring format, journalists pose as minors in online chat rooms to entrap adult men in "stings." So extensive was coverage of this beat that one journalist joked that his own network was "all pedophiles, all the time" ("Pariah" 2006). Meanwhile, the *New York Times* got in on the act with extensive yellow journalism around the case of Justin Berry. Berry began operating his own sexually oriented web cam at the age of thirteen, garnering hundreds of thousands of dollars of income over the years. At the age of nineteen, he got out of the business to begin denouncing his customers to the FBI under the heavy-handed tutelage of the *Times* reporter. The video file of the Berry interviews is redolent of an abusive relationship: the young man can exonerate himself of agency and volition in violating child porn laws only by constantly reiterating the coached accusation that "the pedophiles" made him perform a variety of sexual acts on video. *Times* editors have given this story, which erases any imaginable boundary between journalism and policing, prominent newspaper and Internet placement (Eichenwald 2005a, 2005b, 2006).

PITY THE POOR PEDOPHILE, SUBJECT TO EVER MORE SWEEPING DEFINITIONS AND EVER MORE DRACONIAN PENALTIES

Not so long ago, in more enlightened times, rehabilitation was the normative goal of criminal justice. The need for procedural barriers against police brutality, forced confessions, prosecutorial misconduct, and invasions of privacy was widely acknowledged. Pity, not panic, was the prevailing professional attitude toward nonviolent sex offenders during the 1960s and early 1970s. Of course, Americans no longer give even lip service to such enlightened ideals; they aspire to measures that protect, punish, and preempt. Still, even by these diminished standards, a logical approach to crime of any sort involves a dispassionate assessment of harm, along with informed judgments about risk. Reason, judgment, and measure are precisely what are lacking in the current panics around sex.

In the early years of the twenty-first century, hysterical reportage and overwrought calls to action encouraged widespread acts of vigilantism, and not just in Frederick County, Maryland. Signs posted at my sister's YMCA in North Carolina urged perpetual vigilance: "If you have any reason whatsoever to believe that any child is being sexually abused here, remember—you don't have to 'prove' anything. Just report your suspicions to us and we'll take over from there." The solicitation of "suspicions," to be investigated by Y staff, is quite alarming. I have heard professional educators, no less, express the belief that a child was being abused on evidence no more substantial than a vague sense that the minor seemed inexplicably "sad"—usually in proximity to a stepfather whose race or ethnicity was different from that of the minor's mother. Anonymous broadsides posted in Washington, DC, bilingually identified a registered sex offender as "Child Molester"/"Abusador de Niñas." Actually, the man had been convicted not of molesting a "child" but of having noncoercive sexual relations with a fifteen-year-old minor, less than one year short of DC's age of consent. In Florida, a disabled thirty-eight-year-old man committed suicide after neighbors distributed flyers labeling him a "child rapist." Physically, mentally, and socially impaired, the man was not actually a rapist: he had exposed himself to a nine-year-old girl eighteen years earlier (Associated Press 2005). It goes without saying that the leafleteers expressed no remorse over their actions. In Maine, two registered sex offenders were tracked to their house, using the Megan's Law listings on the Internet, and shot to death. Their murderer got into the house by pretending to be a policeman who had come to warn them of a vigilante plot (Bazar 2006). Acts of arson against registered sex offenders were reported in various states.

The result, too, was yet another sedimentation of sex offender laws and statutes: in 2005, forty-five states passed 150 new laws, with more slated for 2006 (Koch 2006). A stigma has always attached to criminal conviction, but modern sex offender laws represent a major breach of civil liberties. They prescribe ever more exacting forms of punishment and surveillance, in addition to those already applied by judges and juries, thus creating a new class of criminals whose sentences can never be fully served. Megan's Law, passed in 1994 and named for the victim of an especially brutal child murder, had already established public sex offender registries in every state. The public list of registrants—which, contrary to the original intent of the law, to target "violent repeat offenders," now includes those convicted on both felony and misdemeanor charges, violent and nonviolent offenses—currently approaches six hundred thousand and is growing. Since 1994 forty-four states have passed (or currently have pending) laws that would require some sex offenders to be monitored for life with electronic bracelets and global positioning devices (Bolton 2006). The "land of second chances" is rapidly becoming the land of perpetual surveillance. Nine states now allow or require castration before some sex offenders can be released from prison (Sluss 2006). Civil commitment procedures (a modern revival of mid-twentieth-century sexual psychopath laws) in many more states allow for the perpetual incarceration of adults—and sometimes minors—after the completion of their sentences: because they insist, even after being convicted, that they have committed no crime or because of a psychologist's vague surmise that the convicted person was "manipulative," "egocentric," or "unrepentant," and so on (Mansnerus 2003).

Supposedly, the most draconian of these penalties apply to those convicted of the most violent offenses; in practice, they are applied against ever less serious crimes. Indeed, part of what defines the current wave of sex panics is the desire to reveal, publicize, and perpetually punish even minor infractions. There is pressure to continue expanding the original Megan's Law listings to require lifetime public registration of *all* convicted sex offenders, including those busted for soliciting sex in public restrooms or parks. In 2005 the Maryland state legislature considered a bill that would require electronic monitoring of virtually all sex offenders, and New York governor George Pataki issued an executive order (later ruled illegal) remanding all sex offenders to civil confinement in locked mental asylums upon their release from prison (Hartocollis 2005; "Pariah" 2006).

Assorted laws in many states and municipalities restrict where a sex offender can live, work, or walk. In post-9/11 sex panics, this proved an especially popular panacea, promoted by citizens groups, victims' rights advocates, crusading journalists, and politicians everywhere. A number of cities and states passed ordinances prohibiting registered sex offenders from living within 1,000 feet of schools or parks—effectively evicting them from many towns and communities. In some regions, states and municipalities actively competed with each other to pass ever wider perimeters of exclusion (2,000 feet, 2,500 feet) and ever more comprehensive definitions of which offenders would be evicted from their homes.

Consider the scene from Iowa, where a new state law bars virtually all sex offenders from living within 2,000 feet of a school or day care center: twenty-six registered sex offenders crowd into twenty-four rooms at the Ced-Rel motel in Cedar Rapids, one of the town's few residences legally available to them. Some have been driven across state lines—where neighboring states and municipalities now rush to pass similar ordinances. One shuffles into the sheriff's office because he knows nowhere else to go. Others, thrown out of their homes, have been driven underground. They sleep in cars, under bridges, or in abandoned buildings (Davey 2006). The teenager who had sex with his underage girlfriend; the harmless chicken hawk fond of giving blowjobs to seventeen-year-old men; the flasher, the masher, the social nuisance alongside the real menace; the wrongfully accused beside the rightfully convicted: These have become a phantom, fugitive population, shadowy flickerings in the deepest night. Such scenes might be "darkly funny" if staged in a black comedy, a psychological fantasy, or a dystopian novel about the coming of a totalitarian police state. Alas, they are anything but funny. Played out in towns and states across America, they show that something is profoundly broken in American culture, law, and democracy.

REPUBLIC OF FEAR: UNDERSTANDING THE POLITICAL ECONOMY OF PANIC, THE MEANINGS OF VICTIMOLOGY, AND THE LOGIC OF PUNITIVE GOVERNANCE

In *The State of Exception*, Giorgio Agamben (2004) theorizes executive power in modern states as the power of exception: the power, in an emergency, to bypass normal laws, to suspend constitutional rights, and to issue impromptu laws. In this context, the author ominously notes "a continuing tendency in all of the Western democracies": "the declaration of the state of exception has gradually been replaced by an unprecedented generalization of the paradigm of security as the normal technique of government" (Agamben 2004:14, also 6–7). By degrees, exception becomes the norm. Modern democracies are becoming "protected democracies."

Agamben's exposition is a useful starting point. Much of what happens in the realm of governance today is premised on the existence of this or that emergency: some state of affairs so menacing that measures at once protective, punitive, and preemptive are in order. But *The State of Exception* is marred by gaps and haunted by absences. Curiously absent from Agamben's analysis is any real reckoning with the irrational, imaginative, or phantasmic element in the developments he describes. Failing that, Agamben also fails to elicit the flesh-and-blood mechanisms whereby a state of emergency is inculcated in the public, such that undemocratic suspensions of rights can be achieved by formally democratic means—by popular demand.

Above all, what Agamben's textual study of legal documents and political theory fails to disclose is how deeply embedded these trends are in the neoliberal political economy. Far from being restricted to the presidency, the "security paradigm" and its associated forms of action are spread across executive, legislative, and judicial functions of government. And far from being a universal tendency of all governments everywhere (as the frequent recourse to Derridean boilerplate, Roman precedents, and functionalist rubrics like "anomie" might suggest), the passage of ever more exacting and ever more lawless laws in the name of security has to be understood in the context of the new paradigm of economic *in*security. As real economic conditions become more insecure for more people, the masses are more vigorously induced to clamor for imaginary forms of security. The resulting "Law" functions as an imaginary world of Justice, a fetish object, a privatized and moralized substitute for any form of collective social action that might realistically make the world more secure for more people. The old empire had Bread and Circuses; in the new scenario, Court TV serves as Circus—but you are on your own as far as Bread is concerned.

I derive the term *punitive governance* from historian Michael Sherry's (2005) essay, which likewise shows how the Bush administration's post-9/11 actions projected an American "culture of vengeance" on the global scene. I have emphasized the role of sex panics in setting the basic template for punitive governance. The vivid portrayal of statistically uncommon events is invoked to foster the public perception of an emergency, to urge the suspension of procedures embodied in established law, and to pass broadly punitive measures. In these regards, modern sex panics are extreme but not unique; they resemble (and are a subset of) other ongoing panics, around crime in general and perhaps especially the drug scares (Dyer 2000; Garland 2001; Parenti 1999; Wright and Herivel 2003). Overlapping panics around sex, crime, and drugs occupy the same post-1960s epoch; they fashion roughly equivalent, socially acceptable "backlash" politics (condensing heterosexual anxieties in one case, white racial animosities in the others). In tandem, they have contributed to a long-term erosion of civil liberties, a dramatic burgeoning of the prison population, an unprecedented expansion of state powers associated with detection, policing, and surveillance, and—not least of all—the consolidation of new, broadly distributed, punitive norms. A mean-spirited approach has thus saturated not just law enforcement but also the provision of social services (Roberts, chapter 8, this volume) and welfare (Collins, chapter 7, this volume), as well as understandings of governance generally (MacLean, chapter 2, this volume). Responses to the terror attacks of September 11, 2001, greatly accelerated such trends, but they did not inaugurate them.

Whether sex, crime, drugs, or terror is involved, four elements seem crucial to this configuration in America. First, the cultivation of a perpetual state of panic is embodied in a certain style of journalism. "News," by definition, traffics in the novel, and journalism is therefore perpetually drawn to the sensational (Gitlin 2002:51). Once upon a time, the adjective *yellow* affixed to stories that strictly treated of the sensational, prurient, or incendiary. Today, by contrast, even "newspapers of record" wallow in tabloid techniques. The historical sources of this "tabloidization" are complex. Sometime after the Watergate era, investigative journalism took a wrong turn and lost its way. Rather than investigate social problems resulting from the systemic, regular functioning of business or government (the liberal, social-democratic approach favored by Edward R. Murrow and New Left reporters), muckraking journalists began probing high crimes and misde-meanors. This approach, which implicitly depicts social problems as the result of personal misdeeds, fit well with the conservative turn of the late 1970s. Henceforward, crusading journalism takes an anti-crime approach, fusing seamlessly with nascent variants of conservative populism. "News" hitherto will arouse the public to some criminal outrage, forging, in the long term, a redefinition of what will count as "public" or as "a public." Mass communication becomes mass manipulation: this is essential to the state of panic.

Second, a new mode of citizenship and civic participation emerges alongside (and in relation to) such journalism. The victims' rights move-ment is paradigmatic of this approach (Shapiro 1997; Sherry 2005:9–11). Tethering the rhetoric of grievance (much of it derived from decayed New Left and especially neo-Victorian feminist sources) to a law-and-order pol-itics, it has provided the basic organizational template for scores of move-ments over the past thirty years (for example, Mothers against Drunk Driving, the Center for Missing and Exploited Children, the incest sur-vivors movement) and is now fully integrated into policing, sentencing, and the provision of social services. This movement's techniques are well established: its "poster children" (who are often literally children) are the victims of gruesome crimes. The more horrific the crime, the greater will be its power to stir outrage, draw contributions, and stimulate durable political organizations.

This is another way of saying that the less typical the offense, the more loudly its news will resonate with the machineries of the mass media. Victims' rights groups essentially exist to stir up this sort of publicity in per-petuity, to provoke in the public a constant state of fear, terror, and agita-tion. In a speech before the 1997 Victims' Rights conference, US attorney general Janet Reno captured something of this movement's cultural and political capital, the identity work it performs, and especially its sanctifica-tion of victimization *as* American identity: "I draw the most strength from the victims, for they represent America to me: people who will not be put down, people who will not be defeated, people who will rise again and stand again for what is right....You are my heroes and heroines. You are but [a] little lower than the angels" (Shapiro 1997:11).

Third, active collusion between sensational journalism, victims' rights activism, and political grandstanding creates and reinforces a distorted def-inition of what might count as public good. Much of this distortion revolves around the concept of risk (Douglas 1992). The public is coaxed to obsess over statistically insignificant risks (for example, stranger abduction) and is effectively urged to ignore the far more salient, quotidian risks associated with the neoliberal economy: unemployment, uninsured medical expenses, flimsy retirement benefits, widespread environmental pollution. Ever more expansive bureaucracies are complicit with this falsification. For instance, the continued expansion of policing and prisons relies on the perception that crime is getting "worse," that acts of violence are becoming more vicious, that criminals are becoming more intransigent, and so on.

These misperceptions are, in fact, carefully cultivated by a parade of institutional actors: police chiefs, police associations, prison guard unions, citizens groups, crime-watch organizations, aspiring politicians, and crusading journalists. Meanwhile, victims' rights groups, which enjoy official government standing with the Justice Department's Office for Victims of Crime and receive millions of dollars in annual federal subsidy through that office, work to keep sensational crime stories in the news. They also lobby the government that funds them for the passage of ever more punitive laws. Thus, crime panics continue apace, even accelerate, in an era of declining crime (Dyer 2000).

Fourth and last, because the protection of imperiled innocents now defines citizenship (Berlant 1997), to the exclusion of other interests that might come into play, and because social ills are attributed to moral shortcomings, rather than sociological or political-economic causes, the mechanisms heretofore described will admit only one variant of civic action: the passage of new laws to punish, new statutes to surveil; the application of new, more exacting definitions of infraction; the devising of new policies to reduce already negligible risks—in short, endless calls for ever more punitive forms of governance. These discursive technologies and modes of action form a closed, self-reinforcing system. When one takes exception to or resists this immoral morality, one is not being "civic"; one is not being "neighborly" or a "member of the community" but something else. A "public" shaped on this lathe can only speak and act in this manner. The citizen has only to choose his or her allotted role: victim, potential victim, or victim's advocate. Citizens, so defined, clamor for repression; the most repressive elements of the state ventriloquize the citizenry.

DE TOCQUEVILLE, IN REVERSE

Ever since de Tocqueville, observers of the American scene have admired the vibrancy of its voluntary associations (Offe 2006). Such admiration often appears alongside recognition of the role of a feisty, muckraking press in keeping politics "clean." In a recent run of liberal theory, this American social model—the promulgation of a robust civil society, the promotion of a free press—has been upheld as an effective means of shaping active citizens, as a guarantor of democratic participation, and as an effective check on excesses of state power. Even Marxist critics of unfettered market capitalism might find something useful in this picture. When civic groups facilitate the development of cosmopolitan modes of social solidarity, they enrich democracy. And when newspapers and electronic communications allow real debate, democracy is doubly enriched.

But what if, in the toss and tussle of events, some distorted permutation of civic engagement fostered an essentially negative citizen identity: the aggrieved citizenry as an abject, vulnerable class in need of protection? What if this worldview were to become planted squarely within the routine machinations of the mass media, tightly circumscribing public debate? What if groups, organized under this rubric, allied with the nation's most reactionary political factions and struck up a semi-official status with the most repressive apparatuses of the state? And what if the modes of political action thus engendered served not rational aims but increasingly irrational ones? Would the resulting social form still be "democratic"?

A democracy rigged up in this fashion begins to resemble a lynch mob. Of course, the lynch mob is as American as apple pie. But its slow eruption into politics on so many fronts prods profound questions about the direction of American democracy and emergent forms of class rule. Does the bureaucratic modernization of characteristically American forms of authoritarianism—electronic scarlet letters, televised public pillories, an old-fashioned penchant for sending black and brown men to prison— signal a regression to earlier forms of social control, or does it augur the advent of a new form of totalitarian society?

Notes

1. The Stewart case is disconcerting in many ways. In the trial, prosecutors played secretly recorded conversations between the attorney and her client and, moreover, charged the radical lawyer with interfering in their efforts to tape these privileged, confidential conversations. See Cassel 2004.

2. See Robertson 2001 for a somewhat different account of psychiatry's role in these matters.

3. I derive these numbers from various studies produced by the US Department of Justice's National Incidence Studies of Missing, Abducted, Runaway, and Thrownaway Children. See NISMART 2002a and 2002c; see also NISMART 2002b, 2004.

4

The Precipice of Debt

Brett Williams

When Americans imagine debt, they often use two contrasting metaphors: a swamp, quicksand, or a quagmire they are stuck in and a pile or mountain they cannot pare down or dent. More and more, I think of debt as something like Disney World's "Ghost Mountain": a roller coaster roaring up and plunging down sheer inclines, careening around jagged turns where banshees may grab you or suck you up but remain unseen. This Ghost Mountain of debt is equally unsettling because it is haunted in my imagination by the ghosts of the dispossessed. Seductive as this metaphor may be for me, partly because it speaks to the power of industry and government to redefine citizens as consumers, *precipice* captures in a less commodified way the current moment, not just because it is so perilous but also because it resonates with the sharp rise of wealthy borrowers, the steep slide experienced by many in the middle, and the disastrous fall of poor people who may need living wage jobs but receive usurious loans instead.

In this chapter, I offer four examples (out of many possibilities) of the relations between the surge in financial services and the varied life experiences of people as they soar through the opportunities provided by easy credit or struggle with the debt that those who received that easy credit resell to them in life-changing transactions. Each time government issues a tepid regulation, the industry discovers or invents a new market for debt. Each shift has profound implications for people's lives. I explore payday lending, subprime mortgages, and buying, selling, and collecting debt, as well as reporting, scoring, or trying to repair our human worth as established by credit reports. In each case, I discuss the relations between citizens, industry, and the state, as well as the tensions between peoples' needs, government responsibility to protect them from predators, an occasional, lackadaisical poke at oversight, and shifty maneuvers by the financial services industry to evade regulations and respond to new laws by creating deeper, broader, innovative new niches for capital accumulation. The wealthy and powerful disappear, at least from local view, as larger, less accountable, ghostly investors acquire more transparent local players.

I have been writing about credit and debt for ten years (Williams 1998, 2001, 2004), not because I find it entertaining, but because it is so central to modern life yet so hard to see and understand and also because industry strategies shift nimbly, government readily complies with these strategies, and debt drastically transforms people's lives. Each time I write about debt, the plotline has already started a new, zigzagging trajectory. In this chapter, I refer briefly to some of my previous work, but my purpose is to document the hardly believable changes that have occurred since the publication of my *Debt for Sale* in 2004 and to offer a new analysis suggested by these changes that affect us all in different ways. The precipice of debt looms over the new landscapes of inequality, bombarding us with schemes, seductions, disciplines, penalties, and evaluations of ourselves and shaking up our lives, enriching a few, rewarding some, and immiserating many more. As the layers of profit from debt stack up, they reproduce longstanding inequalities, create new, harsh relations between individuals and corporations, divert capital from productive investment, and shatter communities. We are awash in commodities but drenched in debt.

ACCUMULATION BY DISPOSSESSION

Marx described primitive accumulation as the original seizure of common, collective resources by industrialists who required peasants displaced from those commons to sell their labor to the owners of emerging factories. David Harvey argues that primitive accumulation recurs, perhaps not in its original form but through modern plunder ("accumulation by dispossession"), to solve crises of capital overaccumulation in harsh and violent ways. In many parts of the world, capital reaches into underfinanced places, pushes them into development projects by destroying more communal economies and taking land and resources for new projects, and then, to legitimize these projects, devalues the people and places. Constructing the dispossessed as loathsome others renders them unsympathetic and unworthy while making speculation wildly lucrative and ostensibly for their own good. Capital produces new spaces for investment, new grounded and bounded divisions of labor, and new, cheaper resources by penetrating preexisting social relations and transforming them into the institutional arrangements of a capitalist economy. And when capital moves on and out, it leaves devastation and debt (Harvey 2003). Accumulation by dispossession offers a useful lens for understanding why and how debt is so profitable and how capital accumulation escalates to dispossess people of their homes, their communities, their access to goods and services, their rights and duties as citizens, and even their identities.

Paul Smith (2007) argues that to describe the current moment, we must understand the purposes and consequences of modern forms of dispossession and expropriation that help solve crises of overaccumulation by unclogging those spots that stop the circulation of capital. To solve crises of excess idle capital, Smith attests, those obstacles must be removed, for example, through what Smith (2007:55) calls "wars of privatization [in Afghanistan and Iraq]," which offer opportunities to invest and accumulate capital and to draw all people into imposed international wage markets. In this chapter, I argue that the precipitous rise of capital investment in all kinds of debt is also a modern form of dispossession through accumulation, drawing profits from people who are strapped for cash and unable to participate fully in a capitalist society unless they buy the debt that circulates like a commodity through their communities.

Dispossession through Debt

Contemporary inequalities in the world of debt stem from the American economy's shift from manufacturing to finance capital in response to the 1970s crisis of overaccumulation. OPEC merchants chose American banks to hold their windfall, American manufacturers grew tired of mollifying organized labor, the rise of Asian manufacturing threatened their dominance of production, and technology made capital hypermobile. Finance capital offered new possibilities for investment by trapping debtors: selling debt to those struggling to make ends meet or needing credit.

The deindustrialization of America released our financial power throughout the world, and our seemingly boundless domestic market, buoyed by debt, allowed us to import inexpensive commodities produced by poorly paid workers from other countries. The United States became a sink for commodities, and our ever increasing debt fueled consumption (Harvey

2003; Ince 2006; Ranney 2003). Financial institutions redirected funds to the sale of debt, to citizens, collection agencies, other financial institutions, and Wall Street. Debt does not always mean dispossession; in fact, debt frequently finances the indebtedness of others. And debt is not static: as governments, corporations, individuals, and households increasingly live and die by debt, resourceful entrepreneurs have created problems that they then solve through more investment in selling and repackaging debt. They create niches in high-risk investments, online technologies, or poor communities and extract profit through usurious interest; they track potential debtors, identify their worth through imaginary lifeways, and score and sell their worth to prospective creditors who enable or debase them. Dispossession through expensive debt sold to devalued others demands easy access to deregulated credit for those who sell that debt.

Along with other critics of the rise of credit and debt, I tried in *Debt for Sale* to track the rise of household and student debt (Pollin 2003; Ranney 2003; Warren and Tyagi 2003). I have interviewed many debtors, puzzling over a state of affairs that one white woman described as "buying things that are already gone" by the time you "work long enough to pay for them" and that a twenty-five-year-old black man described as "the whole concept of free money. It's a disincentive to get a job. It's the whole idea of getting things without having to pay for them" (author interviews with Judy Watson, July 2000, and Luke Barnes, April 2007, respectively).

Scouring banking and financial services journals, I documented their evolving strategies to wrench profit from debt as they ploughed through "convenience users," who paid off their balances and thus, in essence, received free loans every month, and "revolvers," who carried a balance and paid interest; then into the college market, which each year brought new lambs into the fold, who did not know much about interest and fees but who would be potential "customers for life"; and, finally, into even higher interest gambits for the very poor through predatory lending (Williams 2004:65).

Like almost everything I documented in my book, the situation is changing so quickly that it is tricky to track: for example, student loans are in crisis. Student debt has received widespread media attention, but the many predators taking their cut off the top had slithered under the radar until the recent eruption of scandals documenting that lenders bribe university financial aid officials to recommend their companies to students. The student loan scandals are but one example of how quickly, sinisterly, and secretly the financial services industry develops new schemes and moves into new sites for accumulating profits (Davis 2006; Gaus 2006;

Gaylord 2006; Gertner 2006; Hadley 2006; Kamenetz 2006; Paley 2007; Rall 2007; Schema 2007; Wolff 2007). The student loan industry also illuminates the complicity of government in exacerbating, not easing, the harsh inequalities that emerge from allowing the operations of credit and debt to wreak economic, social, and emotional havoc.

Predatory Lending and the Dispossession of the Poor

In *Debt for Sale* (2004), I pointed to some of the worst abuses in predatory lending: that it filled the void when banks abandoned retail services in poor neighborhoods, quickly became the only game in town, charged usurious interest to the people who could least afford it, and exacerbated the already harsh inequality in American life (Hacker 2006; Lears 2006). I also noted how profitable predatory lending is for capital. Rent America and Cash America, for example, were among the fastest growing stocks on Wall Street (Williams 2004:101, 104).

As banks abandoned retail banking in poor neighborhoods, leaving behind gritty ATM machines dispensing crumpled bills in carryouts and gas stations, a flood of fringe banks gushed through the abandoned neighborhoods. These became the only places where poor people could cash checks, file tax returns, rent appliances, or get small, steep loans.

Since 2004 these grimy storefronts increasingly occupy transitional real estate, apparently warehousing properties for a wave of reinvestment and gentrification. Predatory lending shops glut poor but gentrifying neighborhoods in Washington DC, jammed into pockets of poverty and main avenues such as Georgia Avenue NW and H Street NE. The stigma of their presence appears to keep property values temporarily low; they warehouse property for speculation while signaling that this is a devalued place occupied by devalued people. We need to learn more about who owns these properties, when they purchased or leased these, and what their plans are, for developers take a long view of abandonment and investment and are expert at warehousing and speculative flipping. In many cities, we know that predatory lenders are sucking money out of neighborhoods, but we know little about what their occupation of urban real estate augurs.

Georgia Avenue in Washington is deeply contested and variably viewed as a culturally rich stretch of road along which the whole world is present through Trinidadian carryouts and bakeries, the liveliest go-go and reggae clubs in the city, Afrocentric health food stores, Latino-owned groceries, and evangelical storefront churches. The avenue is also littered by liquor stores, pawn shops, check cashers, and payday lenders, which, in the past few years, have attracted public notice as symbols of a neighborhood where you would not want to live or go. Thus, the location of these shops contributes to the devaluation of a place and may aid capital accumulation through stalling reinvestment in real estate, warehousing potentially valuable real estate with the intention of flipping it for luxury condominiums when the time is right. Corporate ownership is disguised by Plexiglas shields, tacky block letters in creatively misspelled words promising easy money, gritty linoleum floors, blank interiors without tables or chairs, and brochures and signs promising opportunities to purchase the debt that industry analysts describe as a product.

In 2004 these shops were owned and operated by national chains and corporations, which reaped titanic profits in interest and fees and savings on low wages and benefits. Residents living just east of Georgia Avenue, as I do, have watched these shops propagate and been besieged by fliers, junk mail, and online spam hawking rent-to-own furniture, instant cash advances, or "Cash for Houses" (Koprowsky 2006).

While annoying, the blight and spam spewed out by fringe banks are the least of regular people's problems. If a worker is paid by check, there are no local banks to cash it, and with bad credit, one cannot open a checking account in most banks. Thus, that worker is forced to rely on check-cashing services, which take a great chunk of interest off the top for the big capital that owns these establishments. Although check cashers have been around for almost twenty years, the most striking change in the past few years has been the ascendancy of the worst of the lot: payday lenders.

Payday lenders require you to prove that you are employed and hold checking accounts. To obtain a loan, you must provide a postdated personal check or an authorization for automatic withdrawal from your bank account. The lender provides the cash promised by the check, subtracting obscene interest.[1] The lender advances loans in increments of $100, usually for two weeks or until you receive the next paycheck. The largest loan is $500. The payday lender charges $15 for every $100 borrowed for two weeks. If you cannot repay the loan in full after the two-week period, you have to flip it for an additional term, paying interest again, so fees quickly exceed the amount borrowed. Typical borrowers flip or roll over their loans eight times, usually to pay for necessities such as medicine, car repairs, or emergencies (Center for Responsible Lending 2007).

Borrowers know that if they do not pay their interest, the payday lender has the right to pass their postdated checks through their bank accounts again and again, so the borrowers rack up bounced check fees both from the bank and from the lender. Payday lenders also threaten to garnish borrowers' wages or press criminal charges for writing a hot check. To avoid default, the person who has borrowed, say, $300, must pay another $45 to keep the loan outstanding. Sometimes borrowers pay the full amount owed on the original loan and then immediately take out another one with another fee. Whichever path they choose, they will pay $45 every two weeks to float a cash advance of $255, just to keep a loan out of default. The average borrower pays back $793 for a $300 loan.

From the perspective of capital, the interest and the hefty fees for over-drafts, rollovers, and late payments on predatory loans offer a thin, expansive sink for excess idle money, with wondrous returns from very little investment in inexpensive real estate, shoddy shops, and minimum-wage labor. Predatory lenders are virtually unregulated. The state ignores its responsibility to mediate the inequalities that inevitably arise as wealth and pauperism grow (Chen 2006; Mohl 2007; Singletary 2005; Wolff 2006). Payday lenders gain 90 percent of their revenue from the fees they strip from borrowers trapped in debt, and payday lending costs American families $4.2 billion in excessive fees (Center for Responsible Lending 2007). The gap between what a person borrows and has to repay, so harsh for a poor household, means little to lenders, who may or may not know what interest means in people's lives: a monstrous waste of limited resources, less to give to friends and family in need, and, often, depression and despair. As with many other commodities, the poor pay more for debt, and money is sucked out of their neighborhoods to enrich people who seem so far away, they might as well reside on the moon.

Payday lending depends on making loans borrowers cannot afford to repay. Lenders require payment in full at the end of two weeks, knowing that most borrowers cannot comply. As borrowers return and re-pay fees on the same small amount of money they borrowed, loan-flipping fees constitute the source of most of the payday lenders' profits, which are both deep, making multiple loans and collecting obscene fees in the same communities, and broad, reaching into poor neighborhoods all over the country. One borrower, Tanya Willis, testified before the DC city council on July 2, 2007: "They get you hooked, like the crack man. He has you, and he won't let you go. They held my check hostage and told me I could go to jail for writing a hot check."

ACE CASH EXPRESS: THE BIGGEST AND THE BLEAKEST

ACE Cash Express (formerly America's Cash Express and sometimes ACE Cash Advance) emerged in 1988 from Irving, Texas, to "take care of bankless Americans" (Hoover's 2007:1).[2] In addition to payday loans and check cashing, ACE offers multiple products—fax machines, prepaid phone cards, stamps, money grams, payment of utility bills—which gives them unwarranted credibility.

Predatory lenders themselves are borrowers: they raise money to open or acquire new stores and to fund their loans. In 2003 ACE refinanced its bank loan with a revolving loan of $165 million financed by a syndicate made up of nine banks (Raghunathan 2003). ACE bought 21 stores in Memphis, 10 in Arkansas, 5 in Louisiana, and 3 in Kentucky (*American Banker* 2004). By March 2004 Ace had acquired 39 more stores and owned 1,012 shops in thirty-six states and Washington DC. Loan fees and interest accounted for 34.2 percent of ACE's revenues of $268 million in FY2005, out of national revenues of $55 billion from cashing 190 million checks. In 2005 ACE borrowed funds to acquire 111 stores owned and operated by Popular Cash Express, which was based in Puerto Rico but operated shops in California, Arizona, Florida, and Texas as well. Popular CEO Richard Carrion expressed relief and anticipation: "We have been constrained in our ability to compete fairly against non-bank owned cheque cashing operations" (Sabatini 2006:1; Electronic Payments International 2005). By 2007 ACE was the largest payday lender in the nation, with more than 1,600 stores across thirty-seven states and Washington DC.

But 9/11, the Patriot Act, and the Enron scandal spurred a brief stab at federal regulation. The Sarbanes-Oxley Act of 2002 is supposed to hold business to seemingly reasonable standards of accuracy, honesty, accountability, and transparency; it wreaked panic and turmoil in the payday lending industry (Fuller 2007; Wirth 2007). Also in 2005, the FDIC issued rules restricting payday lenders' banking partners to six loans per borrower per year. Mike Loughran, an equity analyst with the Robins Group, drew on a well-worn analogy of substance abuse to describe new FDIC regulations: "What they are saying is you have to be payday loan-free for nine months of the year. It's still a profitable product, even at six loans per person a year" (Bergquist 2006:1; Augstums 2005; Hoover's 2007). But many banks bailed.

This panic and turmoil created yet another opportunity, however, for accumulation by dispossession. Private equity firms, whose executives worry less about negative publicity and the risk of new regulations, entered stage right. Between April 2005 and June 2006, nine private equity firms sought to buy ACE Cash Express. Private equity firms raise (borrow) money from pools of investors, including pension funds and wealthy individuals. In 2006 JLL Partners took ACE out of public trading by paying stockholders $30 a share, for $420.9 million altogether, and sheltered ACE under its umbrella as a private equity firm, where it relends its borrowed money at

ACE's exorbitant rates. This acquisition was considered a great deal and a discount because, although ACE was prospering in 2006, with a net income of $25 million and a growth rate of 8.5 percent, buyers were concerned that its demographic might be glutted. But they also knew that they could evade the new federal scrutiny of publicly traded companies (Bergquist 2006; Hoover's 2007; Terris 2007:1).

Many private equity firms are eying the space inhabited by "the unbanked," the industry's euphemism for the poor. Mark Sproule, industry analyst with Thomas Weisel Partners in New York, noted that "payday lending is a nice, recurring cash-flow business in a situation where there is significant demand from a customer base" seeking an alternative to bank overdraft fees (Bergquist 2006:1). Most industry analysts advise investors to expand slowly after a leveraged buyout and to pay off the financing through the cash flow of existing stores, digging deep into the resources of impoverished communities by offering more products to the payday lending monoline (Bergquist 2006).

For residents, this sweep of acquisitions distances them even more from the people taking their money, and the takeover of ACE by JLL illustrates these convoluted connections. In 1988 Paul Levy (former CEO of Yves Saint Laurent) founded JLL Partners (Fuquay 2006). JLL has a capital fund of $3.2 billion and moves nimbly enough to outperform more supersize firms, at least for now. Some of its fat profits come from J. G. Wentworth, LLC, which started up in 1991 to acquire health care providers, then migrated into purchasing "structured settlements" from people who win malpractice suits. Structured settlements allow the defendant to pay the plaintiff in installments, ensuring a steady stream of income over time for victims. But when plaintiffs decide later that they prefer, or need, a lump sum, Wentworth offers them "discounted settlements," a portion of what they have won, and then Wentworth collects the installments for a stout profit (Carey 2005:1). JLL CEO Shipowitz expressed his pleasure at the addition of ACE to this collection of takeovers, because of its "highly scalable, control-oriented operating model" and the potential for JLL to "accelerate growth through numbers of store openings" (*Fair Disclosure Wire* 2006:2).

JLL's acquisition of ACE enables it to thwart federal regulations and signals a reversal of the 2004–2005 trend, when predatory lenders went public to be traded on Wall Street. This acquisition could also foreshadow more consolidation as larger payday lenders and private equity firms acquire smaller chains and keep the transactions fairly secret because of the growing stigma and regulation payday lenders experience. For example, in

2006 California Check Cashing Stores LLC acquired thirty-three FastCash Stores to grow into ninety locations in northern California, Cash America paid $35 million to acquire Check Giant LLC, and Diamond Castle Holdings LLC bought Buckeye Check Cashing (Terris 2007).

In 2007 there were about twenty-two thousand payday lenders in the nation. Most of the companies began to slow plans for store development, because to raise the revenue that will produce the profits they desire, new stores usually experience losses until they have developed a profitable customer roster. So the industry is stuck in a contradiction: the importance of economies of scale—which demands that they move quickly to open as many sites as possible—and the need for efficient shops on the ground—which means digging deeper, offering more high-cost products to poor people, finding new markets while looking for new initiatives in a small place. For example, Cash America bought an online lending platform to barrage Internet users with cash advance spam. Thirty states and Washington DC require that payday lenders be licensed at a small payment of $500 a year. When more wide-ranging private equity firms acquire them, payday lenders and check cashers like ACE can still receive licenses if their on-the-ground shop in a particular place sells debt to residents. They are more than ripe for increasing, even transnational consolidation (Bergquist 2006; Terris 2007:1).

By 2006 hedge funds had joined the fray. Hedge funds also raise their capital from institutions that invest pension funds or endowments and from very wealthy, accredited investors for high-risk adventures that promise hefty returns. Their equally hefty management fees deserve note. James Simons of Renaissance Technologies, for example, made $3.7 billion in 2006 (Kuttner 2007). However, hedge funds buy and sell investments at warp speed, whereas private equity firms take a long view, which involves taking companies out of public trading and stripping them of expenses like workers, offices, factories, and advertising, as well as research and development, in order to resell them or take them back on the stock market (Henwood 2007). Private equity firms tend to invest for a longer time period than do hedge funds, which "shoot for quicker game." Hedge funds borrow huge sums, use that borrowed money to purchase companies, collect large dividends, cut the costs of labor, sell off the money-making assets, and unload the detritus. The interest they pay for their leveraged buyouts is tax deductible. They are taxed at a "partnership rate" of 15 percent, which is less than half the standard corporate rate, and they evade the disclosure required of corporations traded publicly. They also invest heartily in political campaigns (Henwood 2007).

In 2007 these companies worked together happily, helping each other in a massive buyout of debt-selling institutions. But tensions loomed. "It's not like the old days, when banks held most of the debt," said John Danhaki, founding partner of a private equity firm managing investments valued at $3.7 billion. "You don't know who the lenders are and whether you can get waivers if you need them. Hedge funds can blow up your company" (Sender 2006:C1). Private equity firms are increasingly wary of borrowing from hostile hedge funds and concerned that their portfolio companies might fall to hedge funds, for hedge funds are less predictable and more ruthless than banks. Meanwhile, hedge funds carry such wide-ranging portfolios that they rarely worry that a single company might collapse or that poor people ultimately pay for their loans (Sender 2006). As competition increases among private equity firms and hedge funds, they take ever greater risks with borrowed money, which increases the potential for larger damage to the economy at the same time that it fuels inequality. The payday borrower, who experiences the highest interest rates of all on very small amounts of money, is connected through that loan to financial titans who borrow from other wealthy people to relend it to the poor at usurious, high-profit interest rates (Kuttner 2007).

But a problem, and therefore another opportunity, looms: the prepaid debit card. Payday lenders offer these in their stores, but several companies urge employers to free themselves from paper altogether by making prepaid debit cards available to "progressive employers looking to streamline payroll operations" (TFG Card Solutions, Inc., http://www.tfgcard.com/index.php, accessed July 2007). Promoted as assistance to "un-banked employees," the prepaid card offers employers the opportunity to pay by direct deposit and "realiz[e] significant savings while helping their employees avoid the escalating costs associated with check cashing fees" (TFG Card Solutions, Inc., http://www.tfgcard.com/index.php). In 2004 TFG Card Solutions rolled out a full line of the following on its website:

- Prepaid debit card cost cutting/Benefit enhancing objectives by US employers

- Increased security measures around elimination of fraudulent activities associated with paper checks by increasing use of payroll cards

- Alternative offering of payroll cards to "bridge the gap" which extends direct deposit to every employee

- Growing need of disaster preparedness programs—greatly reducing delivery issues in a heightened time of need

In 2006 Sueldo Paycard, Inc., began to provide the following on its website (http://www.sueldocard.com/welcome.html, accessed July 2007):

- Prepaid debit card cost cutting/Benefit enhancing objectives by US employers
- Increased security measures around elimination of fraudulent activities associated with paper checks by increasing use of payroll cards
- Alternative offering of payroll cards to "bridge the gap" which extends direct deposit to every employee
- Growing need of disaster preparedness programs—greatly reducing delivery issues in a heightened time of need
- Worldwide acceptance and increase access points for employees to access their pay

Thus, another ghostly, clone-like, mysteriously consolidated firm rises from the constructed obsolescence of checks and the plight of check cashing companies.

QUE SERA, SERA: WHAT EVER HAPPENED TO GOVERNMENT?

The Community Reinvestment Act (CRA), passed in 1977 and still the law of the land, requires banks to invest productively and make affordable loans in the neighborhoods where they do business. Whenever a bank contemplates change, the CRA kicks in, and activists can challenge the bank's compliance with the act. Aimed at curbing redlining and abandonment of poor neighborhoods by banks, the CRA should have precluded problems of predatory lenders, but the latter have found many ways to defang it. Activists have almost never won a challenge. When invoked at all, the CRA has often simply fueled gentrification. Most important, bank mergers and acquisitions have made companies so large that it is hard to define what their "community" is. They appear to be nowhere, owned by phantoms.

The Supreme Court's Marquette decision in 1978, however, has reverberated powerfully throughout the business of selling debt. This decision held that credit card issuers could charge the interest rates allowed in their home states to debtors living in other places. In the early days following the decision, banks raced to South Dakota and Delaware, where usury caps were highest. When the high interest rates of predatory lenders violate state usury laws, the resourceful lenders simply partner with banks from other states. Until 2005 payday loan–bank partnerships were everywhere: ACE, for example, offered payday loans in partnership with the Republic Bank of Kentucky and with First Bank of Delaware in Texas, Arkansas, and Pennsylvania. In Ohio and Florida, payday lenders issued loans through Goleta, a bank in California (Cassell-Low 2003).

Some states have been more vigilant in trying to regulate payday lenders. Massachusetts and North Carolina threw the bums out. Georgia has made it a felony to issue a payday loan, punishable by up to five years in prison and a $10,000 fine (Kiser 2006). Illinois tries to regulate payday loans, through a law that reduced interest from $22 to no more than $15.50 on $100 borrowed for two weeks. Illinois also restricts interest to $44 for month-long loans of $100. The law caps total loan amounts at $1,000 or one-quarter of a borrower's monthly salary, whichever is less. The most important change may be a provision prohibiting fees from kicking in each time a loan is rolled over.

The pathetic history of credit card regulation teems with hyperbole and disingenuousness, and the Illinois case is no exception. Laws like this will boomerang, argued its opponents. Smaller loan outlets will be forced to lay off employees, and larger ones will do so simply to maintain high rates of profit. These misleading arguments play on myths of mom and pop lenders offering storefront cash to residents in neighborhoods where major banks are unwilling to play ball. In opposition to the Illinois bill, the president of the Illinois Small Loan Association argued, "What happens now to someone who needs a loan to fix their car? I can't give it to them because maybe they're a bigger credit risk and then they lose their jobs because they don't have their car" (Chase and Noel 2005:1). Indeed. The military offered significant support in all four states (Illinois, Massachusetts, Georgia, and North Carolina); they believe that debt harms soldiers' readiness to fight and to resist corruption (Paletta 2007).[3] In Washington DC, a vigorous grassroots campaign persuaded the city council to vote unanimously to cap payday loans at an interest rate of 24 percent (with Marion Barry abstaining and the industry pouring unprecedented resources into lobbying the council and the Congress to reverse the vote).

But in 2005 payday loan stocks dropped after the FDIC tightened guidelines for the banks that had partnered with companies like ACE. The FDIC began to require banks to ensure that payday loans were really what they claimed to be—short-term emergency cash instead of a regular stream of interest-laden income. The FDIC argued that customers taking out these very high-cost loans really needed longer-term credit. ACE stocks plummeted, and JLL bought it at a discount. The FDIC regulates banks but not payday lenders, except to require that they be licensed in the jurisdictions where they operate, but they and their bank partners have been resourceful at evading those regulations as well (Chen 2004; Dash and Labaton 2006; White 2006).

For example, ACE sought safe harbor in Texas by proposing a credit service offering product with its banking partners: essentially, an installment loan that allows the customer to make ten payments over twenty weeks (*Fair Disclosure Wire* 2006). "While it is frustrating that the FDIC appears to be seeking the elimination of a product that many Americans desire, we remain committed to our mission of delivering products that our customers want," vowed Jay Shipowitz, CEO of ACE (*Fair Disclosure Wire* 2006:1). Shipowitz expects that the CSO rates of 20 percent will offset the loss of fees from payday loans.

FORECLOSURE FREEFALL

Until the summer of 2006, the housing bubble propped up the credit economy as the value of houses increased by 70 percent in the country at large, sometimes as much as 100 percent on the coasts. For middle-class home owners, the housing bubble was a godsend, offering them access to home equity loans, which, unlike other kinds of debt, are tax-deductible. Many middle-class home owners used their houses as ATM machines or honey pots (Henderson 2007). Home mortgage debt increased by $3 trillion between 2001 and 2006 as home owners refinanced their overvalued houses through home equity loans. As housing prices were bid up, home owners' equity in houses rose, and many borrowed more, not for property, but for "equity extraction," which allowed them to pay off other debts at a tax-deductible, lower interest rate. Equity extraction is problematic and worrisome, however. Home owners with adjustable rate mortgages may find that their mortgages become too high to pay. Middle-class baby boomers may face retirement with fewer assets than they expect (Ernst et al. 2006).

The subprime housing market and its consequences are very different. Subprime mortgages lured buyer/borrowers with low introductory teaser rates. Sometimes they promised borrowers a second mortgage to help pay the first. Lenders, in turn, relied on financing that bought the loans as part of packages of small pieces of many loans, which are riskier but relatively unregulated. Subprime mortgages fueled the economy. Many unlikely people were able to buy houses, nurturing a boom in real estate that, in turn, released easy credit to investment firms, whose capital bolstered stock prices and corporate profits and fueled buyouts such as those engulfing payday loans. The mortgages they offered were creative and suspect: they included no-documentation and no-down payment loans, prepayment penalties (making it more expensive to refinance), inflated interest rates after the first two years, balloon payments and refinancing plans that were impossible for people to meet, and costly, worthless add-ons like credit insurance and shady underwriting practices (Bloice 2007).

The subprime housing market is a well-known predator in poor neighborhoods and, like the old redlining, appears to target people of color. A colleague of mine, a well-regarded anthropologist, described his encounter with a subprime lender:

> About three years ago, I decided to buy a house in Philly. I was done with school, makin' some good money, and had decided Philly was where I wanted to settle. I started looking at listings and was just about to go and start talking to agents when I said, "You know what? I'm gonna be living in a neighborhood of color. I'm a black man. Let me make sure I give my business to my people." So I went to a realtor in my neighborhood that was black owned and operated. On a side note, I am a pretty unassuming guy (I hope). I don't wear my credentials on my sleeve, and I kick it clothingwise like most folks from the neighborhood. So when I entered the office (which was crowded, I tell you, crowded with people wanting to buy houses, all people of color), I was any other brother off the street, thirty-one years old at the time, tryin' to buy me a house. Without asking my financial situation, my income, or anything, I was given a sheet of paper of houses. Now these, if you looked closely, were all owned by the realtor. They all were for sale, and they all could be had for an interest rate of about 18 percent!!! At this point, I didn't blink because I could tell this was going to be a rich experience and I wanted to play it out.
>
> They tried to force me to sign an agreement with them that would guarantee that they would receive $6,000 agent fees whether I found a house or not through them in six months. And before they would even show me any additional listings or any of their houses. Keep in mind, most of the houses they were selling were in the $30,000 to $50,000 range (Philly rowhomes), so this $6,000 fee would be anywhere from a 12 to 20 percent agent's fee, as opposed to a standard 6- to 7-percent fee.

> The point being, they had a captive audience that was gener-
> ally over a barrel, and they had figured out every way to screw an
> uninformed public. I have all sorts of stories like this with real-
> tors, tax preparers, and so on, that I have experienced by going
> into situations and letting people assume what they wanted
> about me, and me, with my curiosity, letting it play out.

In the subprime mortgage market, borrowers pay about two percentage points more in interest for their loans. Their two-year adjustable rate
mortgages (ARMs) have grown harder to refinance at rates they can afford,
and many will lose their houses to foreclosure. In 2006 one in five home
loans was subprime, and blacks and Latinos were 30 percent more likely to
pay this higher interest rate (Bloice 2007; Eckholm 2006). In Boston, 70
percent of African American and Latino borrowers who earned more than
$100,000 in 2005 received subprime loans (Callahan 2007). In May 2007,
176,137 homes were foreclosed on, and in neighborhoods with many foreclosed homes, house values drop more severely because foreclosed houses
sell at lower prices. These drops slash home owners' equity, or wealth, in
their houses and make them, in turn, more likely to foreclose because they
cannot sell (Baker 2007; Blanton 2007c; Morgenson and Bajaj 2007).

The poor are often the bellwether of debt-produced havoc in the
American landscape of inequality. In business as usual, the first to experience foreclosure are the poorest home owners. Working with citizen
activists' ONE (Organization for a New Eastside), Susan Hyatt and her students have explored foreclosure rates in the Eastside neighborhood of
Indianapolis, where the median income is approximately $25,000 and the
mortgage foreclosure rate was the highest in the country in 2005. Hyatt
calls Eastside "Ground Zero in the fight against vacant and abandoned
houses resulting from predatory loans and fast foreclosure schemes"
(Hyatt 2006:2). On every block in the neighborhood, researchers found
one-third to one-half of the houses vacant, abandoned, and sometimes
deteriorating, although remaining residents described a once tightly knit
neighborhood (Hyatt 2006:2).

The roots of these problems lie not only in lost jobs and an abyss in
social services and health care, but also in the activities of subprime lenders
who trawl neighborhoods like the Eastside to peddle new roofs or siding
and offer home equity loans based on a grossly exaggerated market value
of the home, bearing high interest rates and hefty fees for late payments
and for rolling over the loans. In 2006 subprime loans grew into a $500 bil-
lion industry, snagging three times the volume of 2002 and composing one-

fifth of all mortgages. Capital investment flows into properties it once abandoned, pushing prices up and constructing luxury housing. Many places face crises in affordable housing, and these crises also displace people. Friends and kin are then obliged to take them in and, in some cases, ultimately cast them out on the streets if they become problematic. Gentri-fication has squeezed the supply of affordable housing and increased homelessness and doubling up.

Susan Hyatt and her students were prescient; most analysts were surprised by the explosion of defaults beginning in the fall of 2006, which moved from the Rust Belt (West Virginia, Pennsylvania, Indiana, Ohio, Kentucky) to unexpected places like California, Arizona, Nevada, and Colorado (Sherwell 2007). Immigrants have been among the first to be hard hit, partly because they received more than their share of subprime loans. Latinos were sold 375,000 subprime mortgages, and 73,000 of their loans were in foreclosure by 2007. Latino immigrants are particularly vulnerable, not only because of their many subprime loans but also because their incomes are low and many work in construction, which will be decimated by the burst of the bubble (Downey 2007).

Home buyers in the prime market may not feel the squeeze, but the so-called subprime borrowers do. The finance companies that make the loans are not regulated like banks. They borrow money from Wall Street to use for loans and then buy the loans back from the lenders, repackage them into securities and sell them to investors, who get greedy and reckless during a boom, then bail out quickly when they face falling profits. In 2007 foreign investors began bailing out, as did domestic holders of mortgage securities and derivatives. Subprime lenders, starting with New Century Financial Corporation, began to collapse, sparking calls for mild regulations that might forbid lenders from selling houses at interest rates way above going rates to people they know cannot afford these. But donations from the subprime mortgages have bucked up many key political campaigns, including half the members of the House Financial Services Committee and Christopher Dodd, the chair of the Senate Banking Committee (Blanton 2007b; Ordower 2007).

In 2007 delinquencies and foreclosures among owners with weak credit have continued to surge, along with mortgage rates. The ratio of home equity to home value has fallen to about 50 percent. Unsold homes offer prospective buyers a year's abundant supply. Soon this may be glutted by all the homes people lose to foreclosure and auction as alarmingly high interest replaces low teaser rates of subprime mortgages after two years (Baker 2007). Monthly mortgage payments on about $600 billion of subprime loans will increase throughout 2007 by as much as 50 percent (Bajaj 2007b). But business has begun pressing another option: purchasing tax-deductible mortgage insurance (Blanton 2007a, 2007b, 2007c; Peterson 2007).

Higher interest rates do curb spending and raise the cost of borrowing, but debt-driven spending has long fueled our economy. How can the federal government help, with the gross federal debt exceeding $8.3 trillion, each soldier in Iraq costing $299,000 (little of which goes to the soldier), and the large interest on the debt devouring revenue for other programs while that interest transfers wealth from taxpayers to bondholders and debt from present to future generations? "It turns out that George Bush has [will have] the biggest ARM in the world" (Ferguson 2006:50; Hyatt 2006; Trumbull 2006; Uchitelle 2006; Weisbrot 2006; Wolff 2005).

BUYING AND SELLING DEBT

One large agency goes under the disingenuous name of *Asset Acceptance*, which apparently translates as "Taking Your Stuff." Asset specializes in people with such small debts that these once flew beneath the industry's radar as a small cost of doing business. Lenders sometimes hesitated to tail the debtors for a long period of time, fearing that negative publicity overrode the profits from very small debts. As the sheer numbers of these small debts have grown, however, they have come to offer another profitable sink for finance capital. Collection companies like Asset Acceptance buy a portfolio of bad debt that is just a bare-bones list of debtors' names, their social security numbers, the amount owed to creditors, and the date of last activity. They acquire these portfolios at a discount or in a bundle of derivatives, and they keep the costs of these portfolios low by loading up with debts that creditors have given up on, paying, for example, two cents on the dollar.

Asset Acceptance employs a large staff, ranging from attorneys who work on commission to hapless, low-wage workers who make maddening daily telephone calls to hapless debtors. Sometimes collection companies pursue debtors years after they have defaulted on small loans. The debtor may not even remember the loan or the credit card involved, but it has accrued interest and late fees all the while. Borrowers often do not know who these companies are—they seem to arrive from another planet, with names that mean nothing. In debtors' dealings with Asset, they have no right to examine the original credit card bill or even to know which bank loaned them money, because once Asset bundles and buys the debt, it becomes an encumbered commodity owned by Asset and owed by the debtor.

If constant abusive telephone harassment at all hours, calls to neighbors, relatives, employers, and coworkers, threats, and offers to settle at some lower amount do not work, Asset takes borrowers to small claims court. These courts offer cheaper filing fees, require less evidence to start a suit, and impose less onerous requirements for protecting defendants' rights. Small claims judges plow through dozens of claims a day, improving the chance of a quick default judgment. Asset's strategy of going after debtors in small claims court has affected tens of thousands of people around the country and buoyed the burgeoning business of reaping profit from consumer debt. When a debtor enters this collection process, her costs explode: one woman in Phoenix, for example, defaulted on $3,000 to Discover (after a divorce) and then lost a court judgment to Asset, which cost her $9,500 because it included court costs and the collection company's fees. Now the company takes $100 out of her bimonthly paycheck of $635.00 (Chan 2006; Hwang 2004). A nurse in New York who had retired on disability received a bill from Asset for $2,300, including a number of payments for gas—although she has never had a driver's license or a car. The collection agency got a court order freezing her bank account, even though it could not demonstrate that the debt was valid. Another retiree was taken to small claims court for $8,000 in tuition and fees at a beauty school she had never attended (Hwang 2004).

The success of Asset illustrates just the tip of an industry that thrives on buying and collecting debt as growing numbers of creditors—from credit card issuers, to telephone companies, to hospitals and gyms—sell their bad debts as a source of revenue. They file tens of thousands of cases each year and process twenty-six million accounts. Asset alone owns sixteen million accounts, including $4.2 billion in debt bought in 2005, when it went public at $17 a share.

Sometimes collectors play rough. The *Boston Globe* Spotlight Team detailed debt collection practices in a four-part series titled "Debtors' Hell," which can be accessed online, along with audios of people telling their own stories (Rezendes et al. 2006; http://www.boston.com/news/special/spot light_debt/part3/page1.html, accessed June 2007). The *Globe* reporters uncovered frightening collection practices in Boston involving the repossession of automobiles. In one case, a single mother who mistakenly thought that a social service agency had paid an old credit card debt and who had never received notice that she was being sued, lost her car to thugs, who caught her early in the morning helping her small children get ready for school. Thugs came to another woman's house just after midnight to repossess her 1997 Ford Thunderbird for an unpaid credit card debt. Disabled with lupus and Crohn's disease, this woman had lost her cleaning business and defaulted on a $430 debt to Providian. To erase that debt and get her car back, she had to pay $1,758.

These thug-like collectors are actually "constables," a colonial era des-ignation for officials with no training, oversight, or registration responsi-bilities with the state. They can charge whatever fees they like for seizure of assets, including $600 and $900 for towing. The *Globe* team provides the biographies of some—illegal gamers, gin mill operators, convicted felons, and even debtors who have declared bankruptcy. When debtors cannot raise the cash to pay the debt and the seizure fees, their cars are sold at auc-tion, where the proceeds are split among the constable, the tow lot, and the creditor. County sheriffs help out with collections too. Between 2001 and 2005, sheriffs in five counties seized 2,500 cars for collection agencies for a fee of $600 a car.

In another optimistic move during the 1970s, Congress passed the Fair Debt Collection Practices Act in 1977 to prohibit abusive, deceptive, and unfair tactics by collection agencies. But several new laws have undermined this effort to rein in predatory collectors: the 1996 deregulation of penalty fees for late payments, which released lenders from a maximum fee of 25 percent, and the Supreme Court's endorsement of "Universal Default," which allows lenders to change a customer's interest rate without warning. These two regulations hammered borrowers hard enough to sour their debt. The final straw was the new, ineptly named Bankruptcy and Abuse Prevention and Consumer Protection Act of 2005, which, by making it vir-tually impossible for individuals to file for a second chance, empowered an aggressive and abusive debt-collection industry that is freed from the con-cern that borrowers might find reprieve from debt piling up from excessive, unexpected penalty fees and wide-ranging interest. Debt collectors inhabit another layer of transactions in the profits that accumulate from debt.

The Federal Trade Commission (FTC), which enforces the federal law governing debt collection, reported in April 2006 that it had received 66,627 complaints against third-party debt collectors in 2005, more than against any other industry and six times the number in 1999. The National Consumer Law Center, an advocacy group in Boston, reports that com-plaints against debt collectors have risen because of a combination of forces, including the sheer growth in number of collection agencies using aggressive and unscrupulous tactics. In July 2005 the FTC won a $10.2 mil-lion judgment against Providian, whose customers complained that they had been hit with late fees for payments sent in on time but not credited to their accounts for days or weeks and that those penalty fees pushed them over their credit limits, sparking more fees. This was an unusual victory. More often, the Office of the Comptroller of the Currency sends an *advi-sory* letter saying that banks should not raise rates without disclosure in full.

Professor Elizabeth Warren of Harvard Law School testified before Congress that "the controller's office should do more than express discomfort with the practices of credit card companies. The regulators did not say that 'these are unfair practices, they are unsafe and unsound and don't do them.' Instead they said it's a problem. Look, if they think it's a problem, then tell the credit card companies to stop doing it" (Warren 2007:3; McGeehan 2004). In 2004, on a graduated region-by-region basis, citizens won the right to a free credit report from each credit scorer. Jennifer Kingston quipped in the *New York Times* that "*freedom* may be just another word for something else to buy" (Kingston 2004:C4). They will not go gently into the loss of the big business of selling reports, and when you get a free report, you will be spammed with pitches to buy related products with pricey monthly fees. You can also expect to be spammed by swindlers pretending to offer free credit reports but actually seeking personal information for wicked schemes.

SCORING IDENTITIES, MEASURING WORTH, CONSTRUCTING CITIZEN-CONSUMERS

Racial and gendered discrimination was once legally rife in the credit industry. For example, until 1974 a married woman could not hold credit in her own name. This discrimination (as well as bias on account of race, religion, ethnicity, national origin, and disability, but not zip code) was outlawed by the feminist-initiated, cross-class alliance that won passage of the Equal Credit Opportunity Act in 1974.

But sophisticated computer technologies and tracking practices have concealed lenders' blatant racism and sexism. Now, every detail of an individual's income, outlay, borrowing, spending, and paying back is accessible to potential lenders, who can tailor credit offers, credit limits, payment plans, and interest rates to fit each profile. Your credit card becomes your identity, your right to be an adult, your right to be a citizen. Because capital accumulation relies on sinking excess into personal loans, then reaping vast profits through interest, you are dispossessed of not only your resources but also important parts of your self, your goals, and the possibilities for your life.

The Fair Isaac Corporation (FICO) produces a credit score for every citizen, based on information provided Fair Isaac by three agencies (Equifax, Experion, and TransUnion) that monitor credit-related activities. We all bear Fair Isaac's computerized credit scores in cyberspace, sometimes with pride, sometimes like a scarlet A. A FICO score may be as high as 850, averaging out at 720. If yours is below 620, you are a subprime person, charged the heaviest interest rates, if you have access to credit at all. A FICO score is like a thermometer. It may be the most vital of all statistics measuring and evaluating Americans, determining whether you can borrow, how much you will pay for automobile or life insurance, whether you can rent a home, whether you need to pay an extra deposit for a telephone or utility hookup. Credit scoring is such a profitable industry that the Fair Isaac Corporation, which dominates the market with its FICO score, reported $798.7 million in revenue in 2005, and the three reporting agencies are trying to capture some of that revenue by introducing their own scores (Darlin 2006).

Five qualities do matter in measuring your worth: how much you owe, how punctually you pay, how long you have been borrowing, how often you request new credit, and the types of credit accounts you hold. Timely payment of rent and utility bills—which people prioritize because they must— do not count, but eviction decimates your score. Failure to make child support payments does not matter either.

Your original lender monitors your score, and under the rule of Universal Default, this lender can change your interest rate without warning, for a number of reasons: a late payment on a telephone or utility bill; your lender's sense that you are overextended, acquiring too many cards, or easing too close to your limit; making late payments on any of those cards. Your lender can also take away your card for any of these reasons. Your score declines every time another party makes an inquiry about it, because this signals that perhaps you are trying to borrow more money somewhere. Thus, lenders not only monitor but also *predict* your behavior. Employers, landlords, rental agents, car dealers, and insurance providers do not treat credit scores as thermometers, which help caregivers diagnose and heal, but as inscriptions about your value as a consumer so that debt merchants can make decisions about offering you a home, a car, a job, or an affordable interest rate. If you have become a bad debtor because your life is hard, or your partner has died or has battered or abandoned you, or you have taken in an ill or elderly relative, or your wages are low, it does not matter (Smale 2004).

Poor people today are devalued as full citizens, in part, because they have "bad credit," which haunts them and excludes them from transactions that middle-class people take for granted: paying bills and buying books online, renting cars, buying tickets, and reserving hotel rooms are just a few examples. If you have been a customer at a subprime lender such as Household Finance or Rent-A-Center, the lender assumes that you must be a risk. When you shop for a car and the agent asks for your driver's license, he immediately pulls your credit report. Potential landlords check your score, as do potential employers. If you have high-interest department store cards, these cards will lower your score because individuals who charge in department stores are considered subprime chargers. Your car insurance rates vary according to your credit score, regardless of your actual driving record and even though you are required to insure your car. Beginning a debt consolidation program lowers your score, unless you consolidate your debts before you "go bad." Closing out your cards and getting a debt consolidation loan means that you have gone bad.

With bad credit, you are not a full human being anymore. If your lender charges off your account and turns it over to a collection company, you can be ruined financially. This happens with increasing frequency with medical bills, which some people are likely to triage because these come every month but do not appear as frightening as others. Debtors may feel that they did nothing wrong in getting hurt or sick. Credit reports do not show that you are a good person working for low wages, but they do reveal many other things about your lifestyle.

Somehow, magically, more capital comes to the rescue through credit repair. Of the many companies rushing to fill this niche, I offer one example: Professional Independent Contractors Association (PIC), which has a "continued desire to grow through service to others" and whose "marquee service is credit repair" offered by PowerPoint-armed "independent representatives": "In business for yourself but not by yourself....Your entry into our business requires a small one-time investment of only of [sic] $399.00" (Professional Independent Contractors Association, http://www.picol.com/, accessed August 2007). Do not even try to count the ways people can be exploited by these companies.

Another opportunity has emerged: imparting financial literacy. The Bankruptcy Act requires that all debtors take a one-hour-credit counseling class before filing, but too often debtors never learn about this requirement. Judges' hands are tied—they must dismiss the application if the debtor fails to take the class—and many judges resent the injustice of having to do so (Rogal 2006). These policy initiatives appear to hold that if debtors were financially literate, they would not have financial problems. Susan Hyatt writes:

> On March 21, 2006, the *Indianapolis Star* featured an editorial entitled, "Do your homework, then buy a home." It begins: "Our position: Better financial education is key to ending Indiana's status as America's foreclosure capital." Even after acknowledging the effects of factory closings and other macro-economic

trends on foreclosure rates, the editorial then goes on to state: "Yet the rate of foreclosures also is representative of the low level of financial literacy, which leaves many Hoosiers prone to the kind of poor choices that can lead to foreclosures and bankruptcy." [Hyatt 2006:4]

In the spring of 2006, I spoke at the annual meeting of National Student Partnerships, a student-run organization that helps poor clients with everyday problems. I was paired with a speaker who also spoke on credit and debt. After I talked of the horrors of predatory lending, the other speaker instructed students on how to help their clients repair their credit scores. This approach to financial literacy is everywhere, unfortunately, an insidious neoliberal carrot offering false hope that the plight of poor debtors lies in their financial ignorance and that they must learn the vocabulary, repair credit, and save.

And so it goes: crisis generates accumulation. Our whole economy teeters on a precipice of debt. The poor have done the most to mop up surplus capital, in the process, being dispossessed of their resources, their neighborhoods, their homes, their biographies, and their standing as full citizens. If they are incarcerated, they will owe interest on their steadily mounting debts while in prison. And like Marx's reserve army, the poorest people live in the world of cash and barter and do not share in the privileges and opportunities of the shifting, stratified, ghostly economy of credit and debt (Austin 2004; Venkatesh 2006). They simply bear the deadly brunt of unproductive investment in buying and selling debt rather than in providing jobs, affordable housing, and decent schools where children learn to demand justice.

Acknowledgments

Many thanks to Jillian Aldebron, Drew Asson, Amy Belasco, Catherine Besteman, Michelle Carnes, Jane Collins, Samuel Colon, Ariana Curtis, Micaela di Leonardo, Hugh Gusterson, Regina Harrison, Susan Hyatt, Bill McKinney, Christopher Pitt, Roger Lancaster, Elizabeth Sheehan, Emily Steinmetz, Shannon Telenko, and Yvonne Jones for being attentive and thoughtful colleagues who send me helpful articles about debt and commiserate with me about its injustices.

Notes

1. An activist group obtained the business plan from a payday lender that advised its employees not to enter the percentage but just the amount owed, because percentages make customers nervous. Employees are instructed to answer questions about interest rates by saying, "We charge 15 percent on $100 loans," but never to add that this loan comes at an annual percentage rate of 805 percent.

2. CNG Financial Corporation (also known as Check'n Go) is another privately held payday lender, which shares the payday loan market in Washington with ACE. CNG is owned mostly by brothers David and Jared Davis of Mason, Ohio, where Check'n Go began in 1995. Check'n Go is supposed to be a subsidiary of Eastern Specialty Finance, which appears in no database except licensing. By 1997 Check'n Go offered payday loans in seventy stores and six states. Denying his business's role in preying on the poor, Jared Davis explained, "You have to meet minimum requirements to do business with us. We don't deal with poor people" (Sekhri 1997:7).

3. Even soldiers are unsafe from collectors. One soldier leaving for Iraq received a last-minute telephone call informing him that his house, in Fayetteville, was to be foreclosed on. This kind of threat is not unusual, even though soldiers are supposed to be protected by the 2006 Service Members Civil Relief Act, which caps payday loans to soldiers at annual interest rates of 35 percent. Despite this act, Marines have returned to Camp Pendleton to find that their cars have been improperly sold to pay for storage and towing. Wells Fargo foreclosed on the home of a young Army couple in northern Ohio, and Sgt. Michael Gaskins and his wife, Melissa, lost their family truck and $6,000 to a hospital credit union while he was in Iraq (Chan 2006; Henriques 2005; Paletta 2007). The banking industry fought the relief act aggressively, arguing that the act singled out and discriminated against particular sorts of lenders and that, instead, GIs should take financial literacy classes (Kuttner 2007).

5

Integration and the Collapse of Black Social Capital

Nostalgia and Narrative
in the Neoliberal City

Michelle R. Boyd

We've forgotten how strong we were when we were segregated. We forgot the morality of Black people, that we've always been a good people.

—*Phillip O'Bannon, President, South Side Chicago branch of the NAACP*

In February 2006, Chicago's free weekly *N'Digo* published a cover story titled "Segregation—Was It Better?"[1] The piece, which appeared in a special black history month issue, took the deaths of Rosa Parks and Coretta Scott King as the starting point for a consideration of "the good and the bad of segregation" (Muhammad 2006:6–7). Several leaders and scholars discussed a wide variety of troubles plaguing African Americans in the post–civil rights era, but altogether they told a strikingly similar story. The problem, they asserted, was not that integration was incomplete, nor ineffective in attacking institutionalized racism. Rather, the problem was integration itself.[2]

Take Jocelyn Delk, an employee of The HistoryMakers, a company that creates African American oral history videos. She argued that blacks' current problems are "more internal than external" and that "integration has led to a loss of the sense of community. The idea of 'it takes a village to raise a child' is almost completely gone" (Muhammad 2006:6). University of Pennsylvania professor Michael Eric Dyson concurred: "We've forgotten that we are all in the same boat...when we couldn't escape, we understood we had to be each other's keepers. It's important to understand the necessity of what segregation taught—the necessity for communion with one another" (Muhammad 2006:7). These observers argue that fraternization with whites has weakened African Americans' mutual commitment to one another. They suggest that, whatever the problems with racial segregation, it had the benefit of forcing its victims to depend on one another and that this social connection has been lost with integration.

Most interesting, however, is how those who hold this view of integration assign responsibility for the lapse in racial solidarity. Phillip O'Bannon, president of the city's South Side branch of the NAACP, echoes the comments of others: "Integration stripped the Black community of its most prominent citizens, leaving an underclass to maintain the community" (Muhammad 2006:7). According to O'Bannon and others, integration fostered intraracial discord by robbing blacks in the middle class of their collectively oriented values, luring them away from the central city, and leaving poor blacks bereft of their example. Thus, blacks are the perpetrator of racial disunity, but racial integration is its driving force.

This view of integration is important because it contains a moral tale about the rise and fall of black social capital—its cultivation during segregation, its corruption by integration, and its recovery through black gentrification.[3] Scholars have defined *social capital* in multiple ways, but the term generally refers to a set of social networks that individuals can draw upon to enhance their status and access to additional resources (Putnam 1995).[4] The narrative of lost social capital argues that the problems besetting blacks in the post-segregation era are a function not of continued structural discrimination, nor of individual moral failing, but of the distortion of collective social values and networks that followed from racial integration. In particular, the narrative names blacks as responsible for urban decline, but only because of their contact with white culture. Thus, it simultaneously condemns blacks for contemporary racial inequality and absolves them of ultimate responsibility.

N'Digo's expression of the lost social capital narrative is not an isolated incident—indeed, this tale is retold in cities throughout the country, where community revitalization plans are explicitly and implicitly linked to the recovery of segregation-era life and culture (Boyd 2000; Jackson 2001; Moore 2002, 2005; Prince 2004; Taylor 2002). Chicago has been an important source and center of this social myth. Over the past thirty years, the primary tellers of this tale have been development advocates in Douglas/Grand Boulevard, two contiguous black community areas on the city's south side. By developing Douglas/Grand Boulevard into a tourist destination, community development corporation (CDC) leaders hope to attract the black middle-class business owners and residents whose departure supposedly led to neighborhood decline. Their efforts to re-create the physical and social structures of the Jim Crow period constitute both the ideological and concrete expressions of the lost social capital narrative.

This chapter examines the emergence of this narrative in Douglas/ Grand Boulevard to explain its recent and widespread articulation in US cities. I argue that its adoption is neither accidental nor the natural response of old-timers lamenting their lost youth. Rather, it is a deliberate political response by black middle-class elites to the neoliberal assumptions undergirding development in urban areas. Proponents of neoliberalism understand racialized urban inequality as the result of individual behavior instead of uneven development. As a result, they advocate gentrification as the appropriate strategy for revitalizing urban space and rehabilitating poor African Americans. Black CDC leaders adopt an explicitly racialized version of this strategy by attempting to attract the *black* middle class to African American neighborhoods.[5] The point of this tactic is to make black communities more competitive in the residential and tourist marketplaces. The lost social capital narrative positions neighborhood blacks as morally deserving participants in that competition.

In what follows, I illustrate first how economic and policy shifts have shaped the goals and tactics of Douglas/Grand Boulevard's neighborhood organizations, encouraging them to adopt economic development strategies that mirror the neoliberal policies of the City of Chicago. I next describe the racial nostalgia used to market the area to middle-class residents and tourists, and I analyze its depiction of black segregation-era culture. Finally, I examine the lost social capital narrative embedded in this nostalgia. Specifically, I illustrate how its explanation of economic decline both accepts and rejects dominant interpretations of black cultural inferiority—blaming blacks for neighborhood poverty, but in a way that portrays them as members of the "deserving poor." I conclude by suggesting that, although black elites have attempted to use neoliberal development strategies to their own advantage, their efforts have served to depoliticize and deradicalize community development in black neighborhoods.

FROM FACTORY TO FANTASY: POST-WAR DEVELOPMENT IN DOUGLAS/GRAND BOULEVARD

Douglas/Grand Boulevard is located just two and half miles south of the Loop—Chicago's central business district (figure 5.1). The neighborhood's northern border lies at 26th Street and stretches south for twenty-five blocks to 51st Street. The Dan Ryan Expressway forms its western edge, and to the east lies Lake Michigan. Its contours closely approximate those of the city's "first ghetto," whose borders were initially determined by white

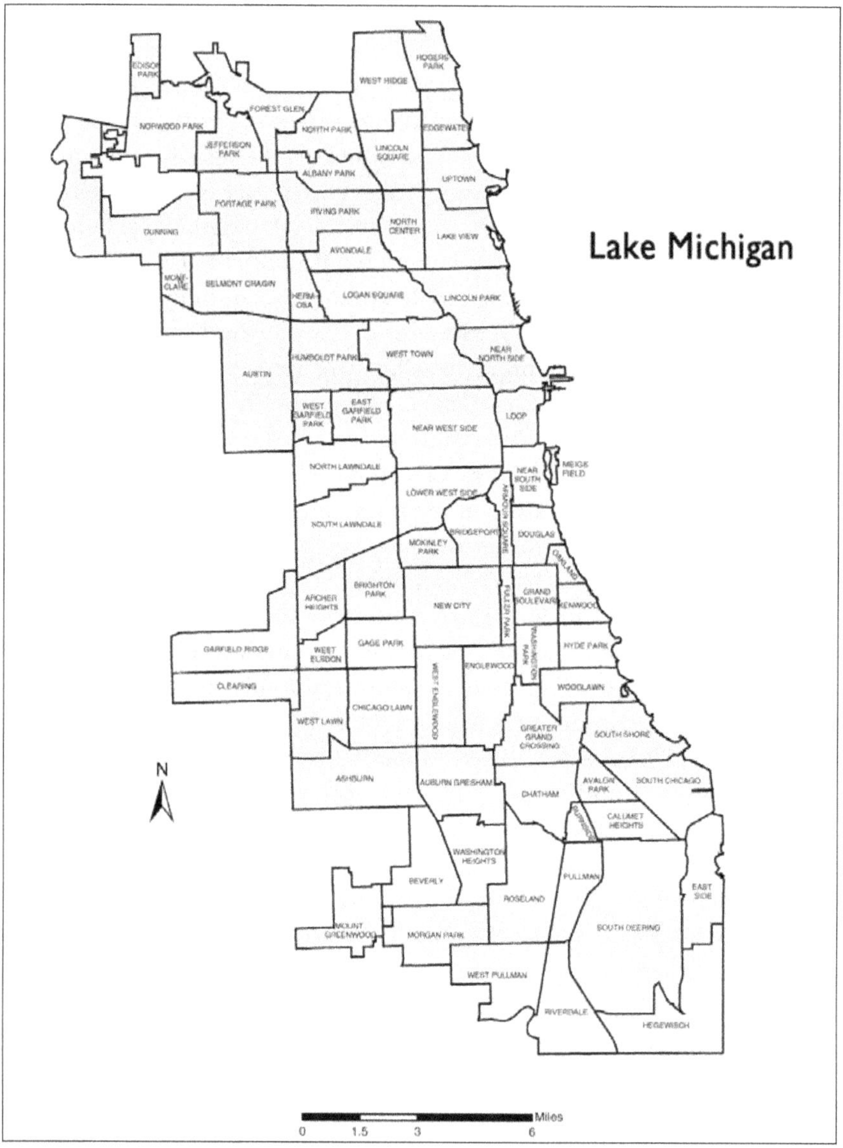

FIGURE 5.1.

Chicago community area map (adapted from the City of Chicago Department of Planning map).

resistance to black migration (Drake and Cayton 1993; Philpott 1991; Spear 1967).

Although individual-level racial hostility shaped its outlines before World War II, urban renewal and public housing programs were the biggest factors in neighborhood development at mid-century. These projects fostered untold amounts of residential and business displacement (Hirsch 1983:122, 259). They also served to concentrate poverty in the community and give spatial articulation to the class cleavages previously expressed in social organizations (Drake and Cayton 1993). Since the 1970s, however, the revitalization of Douglas/Grand Boulevard has been profoundly shaped by the restructuring of the urban economy. Political-economic shifts have redefined the nature of black political action, encouraging African American neighborhood leaders to adopt economic development strategies that mirror the city's own neoliberal policies.

Globalization and Economic Decline

Chicago was the destination of millions of black migrants in the post-war period (Kleppner 1985). These new residents enjoyed an economic boom that initially buoyed the transportation and manufacturing industries in Chicago, including steel, heavy machinery, consumer appliances, and food production (Bennett 1989:163). Like other older industrial cities, however, Chicago suffered from the restructuring of the economy that closely followed the post-war prosperity of the late 1940s. Not long into this wave of black migration, manufacturers began moving from the city to the suburbs, and "between 1947 and 1982, factory employment in Chicago dropped from a twentieth-century high of 688,000 [jobs] to 277,000—a decline of 59 percent. At the same time, suburban Cook County manufacturing jobs increased from 121,000 to 279,000 (a 131 percent increase), and factory jobs in the other SMSA [Standard Metropolitan Statistical Areas] counties jumped from 64,000 to 189,000 (a 195 percent increase)" (Squires et al. 1987:27). As these numbers show, the loss of industrial work was important not only for its impact on the city but also for the way it positioned Chicago relative to the surrounding area. Industrial work was relocated in the nearby suburbs, making the city the loser in regional economic competition.

These population and job shifts were partly a function of policy and politics at the national and municipal levels. Federal highway programs and FHA mortgage policies exacerbated the decentralization of population and industry by easing access to the suburbs (Hirsch and Mohl 1993). At the local level, post-war mayors adopted a pro-growth strategy that converted the Loop from a manufacturing center into a space for offices and high-priced residences (Rast 1999). The first to implement this strategy was Richard J. Daley, who, soon after his 1955 election, established alliances with the city's business leaders and began using economic revitalization projects as the primary vehicle for rewarding Democratic Party allies. These projects ringed the central city with developments, including the McCormick Place convention center on the near south side, Watertower Plaza on the near north side, and the University of Illinois at Chicago on the near west side (Ferman 1996:60–61). These policies drew resources away from failing neighborhoods and added to the city's employment loss by displacing smaller-scale industries from Chicago's central area (Rast 1999:22; Squires et al. 1987:29).

Chicago's declining economic fortune was also driven by the decisions of international corporations, which responded to decreasing profits by shutting down or relocating plants in the 1980s. According to David Ranney (2003), 60 percent of the companies responsible for manufacturing job loss in Chicago had international operations, "and in the majority of these cases the corporate parents were expanding overseas while closing down Chicago operations" (Ranney 2003:80). In the wake of these plant closings, city planners turned to the industrial and non-industrial corporations located within its borders to make up for employment, population, and income losses (Squires et al. 1987:38). Because of Chicago's diversified economy, service-sector employment has replaced industrial and manufacturing jobs. Nevertheless, the city has experienced an overall loss in employment, and "the gains in service-sector jobs (57,000 between 1963 and 1982) did not offset in numbers or salaries the 232,000 manufacturing jobs lost during that same period" (Ferman 1996:28). Particularly in comparison with the counties that surround the Chicago metropolitan area, the city continues to lose out, even through the current period (Abu-Lughod 1999:326).

Changes in federal funding exacerbated this drop in the city's tax base. Traditional federal support for urban economic development was replaced by policies emphasizing the competitiveness of individuals and places and abdicating responsibility for urban economic development. Most notable have been the decrease in federal funding for urban areas and the devolution of policy development and administration to local authorities (Bennett 1999; Eisinger 1998).

In the past twenty years, Mayor Richard M. Daley has responded to economic decline by trying to attract middle-class consumers and residents back to the city. The administration's focus has been on developing Chicago as a site for national and international leisure and tourism. To this end, municipal planners have relied heavily on a four-pronged strategy of school reform, upscale residential development, public housing demolition, and cultural and tourism development (Bennett, Smith, and

Wright 2006; Chicago Housing Authority 2005; Grazian 2003; Lipman and Haines 2005; Stovall and Smith 2005).

Douglas/Grand Boulevard, as a result of its proximity to the Loop and its status as a target of previous disinvestment, is one of the most attractive and underdeveloped areas of Chicago. Therefore, much of the new policy is centered within that neighborhood, and initial analyses reveal that the area is experiencing some degree of gentrification (Manley, Buffa, and Dube 2006). Some scholars have argued that gentrification in Douglas/Grand Boulevard is the result of city policies (Manley, Buffa, and Dube 2006), but these analyses minimize neighborhood organizations' role in initiating and, more important, legitimizing neighborhood change. Although they cannot be characterized as having friendly relations, neighborhood organizations have nonetheless adopted an economic development strategy that, to some degree, meshes with that of the city.

Community Development in the New Global Economy

According to Bennett (1999), these shifts have had significant implications for politics at the neighborhood level, changing the players, roles, alliances, and agenda in Chicago's community development conflicts so that community organizations are more likely to cooperate with development than challenge it. First, as federal funding streams have dried up, the city has lost its place as the chief *initiator* of economic redevelopment. Private developers and institutions such as universities and hospitals are increasingly likely to be the source of unwelcome community-revitalization initiatives. They are therefore more liable to be the object of neighborhood residents' hostility and protest, which takes some political pressure off the city. A second and related change, the retrenchment of federal funding has meant that the city is not the only *funnel* for public funds for neighborhood development. Instead, community groups are relying more heavily on businesses and philanthropic organizations for financial support, many of which require community organizations to pursue economic development in partnership with private institutions.

Finally, these shifts change the agendas of black organizations, thus diminishing the likelihood of political confrontation and contestation. Neighborhood organizations, like the city itself, are increasingly being forced to find alternative engines of economic growth. Deprived of federal support, they are relying on culture, leisure, and entertainment tourism to drive their community initiatives. To the extent that these changes have turned community organizations' attention away from making demands on city government and toward making requests of private businesses and funders, they constitute both a privatization and a depoliticization of community development politics (Goode and Maskovsky 2001; Ranney 2003). The lack of federal funds, in combination with "newly rigid interpretations of IRS restrictions on political activity of nonprofit groups, the necessity of seeking funds from and joining in partnerships with private-sector leaders, and the orientation of the CDC approach to economic investment and development decisions, all pushed CDCs away from politics and an analysis of power" (Fisher 1994:14). Therefore, as many scholars have pointed out, Chicago has not fit the traditional "city hall versus the neighborhood" model of urban conflict (Bennett 1999). Instead, black community organizations have found that in an ever more competitive and global context, their own agendas and tactics have become more tightly aligned with those of the city and private institutions.

Such was the case in Douglas/Grand Boulevard, where development organizations were first established in the 1980s by middle-class residents seeking technical assistance and city support for neighborhood redevelopment plans (Douglas Development Corporation 1979; Mid-South 1993; Stevens 1982). These organizations did not fear development per se, but the likelihood that it would be controlled by white development elites (Center for Urban Economic Development 1986). Neighborhood elites felt particularly hostile toward the Illinois Institute of Technology (IIT), which in 1989 sought to shut down the local public transportation "el" station at 35th and State streets as part of a larger campus-redevelopment initiative. After initially protesting against IIT's campus plan, Douglas and Grand Boulevard organizations decided to collaborate with it on a broader, community-wide development plan. They did so for two reasons: First, the two sides shared a common concern about the lack of local economic development. Neighborhood groups opposed IIT's plans to disrupt el service, but their middle-class home-owning membership shared an interest in changing the perception of the neighborhood and increasing property values. Second, community residents were particularly keen to be involved in formal decision-making processes. They feared that "another relocation plan was in the offing and that they would have no significant voice in planning nor receive any tangible benefits as community residents," a concern that provided ample incentive for collaboration (Gills 2001:32).

As a result, in 1990 several community organizations began collaborating with IIT and other neighborhood institutions to form a public-private planning group, the Mid-South Planning and Development Commission (Mid-South). The planning partners included the nearby Mercy and Michael Reese hospitals, De La Salle High School, Illinois College of Optometry,

First National Bank, and the Chicago Department of Planning. From 1990 to 1993, Mid-South worked to develop an economic development plan for the two neighborhoods: "Restoring Bronzeville." The plan proposes to combine historic preservation with tourism to develop the area as a Heritage Tourism Destination. It also advocates luring middle-class blacks to the area through the development of mixed-income housing and the establishment of tourist-oriented, black-owned businesses (Mid-South 1993).

These neighborhood revitalization efforts in Douglas/Grand Boulevard have a peculiar relationship to the city's own strategies for wider metropolitan development. Neighborhood plans are *distinct* from those of the Daley administration in that they were initiated by African American organizations trying to avoid white intervention and racial displacement (Boyd 2005). Nevertheless, these two efforts cannot be said to be *independent* of each other: the city has supported neighborhood initiatives, and, to the extent that city plans echo the goals of Restoring Bronzeville, the city's initiatives are legitimized as having "community support." Most important, both programs express the same fundamental commitment to neoliberal anti-poverty policy. That is, each understands poverty on Chicago's south side as a function of individual behavior instead of development policy and broad economic trends. As a result, CBOs (community-based organizations) in Douglas/Grand Boulevard have offered no coherent challenge to the neoliberal assumption that the "return" of the middle class is the solution to neighborhood disinvestment. Instead, neighborhood organizations have tried to beat the city at its own game by attracting black, rather than white, middle-class residents to Douglas/Grand Boulevard. Where the city and the neighborhood differ is in the rhetoric each uses to justify its agenda. On one hand, the city speaks to a broad constituency of residents and businesses, using a language that emphasizes economic competitiveness in the global marketplace. Douglas/Grand Boulevard organizations, on the other hand, draw heavily on nostalgia and the lost social capital narrative to legitimize their agenda to black residents of varying economic statuses.

HERITAGE TOURISM DEVELOPMENT AND NOSTALGIA FOR SEGREGATION

The narrative of lost social capital depends on the idea that the first half of the twentieth century represents a kind of golden era in Douglas/Grand Boulevard's history. As noted elsewhere, this vision of black community is highly problematic because it minimizes historical intraracial tensions and spit-shines a period of vicious, state-sanctioned political subordination (Boyd 2000; Reed 1996; Williams 1999). It is true that Chicago's black residents were successful in establishing a wide array of economic, political, and social institutions to ease their adjustment to urban life during the early 1900s. Yet, the strategies adopted by migration-era leaders were no match for the physical segregation, economic marginalization, and political exclusion that African Americans faced at the time (Drake and Cayton 1993; Spear 1967). Nevertheless, public descriptions of that history—including promotional materials, tours, development charettes, and public education meetings—emphasize blacks' accomplishments at the time and claim that Bronzeville was marked by four principal characteristics.

First, these descriptions suggest that Douglas/Grand Boulevard was home to an enormously successful black elite. Development advocates often refer to historic Bronzeville as the "economic capital of black America" and are quick to recite the achievements of the early twentieth century's black elite. These sources are most likely to mention entrepreneurs like Joseph Jordan, Anthony Overton, and Jesse Binga, men who constructed the buildings and founded the businesses that make up the "Black Metropolis." In the neighborhood paper, *South Street Journal*, Harold Lucas of the Black Metropolis Convention and Tourism Council argued that before the depression, economic institutions in the neighborhood "had become so powerful and prosperous that in 1925, the main business district on south State Street, between 31st and 39th, was known internationally a[s] the Black Wall Street of America" (Lucas 1997:3).

This portrayal highlights the financial success of black business owners, that miniscule percentage of the black population able to establish and sustain an economic enterprise in the early twentieth century.[6] Although promotional materials and event organizers do not often make claims about the number of residents who fit into this category, the disproportionate amount of attention paid to this portion of the black population elevates their importance and gives the impression that affluent blacks were numerous and their impact far-reaching. In the swell of enthusiasm, supporters implied or even stated outright that "black-owned and black-operated businesses were the norm, not the exception" (Davis 1996).

The emphasis on black entrepreneurship is related to a second claim about Bronzeville—that it was independent of white control. Bronzeville supporters commonly refer to the area as "a city within a city." Development advocates often assert that the community was nearly self-sufficient during its golden age because, as the Restoring Bronzeville plan argues, "the goods and services to support the black population were...supplied from within the community itself" (Mid-South 1993:19). According to some older residents, leaving the community was neither necessary nor desirable. Steven Anthony, a long-time resident and lay historian, mentioned on one community tour that "there was the foundation of the economic, political, and social system inside the larger community. It wasn't necessary to leave the community, other than to go to your job....We didn't have to go downtown, we could stay in the neighborhood, we had everything we needed right here" (author's fieldnotes, January 1998). This perspective suggests that Bronzeville was not only independent from white control but also economically self-sustaining, a racial separatist's dream.

Community organization leaders depict the financial and political independence of Bronzeville as being complemented by a third characteristic, a tradition of cultural innovation. Mid-South applauds its citizens for having historically "developed their own cultural institutions and forms, built their own buildings, and founded and supported their own businesses" (Mid-South membership pamphlet). Neighborhood promotional materials often mention a long list of artists and musicians who lived and worked in the area. The Restoring Bronzeville plan and other Mid-South literature repeatedly mention "such notables as Joe Louis, Scott Joplin, Jesse Owens, Redd Foxx and Dinah Washington" (Mid-South 1993:2). In addition, music and dancing establishments are some of the most celebrated of Bronzeville's historic businesses. Neighborhood revitalization proponents claim that the entertainment venues lining State Street before IIT's expansion created "a vital and thriving cultural scene and an eager audience for jazz, blues, gospel, literature and visual arts" (Chicago Historical Society n.d.). They also insist that Bronzeville did not just feature this music; Bronzeville was its original source. On one community tour I attended (June 29, 1997), our guide told us that blacks have made "three great cultural contributions to this world: jazz, the blues, and what's the third one? Gospel." Although these artistic innovations are valued on their own terms, they have a particular economic significance in the redevelopment efforts. Steven Anthony complained, "Now we have to go north for BBQ, for Jazz. If you don't retain pride in your heritage, then people make you feel ashamed of it, so you reject it. And then they steal it from you and make you pay for the privilege of experiencing it!" (author's fieldnotes, January 24, 1998). Mr. Anthony emphasized the importance of maintaining black cultural traditions, not merely for the joy of experiencing them but also because these traditions are increasingly commodified in the contemporary marketplace.

Cultural innovation includes not just artistic products but cultural practices as well. In particular, Mid-South portrays Bronzeville residents as having displayed a high degree of social and political cohesion. This racial solidarity is the fourth characteristic that marks the Bronzeville heritage. Mid-South often looks back on the segregation era as a time when neighborhood residents lived and worked together without class tensions. In a 1997 *Chicago Sun-Times* article, Mid-South executive director Pat Dowell-Cerasoli insisted that "the beauty of Bronzeville in its heydey was that it was home to all people from different economic backgrounds who worked together and played together" (November 9:34). This sense of unity is credited with causing, directly or indirectly, the great successes for which Bronzeville is famous. Similarly, Harold Lucas (1997:3) suggested that living in close quarters fostered a deep racial unity, "a greater sense of cultur[al] awareness and self-sufficiency." It was this social capital, this racial unity and class cooperation, that provided the foundation for the financial success of the community. This understanding, of a community void of any serious or lasting class conflict, is widely accepted and often repeated by residents in public forums. According to Byron Williams, a businessman who left the suburb of Naperville for Bronzeville in the early 1990s, "there were millionaires, doctors, entertainers and athletes living with housemaids and railroad porters. Everyone lived together because there wasn't anyplace else in the city where they were welcomed. And the community thrived" (Davis 1996:12).

Taken together, these claims form a coherent picture of the neighborhood's past, one that celebrates early twentieth-century black culture, locates that culture firmly in the black middle class, laments its loss, and wishes fervently for its return. Such nostalgia helps sell the neighborhood by imbuing its residents with heroism and historical significance. It also serves as an ideological alternative to urban frontier rhetoric that requires the removal of poor, black populations from revitalizing neighborhoods (Boyd 2005).[7] Yet, it does so by screening from contemporary view the cruelty of segregation, the venom of intraracial class tensions, and the way that each weighed on the lives of everyday black Americans (Drake and Cayton 1993; Grossman 1989). Elsewhere, I have described the political implications of retrofitting the past in this manner (Boyd n.d.). Here, I focus on how the nostalgic portrayal of the past serves as a starting point for a narrative about the present: a story that details the loss of black social capital and, in doing so, mirrors conventional ideologies of neoliberalism.

INTEGRATION AND THE NARRATIVE OF LOST SOCIAL CAPITAL

The nostalgic portrayal of black life during segregation is the starting point for a narrative about the loss of black social capital during integration. According to neighborhood development advocates, the neighborhood's fall from grace has two sources: The first, less frequently mentioned but still relevant, is the urban renewal initiated by the nearby Illinois Institute of Technology. The university liked to paint itself as being responsible for "revers[ing] the blight" that plagued the neighborhood in the 1950s and taking responsibility for rejuvenating its environment (Long 1996). But urban renewal was a not-so-distant memory for some community members, who recalled things differently. In addition to commercial property loss, residents remember the role of white institutions in displacing blacks. On a tour of the community, one long-time resident pointed out that several apartment complexes were "the result of black displacement. A lot of black people lived in Douglas. Maybe the area wasn't pretty, but …then New York Life Insurance Company and Michael Reese Hospital decided that they wanted the land. As a result, forty-five to fifty thousand people were displaced" (author's fieldnotes, January 1998). Despite these institutions' responsibility for much of the recent neighborhood disinvestment, this external source of decline is mentioned much less often than the second: the physical and psychological abandonment of the neighborhood by the black middle class.

A story told habitually and almost universally is that desegregation destroyed Bronzeville by allowing its more affluent residents to move away. Consider, for example, the comments of Isaac Naples, the owner of several small businesses in Douglas/Grand Boulevard. He expressed this widely held interpretation of the neighborhood's decline:

> ISAAC: Well, you know, what hurt us out here is the integration, you know. Before that, I mean, the Ritz [Hotel] was doing real good back in the 50s and the 40s, and, I mean, if I talk to the guys before my time, they say, "Oh, the entertainers that used to stay at the Ritz," 'cause they could not go downtown. They could *entertain* downtown, but they could not stay at the motels downtown. Like Little Richard, used to stay at the Ritz. Louie Armstrong, used to stay at the Ritz. Earl Fatha Hines was the house band of the Ritz. Yeah, he was the house band. I'm trying to think of a few others off the top of my head, but, but Little Richard, Sarah Vaughn, Louie Armstrong, it's a bunch of them. They would entertain downtown, and when they would go to entertain, they had to take the freight elevators. They could not even take a passenger elevator to go up and down to entertain. They had to go in the back door, take the freight elevator, get

substandard pay. Then they'd have to come back to the Ritz to stay, you know, and it was a lot of them. Even Nat King Cole.

MICHELLE: But after integration?

ISAAC: Right. And then, soon as we could go downtown, then we all went downtown and we abandoned. And that's what's happened all up and down here. It's abandonment. When we could go downtown, we went. And did we ever go. We didn't plan for it. We didn't say, "Well, you know, yeah, we can go downtown." But let's use a little logic. Let's still support our, you know, our neighborhood, our ma and pa stores, which is the backbone of our economy. [Author's fieldnotes, March 1998]

Mr. Naples' remarks contain the key features of the local version of the declining black social capital story. First, he describes the segregation period as a golden era in black cultural life. Second, Mr. Naples locates the significance of this period in the proliferation of "great men" (and one token woman) who nurtured that culture. In complete accordance with the rhetoric of Mid-South and its Restoring Bronzeville plan, Mr. Naples catalogs the neighborhood's jazz greats in such detail that he becomes distracted and must be reminded of his original point.[8] Third, this description identifies desegregation as the turning point in the golden era, as well as the reason for its demise. Fourth and finally, it identifies the deterioration of racial solidarity as the key loss experienced because of desegregation.[9]

Narrative, Race, and Responsibility

Mr. Naples' story also illustrates several important political functions of narrative more generally. The first, according to Polletta (1998), is that narratives make claims about group identity through the use of plot and personification (the identification and portrayal of different characters). Through this process of personification, of telling "the story of our becoming—as an individual, a nation, a people—we establish who we are" (Polletta 1998:141). The black social capital narrative explains how Douglas/Grand Boulevard became the neighborhood it is today by identifying both explicit and implicit characters, including the whites who enforced segregation, the black neighborhood business owners who provided goods and services to segregated markets, and the black visitors and residents who supported the African American economy. In recounting the story of segregation, then integration and its effects, Douglas/Grand Boulevard residents construct a vision of black community.[10]

Social constructionists often understand narratives and interpretive frameworks as tools for unifying group members—in this case, the black members of the Douglas/Grand Boulevard neighborhood. Yet, Smith (2003: 37) suggests that elites who construct and use narratives "are engaged in political projects that seek to stabilize structures of power." The construction of what he calls "stories of peoplehood" tends toward the hierarchical; that is,

> leaders seek both to prompt constituents to embrace member-
> ship in the community or people they depict, and to persuade
> them to accept as leaders the very sorts of persons who are
> advancing these people-building accounts. That is why even the
> most "horizontal" stories of people are likely to have certain
> dichotomous elements; and "vertical" accounts that define a rul-
> ing class in opposition to various lower ranks. [Smith 2003:53]

Smith's (2003) analysis is useful because it highlights the way that narratives distinguish between members of the same group, even as they construct its members as essentially similar and bonded. It therefore points to a second function of narrative, which is the allocation of blame and responsibility.

The narrative being told in Douglas/Grand Boulevard does not simply tell a story that bonds black neighbors together; it also characterizes them in ways that assign them different roles and responsibilities by class and residence. Specifically, the black social capital narrative defines community members in ways that cast its middle-class members as race traitors who abandoned Douglas/Grand Boulevard for whiter pastures and now seek readmission to the community. Doing so implies that poor residents—those who remained in the neighborhood—engaged in behavior that contributed to neighborhood decline. This story blames all blacks for the neighborhood's demise, but it does so in class-specific ways; that is, it explicitly portrays middle-class blacks as the *cause* of neighborhood decline and implicitly describes poor blacks as its *source*.

This characterization is apparent in the following version of the neighborhood decline story, offered by Steven Anthony, identified above as a long-time resident and local neighborhood historian. Along with many other residents, he claims: "Up until 1970, the land and the buildings in this area was 80 percent owned and occupied by people of color....Eighty percent of this area was occupied by the residents....Many of them were older people whose children moved out to the suburbs...they said it wasn't good enough for them"(author's fieldnotes, June 1997). It is important to note that Mr. Anthony's story of desegregation includes not just a description of black residential mobility but also an evaluation of the motivations of those who moved. Mr. Anthony portrays the decision to leave as a selfish and snobbish abandonment of the community, rather than as an expression of long-denied mobility and access to housing. In doing so, he understands the economic mobility of the black middle class as necessarily elitist.

The black social capital narrative also portrays black middle-class elites as color-struck, wanting so much to imitate whites that they were blind to the rich resources available to them in their own neighborhood. Randolph Jeffries, head of a local social service organization and one of the founders of Mid-South told his community decline story in this way:

> There has been a tendency on our part to think that white is better, and so we're always running. I mean, the reason that this community got so stripped in the first place is that we always thought that something was better outside here…we had it, we had it here, you know. We had the Binga Bank, we had the Overton Building, we had the Supreme Life, all that kinda stuff. But in '54, when they said "Y'all free!" boy, we just, I mean, we lit outta here, and buying up these crummy houses the white folks were selling, we bought churches, and all that kinda stuff. And left all these fine buildings down here to crumble. And that's, that's how they felt. [Author's fieldnotes, March 1997]

Mr. Jeffries agrees with Mr. Anthony, arguing explicitly that Douglas /Grand Boulevard's economic decline is the result of out-migration by middle-class blacks. Yet, his comment goes beyond Mr. Anthony's, suggesting that blacks who left the neighborhood were elitist, not just in economic but also in racial terms.

These explanations suggest that middle-class out-migration left Douglas/Grand Boulevard without the resources necessary to maintain the economic health of the neighborhood. They therefore frame urban job loss, ensuing unemployment, and rising poverty as a function of individual behavior instead of economic processes or urban policy. Such arguments, though common, are shortsighted and incomplete to the extent that they divorce black behavior from the political-economic context in which it takes place. More problematic, however, is what this depiction of the black middle class suggests about poorer residents, namely, that the latter fail when deprived of middle-class role models and that this failure manifested itself in the deterioration of the neighborhood after integration. This understanding of integration is therefore an odd mix of blame and absolution: black middle-class people have indeed committed an error, betraying the race by leaving behind its most benighted members. Yet, they are responsible for neighborhood decline only in the way that a parent is responsible for the actions of her truant teen. The real culprits in this narrative about integration are the low-income residents who stayed behind in the neighborhood and fostered its deterioration.

It is important to point out that this portrayal of poor neighborhood residents is implicit, not explicit. It is inherent to the depiction of middle-class black residents and their retreat from the neighborhood—yet neighborhood development boosters do not often openly criticize low-income residents when discussing the effects of integration and the sources of neighborhood decline.[11] Such a damning portrayal of poor people disrupts the vision of harmonious class relations that is the basis for both nostalgia and contemporary revitalization. It highlights middle-class residents' long-standing reluctance to live near the poor and suggests that mixed-income developments are a risky investment. Thus, the *explicit* role that poor blacks play in the social capital narrative is quite different. Consider the comments of Lerneal Ogden, a staff member of a Douglas/Grand Boulevard community-based organization. He described poor and older residents who stayed in the neighborhood as "the keepers":

> The people who are here are the keepers of the culture, you know what I'm saying? Like the keepers of, the holders of all this history.…And the people who come back, they know about the history, but if it wasn't for the folks who were here, they couldn't have come back.…These folks who kept these homes and stuff, they could have left too, sold their homes…doing all this kind of stuff, but we'll be here. You know what I'm saying? You got some old folks who been here since, I mean, shit, the thirties or something…if you didn't have them to interview, the Etta Moten Barnetts, the, you know, different folks, you know, you wouldn't have it.…They, folks who were here, they maintained. [Author's fieldnotes, February 1998]

In making his comparison between recent (middle-class) and long-time (poor) residents, Mr. Ogden echoes the idea that the former are individualist and elitist. He also portrays poorer residents as having preserved and been devoted to the community, even when it faced desperate conditions.

He argues that their decision to stay in the neighborhood was an expression of community commitment, not a reflection of limited financial ability. Because they "maintained," they have kept alive the neighborhood history that redevelopment advocates are now trying to unearth and preserve.

These implicit and explicit characterizations have a fascinating relationship to the logic of neoliberalism. On the one hand, they echo the idea that individual failings are what make people and places poor, and they accept black responsibility for urban decline. On the other hand, they portray neighborhood residents in such a way that the race is simultaneously responsible and exonerated, with differential burdens and obligations being borne by blacks of different class status. I am not suggesting that neighborhood residents make these arguments in conscious response to neoliberalism; rather, I argue that in their use of the lost social capital narrative, neighborhood elites echo its broader logic in ways that depict blacks advantageously.

The final political function of narrative is the suggestion of a preferred course of action. Narratives "not only make sense of the past and present, but since the story's chronological end is also its end in the sense of moral, purpose or telos, they project a future" (Polletta 1998:140). In holding middle-class blacks responsible for neighborhood decline, the black social capital narrative identifies civic leadership as both the right and obligation of the black business class. Mr. Ogden communicates this:

> For a long time, middle-class black folks left this neighborhood. I mean, they were scared to live in the neighborhood. And now they're coming back. And now they're, you know, calling it Bronzeville, calling it home. They've been down here for five years, and we've made our home and…and that's cool, 'cause they're supposed to come back and, you know, open arms, we're all black, right? But the thing is, though, don't forget the people who've been here for thirty and forty and fifty years, who, you know, who don't have the money to fix up their homes. [Author's fieldnotes, February 1998]

Here, Mr. Ogden repeats his earlier assertion that the behavior of both middle-class and poorer blacks is based in their feelings about the neighborhood, locating the former's decision to leave in their fear and portraying them as having abandoned the space and the race. In addition, he asserts that middle-class residents owe their allegiance to long-time residents, that they should help preserve and protect the cultural custodians in the face of the threats posed by development. Mr. Anthony responded similarly when a resident asked him whether he thought that integration "ruined the neighborhood":

> Yes! Now how to fix that is your task. And we're going to have to make some sacrifices....We've started taking our money out of the community. In the black community, we have fourteen billion dollars worth of income, and only one billion of it is spent in the black community. In the Chinese community, or Chinatown, that same dollar turns over five times....Chicago had more black millionaires and politicians than any place else in the world. When we allowed our community to be diluted, [we started having problems]. [Author's fieldnotes, January 24, 1998]

Mr. Anthony suggests that the solution to neighborhood disinvestment is personal sacrifice and commitment from individual residents. Relying on the well-worn reference to a model minority, he articulates a classic black nationalist argument about the importance of racial commitment, particularly as it is expressed in financial terms. Like other residents, he tells the tale of segregation's satisfactions partly to tell the story of integration's inadequacies and partly to impel race traitors to return home, along with their resources.

CONCLUSION

Culture-based economic development programs, and the narratives that accompany them, illustrate the contradictory ways that urban blacks experience and respond to the globalized political economy and the ideology that supports it. Douglas/Grand Boulevard community leaders have sought to control the revitalization of the neighborhood, hoping to preempt the racial displacement that is a likely outcome of the city's culture-based redevelopment plans. Yet, in shifting their focus from political agitation to economic development, they have accepted the precepts of neoliberalism, which sees gentrification and public-private revitalization as the best strategy for alleviating black poverty.

The narrative of lost social capital is a racialized articulation of that ideology. It is the story through which black elites hope, as Phillip O'Bannon suggests in the opening epigraph, to remind themselves and others of the fundamental "goodness" of African Americans. What is most disturbing about this story is that it seeks to explain conditions that are the consequence of broad economic, political, and policy shifts, by extracting them away from those very forces. They rely instead on explanations that exaggerate the importance of individual behavior as the cause of and the solution to contemporary urban poverty.

The narrative of lost social capital thus follows a broader trend of explaining urban poverty with references to black culture. As Dubey (2003) points out, culture-based explanations for urban poverty are highly problematic, even—perhaps especially—when condemnation of black culture is replaced by its celebration. The emphasis on the "positive" features of African American culture obscures how economic shifts and the considered decisions of political elites constrain the choices available to residents of black neighborhoods. Yet, as cities rely more heavily on tourism-based economic development, African American community elites will turn more frequently to images of race and heritage, both to draw visitors and residents to black neighborhoods and to distinguish themselves in the marketplace of culture. In doing so, neighborhood leaders do not merely rationalize black economic subordination; they accept the logic that prioritizes cultural rehabilitation over political mobilization.

Notes

1. *N'Digo* boasts the "nation's largest African-American newspaper circulation."

2. It is worth noting that these observers are critical of integration, not desegregation: their complaint is with the racial mixing that has presumably taken place between blacks and whites as a result of the passage and enforcement of the civil rights act of 1964.

3. As I use the term in this article, *gentrification* is the entrance of more advantaged populations into declining neighborhoods in ways that diminish existing residents' capacity to remain in the community. Black gentrification takes place when African Americans constitute the entering population, regardless of the race of the displaced population. The use of the racial modifier indicates who is doing the displacing and also highlights the ways that racial ordering shapes the process of gentrification (see Boyd n.d.).

4. The concept of social capital has been extensively criticized. For a thorough review of the literature, especially as it relates to African Americans in urban areas, see Jennings 2005.

5. Gentrification often has a racial character to it—what distinguishes black neighborhoods is their degree of openness about its racial dynamic.

6. Drake and Cayton (1993:434, 522) argue that there were five hundred black businesses before migration, 5 percent of which were upper-class.

7. The urban frontier framework portrays gentrifiers as urban homesteaders act-ing as a civilizing force in an untamed, unexplored urban territory. For more on the urban frontier perspective, see Smith 1996.

8. Mr. Naples is certainly not the first informant to lose his train of thought, and in pointing this out, I do not mean to belittle him. Rather, his distraction is interesting for the way it represents a fundamental problem with the entire racial heritage tourism strategy: in his excitement about the past, he loses his point about the present.

9. Mr. Naples' rendering of this story emphasizes the economic impact of deterio-rating racial consciousness. Other variations may emphasize the loss of moral values or political strength as well.

10. Narratives are similar to collective action frames, the interpretive schemes that mobilize political action by describing problems, assigning blame, and justifying action. Polletta (1998) argues that narratives are more than a type of frame; rather, they constitute one of many important *mechanisms* through which framing takes place.

11. Residents, however, are more likely to openly criticize other public housing residents particularly (see Andrews-McKinney 2005; Boyd 2000).

6

Discipline and Citizenship

Latina/o Youth in Chicago
JROTC Programs

Gina M. Pérez

Actually, it was the discipline [that first got me interested in JROTC].

—*Antonio Gallegos, eighteen years old, JROTC cadet, Bellow Academy, Chicago*

Like many young people in American public schools today, Antonio Gallegos joined his high school's Junior Reserve Officer Training Program (JROTC) with the hope that it would teach him discipline, earn him respect from his peers, and turn him into a leader.[1] Born and raised in Chicago to a Mexican mother and Cuban father, Antonio volunteers regularly at his local public library, earns money painting signs for a local business, and often works at a Mexican restaurant as well. Antonio hopes to attend college one day and explains that JROTC has taught him how to be more disciplined, to be responsible for others, and ultimately to be a leader, all qualities that will help him succeed when he goes to college. In order to pay for college, Antonio has also considered enlisting in the Army Reserves to receive training as a computer specialist. Although his mother is willing to help him with college expenses, Antonio hopes to pay for college himself: "My mom has done so much. And she has already too much to worry about. I don't want her to have me to worry about, so I want to do it myself. I don't want her to be sick taking care of me. I can do this. I don't want her to worry. If I become a computer specialist, there is *no way* they're going to send a computer specialist to war."

Antonio's dreams of attending college and gaining financial independence, his concern for his mother and siblings, and his understanding of

JROTC and military service as key strategies to achieve his goals are shared by many of his fellow cadets in Bellow Academy's JROTC program. Young men and women consistently explain that participating in JROTC enables them to command respect from others; they also describe how it provides them with important skills and values they regard as necessary to succeed.

JROTC's promise of instilling discipline and leadership in its cadets is not new. In fact, since its inception in 1916, JROTC has been regarded by some as a critical feature of revitalizing American military power by focusing on civilians and military personnel alike. As anthropologist Catherine Lutz (2001:33) notes, "preparedness movement" advocates of the early twentieth century advanced the idea that military conscription and training would "solve the problem they saw of American manhood gone soft." Military, popular, and political support for JROTC has waxed and waned over time, but Marvin Berlowitz and Nathan Long (2003:166) argue that since the mid-1970s, JROTC programs have "enjoyed expansion and reform with support from presidents and congressional representatives."[2] Today, JROTC advocates justify increased spending and the proliferation of JROTC programs by arguing that these instill values of discipline, hard work, and honor in "at risk" youth in American public schools. As many scholars have noted, JROTC programs operate with particular intensity in urban school districts largely serving poor and working-class youth of color.[3]

This chapter focuses on a critical feature of the new landscape of inequality wrought by neoliberal policies and ideology, namely, the rise of the punitive state in the form of military programs proliferating in American public schools. These programs are popular with many school administrators because they bring much needed federal monies for financially strapped schools. Simultaneously, they reinforce many public schools' turn to enforcement, surveillance, and discipline in order to meet the standards and accountability policies mandated by national educational policy. At a time when extracurricular activities such as art, drama, music, and even sports have been severely strained and cut, JROTC thrives and increasingly replaces these programs. As Roger Lancaster and Dorothy Roberts demonstrate (chapters 3 and 8, respectively, this volume), such moves highlight the increasingly punitive role that neoliberal governance plays in the lives of those residing within the United States today. Instead of resources and support, the most vulnerable in US society get surveillance, discipline, and punishment.

This chapter draws on interview data with JROTC cadets at Bellow Academy, a public high school located on Chicago's near northwest side, to explore why Latina/o youth turn to JROTC for the discipline, respect, and values they believe that they lack. In what follows, I examine how their lives are structured at school and in their communities by the realities of a punitive state that regards them not only as dangerous but also in need of discipline, surveillance, and reform. Participating in JROTC is one way Latina/o youth navigate the racialized urban landscape; it is also one way they attempt to lay claim to their rights and obligations as American citizens.

GLOBAL LATINA/O CHICAGO

Why do Latina/o youth in Chicago believe that they lack necessary qualities of discipline, leadership and respect?[4] And why do they seek to cultivate these values through participation in JROTC? The experiences of Latina/o youth in Chicago communities and public schools provide an important window into how they come to these understandings. In other words, their experiences are ideal sites for exploring what David Harvey (2005:41) refers to as "the material grounding for the construction of consent" for neoliberal policies and punitive measures shaping their lives in school and in their community. As Chicago struggles for its position as one of America's "global cities," it is increasingly characterized by what Saskia Sassen (1998:xxvi; see also Abu-Lughod 1999) describes as "a new geography of centrality and marginality," in which the extreme wealth and privilege generated by global finance produces low-wage, low-skill service jobs that are primarily filled by immigrants, African Americans, and Latina/o residents. As scholars have noted, Chicago also relies "heavily on a four-pronged strategy of school reform, upscale residential development, public housing demolition, and cultural and tourism development" (Boyd, chapter 5, this volume). How Latina/o youth are implicated in the city's development strategies and its racialized labor market is of great concern.

With more than three-quarters of a million Latina/o residents, Chicago is home to the third largest Latina/o population in the country and one of the most diverse—it is also the only place where large numbers of Mexicans and Puerto Ricans of several generations live, marry, and work side by side. According to the 2000 census, more than a quarter of Chicago's population is now Latina/o, a demographic shift that has contributed to an increase in the city's population for the first time in fifty years.[5] Mexicans and Mexican Americans are by far the largest of Chicago's Latina/o population, at slightly more than 70 percent, with Puerto Ricans constituting 15 percent. Latinas/os also constitute a majority in almost 15 percent of Chicago's seventy-seven official community areas.[6] Like New York City and Los Angeles, Chicago's economic, social, and cultural vitality results largely from its burgeoning Asian and Latin American—and primarily Mexican—populations.

Latinas/os, however, are also some of the city's most impoverished residents; nearly 24 percent of Latinas/os live in poverty. With limited employment opportunities primarily in the low-wage service sector, Puerto Ricans index the highest poverty rates in the city at 33.8 percent, compared with 33 percent for African American families and 26 percent for Mexicans.[7] In contrast with Cubans and South Americans, Puerto Ricans and Mexicans have lower educational and average-income levels and are concentrated in the low-wage service sector and as operatives.[8] Moreover, studies by the Latino Institute, the Chicago Urban League, and Northern Illinois University demonstrate that few of the jobs requiring only a high school diploma —and even many of those that demand some postsecondary education— pay a living wage for a family with dependent children.[9] According to the Latino Institute (1994), more than 75 percent of Puerto Ricans are employed in low-wage sectors of the economy. In short, the loss of manufacturing jobs in the Chicago area has rendered Latinos, in general, much poorer than a decade earlier, and Puerto Ricans, specifically, remain the most economically disadvantaged group in all Chicago.[10]

In addition to their marginal economic position, Latinas/os—like other working-class and working-poor communities in the city—suffer from the city's crisis of affordability and availability in housing.[11] Federal and municipal cutbacks in subsidized housing, the city's fast-track demolition program of older housing stock, and a concomitant rise in private residential development severely limit housing options for many Chicagoans. According to advocacy organization Latinos United, Latina/o residents have been particularly disadvantaged in this area because, until recently, federally assisted housing programs systematically have excluded them by failing to advertise CHA (Chicago Housing Authority) services in Spanish news media and to establish neighborhood offices servicing these communities.[12] Latina/o communities have also experienced some of the highest levels of gentrification in the city, a phenomenon that has had a profound impact on young men, who, within the racialized urban landscape, are regarded as dangerous and suspicious and are under constant surveillance by law enforcement. As sociologist Nancy López notes in her study of second-generation Caribbean youth, their experiences as racialized immigrants shape their daily life, including "[s]eemingly mundane and insignificant social interactions" with neighbors, law enforcement, storeowners, and strangers in public spaces: "At a very early age, second-generation youth learn that they are not viewed favorably in the larger society" (López 2003:16).

These racialized experiences in their communities and in public space affect how Latina/o youth navigate their social world; these experiences are also deeply gendered. Nancy López persuasively illustrates how young women believe that education is key to challenging the ways they are racialized as sexually immoral whereas young men often respond by doubting education as an effective avenue of social mobility for them. In Chicago, participating in JROTC is a means of challenging the ways they are regarded as both dangerous and irrelevant in the Chicago labor market. Latina/o youths' decisions to participate in JROTC therefore need to be analyzed within the material contexts of their schools and communities. Their decisions also need to be contextualized within the Chicago public school system, which is characterized by "a corporatist regime focused on accountability, high-stakes testing, standards, and centralized regulation of schools" and is also touted as a model for reforming America's troubled urban schools (Lipman 2003:81).

NEOLIBERALISM, MILITARISM, AND CHICAGO PUBLIC SCHOOLS

Chicago public schools provide a revealing example of how neoliberal versions of equity, freedom, and justice not only inform school policies but also justify severe punishments and discipline for those who dare to challenge them. Just as neoliberalism holds that the role of government is to create "a good business climate rather than look to the needs and well-being of the population at large" (Harvey 2005:48), the principal charge of the Chicago public schools' CEO is to provide a good learning environment in which students are both "free to learn" and are "held to the same standards" that were allegedly absent before reform (Lipman 2003:97). This ideology of equity and justice is particularly powerful, given the demographics of Chicago public school students. Nearly 85 percent of Chicago public school students come from low-income families and are either African American or Latina/o.[13] They are also increasingly enmeshed in what Pauline Lipman has identified as "stratified academic programs": African American and Latina/o high school students attend schools with "limited offerings of advanced courses and new vocational academies, basic skills transitional high schools," or public military academies, instead of the "[n]ew academically selective magnet schools and programs, mainly located in largely white upper-income and/or gentrifying neighborhoods" (Lipman 2003:81).

Chicago's public schools, for example, lead the nation with more than ten thousand students participating in a wide range of expanding public-school military programs. Chicago is home to two school-wide military academies, Chicago Military Academy and Carver Military Academy, both affiliated with the US Army and located on Chicago's south side; eight military academies within regular high schools (four affiliated with the Army, two with the Marines, and one with the Navy and the Air Force); the Middle School Military Academy, in the predominantly Mexican neighborhood of Little Village; and part-time JROTC in forty-three high schools and after-school programs at seventeen middle schools.[14] Elected officials and school administrators beyond Chicago have paid close attention to the city's expanded military programs. Chicago Military Academy has been nationally recognized as a model for military academies in Washington DC and in Oakland, California. In August 2001, for example, Mayor Jerry Brown inaugurated the Oakland Military Institute with the goal of preparing students to "become leaders in business, government and the arts."[15]

In Chicago, JROTC is part of the Education to Careers (ETC) program; its mission is to "equip students to successfully transition into post-secondary education, advanced training, and the workplace." To that end, ETC's stated goal in 2002 and 2003 is to "increase opportunities for students to explore military career options through JROTC" by increasing the overall numbers of JROTC participants to more than ten thousand by 2005 and, more specifically, to increase the number of JROTC middle schools to twenty-five.[16] High school students may participate in JROTC to satisfy the Chicago public high school career education requirement or, in some schools, to satisfy the physical education requirement for graduation. JROTC also offers many extracurricular activities, including honor guard, competitions, service, field trips, and opportunities to visit military installations. Many students explain that it is precisely these curricular and extracurricular offerings that make the program so appealing.

In addition to meeting graduation requirements and providing extracurricular activities, JROTC offers cadets less obvious rewards and benefits. Almost all the students I interviewed at Bellow Academy cited "being treated with respect" (especially while wearing the cadet uniform) as a reason for joining, as well as one of the greatest advantages of participating in JROTC. Students' concern with respect is no small matter because most reside in poor and working-class (and, often, slowly gentrifying) neighborhoods regarded in local media as dangerous, areas enmeshed in racialized policing practices aimed at containing suspect youth.[17] Latina/o and African American youth are also painfully aware of how their bodies are read—how the color of their skin, their manner of dress, and the places where they live elicit suspicion and fear from law enforcement, business owners, and even neighbors (Flores-González 2002; López 2003:37; Pérez 2004:147). Transgression of norms of dress, class, and ethnicity, Dwight Conquergood (1992:135) observed, "legitimizes official systems of surveillance, reform, enforcement and demolition." Wearing a military uniform is one way of negotiating the racialized systems of surveillance that operate within their neighborhoods and within their own schools.

Some scholars have argued that the proliferation of JROTC programs is only one example of a broader pattern of school security initiatives that justify zero-tolerance discipline policies and reflect "a rising culture of 'law and order' that pervades popular culture, educational discourse, foreign policy, and language" (Saltman 2003:21). Indeed, the emphasis of Chicago's school reform law on "accountability, high-stakes tests, standards, and centralized regulation of schools" has enabled administrators and elected officials to regulate teachers and students and to "'crack down' on African American and Latino youth who are seen as largely superfluous in Chicago's restructured, informational economy and dangerous in the racialized social landscape of the city" (Lipman 2003:81, 82).[18] In short, militarized schooling (despite JROTC's claims to "motivate people to be better citizens" and to develop citizenship) significantly undermines public democratic power by advancing a militarized notion of citizenship contingent upon unquestioning loyalty and obedience.[19]

These militarized notions of citizenship, however, can be extremely powerful and seductive for young people, especially for those who may not be citizens (or whose family members may not be) and even for those who may be legal citizens but whose behaviors, values, and attitudes represent what anthropologist Ana Yolanda Ramos-Zayas (2004) labels "deficient citizenship." If, as Cynthia Enloe (2000) argues, military service is often regarded as "the full path to full citizenship status" and "first class citizenship," then participating in JROTC may be one attempt at laying claim to citizenship rights, obligations, and duties. The students whom I interviewed never directly explained their participation in JROTC as a way of laying claim to citizenship rights and status, but their concern about money, desire for financial independence, hope for educational attainment and social mobility, and enjoyment of the respect that wearing a military or JROTC uniform conferred upon them speak to the social meaning of citizenship that is defined, in part, by the dignity and ability to work and to be paid. Political theorist Judith Shklar (1991:3) persuasively argues that, in the United States, citizenship has been fundamentally a matter of social standing characterized by the ability to promote one's interests (vote) and to make money (earn). Those unable to earn or be economically independent are not full members of society: "In effect, the people who belong to the under-class are not quite citizens" (Shklar 1991:22).

Chicago Latinas/os' precarious economic position, their location within a public school system increasingly espousing neoliberal ideologies of equity, justice, and freedom, and the neoliberal state's increasingly punitive role all shape the range of opportunities available to Latina/o youth. Understanding these constraints, as well as the social meaning of citizenship, helps clarify why Latina/o youth turn to JROTC and military service, even in a time of increasing danger.

DISCIPLINE, RESPECT, AND JROTC

In June 2004 I spent three days observing and interviewing young men and women participating in a Chicago public high school JROTC program. Of the nineteen students I interviewed, ten were Latina, eight Latino, and one African American. Most of the students were born in Chicago; eight were born in Mexico. A majority of those interviewed were Mexican. Only six students were Puerto Rican. Everyone spoke English and Spanish to varying degrees. All but four of the interviews were conducted in English.[20] When I first arrived, the JROTC commanding officer, retired Major Ellis, gave me private office space to conduct interviews, which I tape-recorded. I asked students a range of questions, including how they decided to participate in JROTC, their experiences in "RO" (as they referred to the program), their goals for joining, the challenges and benefits of participating, their career plans for after high school, and whether members of their family had been in the military. Most of the students concurred that one particularly appealing aspect of RO was that it fulfilled the physical education requirement, but they varied widely regarding their plans after high school and their reasons for joining JROTC.

In addition to talking with students, I spent much time with Major Ellis, observed his interactions with students in and out of the classroom, watched student leaders supervise and inspect the class, and spoke at length with some students whom I had interviewed. I also talked casually with students who did not want to be formally interviewed but who wanted to talk about their experiences in JROTC. All spoke very highly of their experiences in RO and of Major Ellis. On these particularly warm, early summer days, the students were clearly distracted, eager to begin their summer vacations. Many spoke excitedly about their summer plans, including employment in construction, restaurants, and city-run community arts programs. Others spoke of the scholarships they received, as first-generation students of color, to attend summer classes at various colleges and universities. One student shared her excitement about attending boot camp in Wisconsin in late June/early July. The atmosphere in all the classes I observed was congenial and supportive, with moments of quiet as cadets were called to attention by their cadet leader.

In the afternoons after school, I had several conversations with Major Ellis, who spoke fondly of his students and their aspirations after high school and of his vision of how JROTC may support those dreams. A father of young adult children, whom he encouraged not to join the military, Major Ellis spoke at great length about his own military career, how at a young age he enlisted in the Army to help pay for his college education, and about his early marriage, the marital strain familiar to many military couples, and his new career as a high school teacher. Major Ellis noted several times how challenging it was to teach in Chicago public schools and how the commute from Wisconsin to Chicago was particularly grueling. But he expressed a deep level of personal and professional satisfaction. I soon understood why the students held Major Ellis in such high regard: He is kind, soft-spoken, and respectful. He is also a thoughtful listener who quickly puts you at ease. Maggie, a young Mexican American cadet who was then a junior, noted: "[The commanders] always encourage us to do good in school. You know, to keep our grades up, because if you go under a C…Major [will] talk to you. They want to know what's happening, what's going on. And then they're always encouraging us.…They talk to us about going to college."

Major Ellis was very clear with me: he did not encourage his students to join the military after high school. In fact, he alluded to recurring tension between himself and military recruiters who frequently visited campus. If students wanted to pursue military careers, he was willing to support them and provide guidance. But, as with his own children, he spoke of different career paths for his JROTC students. Because I was at Bellow Academy immediately following the Abu Ghraib torture revelations, we inevitably (and carefully) discussed military training, the use of torture, and the war in Iraq, which he supported but more out of a sense of loyalty to American troops deployed in Iraq than a belief that the war was right. Although Major Ellis clearly had concerns about the present and future in the military, he was unwavering in his belief in JROTC as a program that supports, directs, and encourages young people to succeed in school and beyond.

My interviews with cadets confirmed these understandings of JROTC. In what follows, I highlight two recurring themes from their narratives:

first, JROTC provides students with skills they believe will be useful to them in reaching their future goals, and, second, JROTC instills particular values that students identify as critical for their future success and which they feel that they lacked before joining JROTC. Students' reflections on the skills and values they cultivate as a result of participation in JROTC are also marked by frequent reference to their families' economic realities, as well as a keen understanding of contemporary US politics' impact on immigrants' lives.

SKILLS AND PREPARATION

When I asked the students how they became interested in JROTC, almost everyone described a particular event that sparked initial curiosity about JROTC. Sixteen-year-old Letty, who was moved to Chicago from Acapulco, Mexico, when she was four months old, recalled seeing a girl wearing a military uniform on the bus and learning about JROTC from her. This conversation intrigued her. I asked her why, and she responded, "They show you how to be a leader…I was mostly used to being a follower. So I wanted to learn how it was to be a leader." When I asked how JROTC teaches her to be a leader, she explained in detail how, as squad leader, she now organizes the cadets in lines and makes sure that her squad is in order and how she can continue to "get rank" ("depending on your behavior and your commitment to RO"):

> Well, I am in Color Guard. And in the mornings, I don't miss a day in the mornings. And I'm always going. If there is an event going on, I'm always a part of it…I've always been the kind of girl that I can't stay and not do nothing. And I always have to do something, and right now, they are giving me the opportunity to do something, so I'll just do it.

Letty explained also how she had remained in school because of JROTC: "It's because of ROTC that I am here. Because all of the responsibilities that we have, it makes us want to come to school so we can finish it. And because of ROTC, it makes us come to school." Many other students shared Letty's emphasis on leadership skills, on the value of the responsibilities given in JROTC, and on the way the program motivates students to stay in school. Marisol, a young Puerto Rican cadet whose father was a Marine, described how JROTC helped her to develop skills critical for college:

> I want to go to college, and I want to get my degree in history. I want to be an archaeologist. I like to study things about the past

and stuff. I would like to go away for college…and they [JROTC] teach you to focus. It teaches you to prepare for anything. It teaches you to take responsibility for what you want to happen in your life. It teaches you to stand your own ground.

Being a leader, focusing, managing others, and getting others to follow were skills the students valued not only in the context of school but also in helping them get into college. Sixteen-year-old Richie, who was born in Guanajuato and arrived in Chicago when he was five years old, spoke force-fully about how the confidence and responsibility he cultivated in JROTC would help him to go to college. Asked what the greatest benefit was for participating in JROTC, he explained:

> Basically, the knowledge that I can do whatever I want. Because right now I'm taking charge of the entire battalion in the school.…I'm the executive officer, which is the highest, the second highest. But now that the seniors are leaving, I'm going to be raised to battalion commander, which is the highest…[he] makes the vision for the entire school. He makes whatever the battalion commander wants to happen. So promotions, demotions, events, basically everything.

When I commented that being in charge is, indeed, a great responsibility and asked whether he believes that having this responsibility will make him more attractive for a job or college later on, he immediately replied, "Of course! Yes. It also helps college applications, knowing that I controlled the entire school program. It always, it never hurts."

Like Richie, other students noted how the skills derived from JROTC would be useful in their lives, especially if they join the military. Students noted, for example, that participation in JROTC will give them some rank if they join the military after high school. And many of them were seriously considering military service after high school, often as a means to pay for college. Maggie explained:

> I want to go into the military. I might want to join the Air Force or the Marines…I want something, I want to experience something new. Like, over the summer last year, I went to Georgetown University to take classes. And I mean, I got a feeling of what college is and how just everyday having to go to school and stuff. And…it was nice, but I wanted something more than just going to school, I guess. 'Cause since I like traveling a lot, I guess that's

why I want to go into the military. And college now is kind of expensive, and I don't want my parents to have to pay for it. So...I guess just ever since I was little, like twelve years old, I kind of, I don't know, like the commercials from the Army, I would say, like, "Oh, that's cool." And I used to watch the commercials...and I just kind of encouraged myself to...I wanted to be in the military ever since I was a little girl.

Maggie referred to many reasons why the military appeals to her: money for college, travel, financial independence; she described how from an early age she was attracted to the military by Army commercials. She decided to participate in JROTC, in part, because her mother encouraged her to do so, but she is also very clear about how participation in the program leads to other possibilities for her after high school. Like Richie, Marisol, and other peers, Maggie believes that the leadership skills she builds in JROTC and the opportunities it might open up after high school are some of the most important reasons to join JROTC.

MILITARY VALUES, HISPANIC VALUES?

Perhaps the most striking feature of my interviews with JROTC students was their unanimous agreement that the program instilled in them important values such as discipline and respect. For some students, their parents had encouraged them to join JROTC rather than take physical education, because they believed that the program would provide structure and discipline. Sixteen-year-old Gabby described her mother as "real strict," saying that originally she did not want to join JROTC but that her mom encouraged her to do so. When I asked her why, she explained: "So they could be strict on me. I don't know. So I could see how discipline is...and [so they could] teach me some of those things." When I asked whether her mom thought that she lacked discipline, she laughed:

> Yeah, because I used to sometimes talk back to her. I don't know....I was, like, "No, I don't want to join it! It's going to be hard. I don't know how to do pushups. I don't want to do nothing. And...if you put me in there, I'm gonna get into trouble. I'm telling you." And she was like, "*No*, you're not. At first, you're gonna hate it, but then you're gonna like it." So then—yeah, I like it. It's nice. It's cool.

Originally, Gabby resisted joining JROTC, but she talked at great length about how much she now enjoys being in the program, what she has learned. She says that she is considering going into the Marines after high school graduation, despite her mother's protests. Like Gabby, Marisol also talked at great length about how she initially became interested in JROTC because of the discipline it teaches you. Eighteen-year-old Antonio also noted that wanting to become more disciplined was one of the principal reasons he joined JROTC:

> Actually, it was the discipline [that first got me interested in JROTC]. Because, I mean, we have to learn so many things. How to mark, the chain of command. But the cool thing about it is that it's not the adults, you know. The people that's in charge are our age....There are people our own age who have rank. So we can get used to that.

That JROTC teaches discipline and gives students an opportunity to be leaders speaks to another recurring theme highlighted in the interviews, namely, that being in JROTC commands respect from their peers, communities, and families and friends. Like Antonio, Carlos explained how his desire for discipline and respect led him to join JROTC: "I wanted discipline. I wanted to be able to respect and to get respect back. And I wanted to get high rank—I like to boss people around!" Both Carlos and I laughed after this last statement, but he was sincere in his desire to receive respect and show respect to others. He also mentioned that he was encouraging his younger sister to join JROTC when she gets into high school, so that she will finally have to listen to him and obey him, because he will have rank over her. He complained that she never listened to him.

According to Marisol, being in JROTC made her more disciplined and taught her how to "take charge." These are important qualities that others now admired in her. Since joining JROTC, she regularly woke up early to go to drill before classes began in the morning, and she was doing more physical exercise. Her mother, who initially objected to her participation in JROTC, was now praising Marisol for being more responsible. Wearing the uniform was particularly important for Marisol and was an important connection she shared with an uncle who was also in the Marines. When I asked whether she liked wearing the uniform, she answered emphatically: "Yes. I don't know, it just...shows people that I'm trying to do something with my life. I'm in JROTC." Many students talked at length about the uniform—how they preferred the Marines' uniform over all other military dress, how wearing it made them feel that they were "somebody," and how being in JROTC made them feel proud. Lorena explained that she enjoyed excelling in JROTC because it gave her a sense of pride: "I really want to be proud of myself, to show other people that I can do something." When I asked whether there were other things she was proud of, she quickly added: "I'm proud of myself because my grades are very good. My GPA is 3.0. So I'm very proud of that. I'm proud of my family, you know, because they're all very successful. My dad owns a company...and I want to follow in their footsteps."

Wearing the uniform, becoming more disciplined, and earning rank and respect are all ways in which many young people said that participating in JROTC was important to them. Seventeen-year-old Wendy explained: "I'm stronger in RO...it made me feel more respectful and stuff like that. Like, I'm not wild and crazy like I was before, running around...I used to...run around the block and be crazy with my friends. Now, I'm just, like, I go home. I volunteer. I go back. I just do my homework, and after that, it's time for me to go to sleep. For me, I'm just busy."

Despite their positive attitudes about JROTC and the military, however, there are critical moments of discontent, frustration, and disillusionment emerging from their attempts to make sense of the ways in which they, as Latinas/os and Latin American immigrants, are located within the American nation. As noted above, Nilda, for example, was extremely positive about the skills JROTC provided her. But she was also incredibly circumspect when she talked about Latinas/os' patriotism. Even though noncitizen Latina/o soldiers demonstrate tremendous patriotism by serving in the military, she observed, they still lack equal rights with other Americans: "[Latinos] are patriotic. Even though they might not be given the same rights [as Americans]. Even though they're actually fighting for that in *this* country, which I still think is crazy that some of them can't vote because they're not citizens. But they're still fighting."

According to a recent *New York Times* article, noncitizen enlistment in the military has actually decreased since 2002, but Nilda's comments are important because they offer a window into how young Latinas/os apprehend and navigate their simultaneous inclusion in the nation and exclusion. Her comments also gesture toward a long history of Latina/o organizing and ongoing efforts to bring about progressive social change within new, shifting, and unequal landscapes in the United States and abroad.

CONCLUSION

Students have complicated, and sometimes contradictory, reasons for participating in JROTC and considering the military after high school. But the degree to which they underscore their desire and need for discipline, respect, and to "be somebody" in these decisions is striking. How do those of us who research these questions remain true to the complicated sentiments students shared with me regarding their thoughts about JROTC and the military, without affirming extremely seductive and, I would argue, simplistic understandings of Latina/o youth, culture, and behavior? And how do we ground these decisions within shifting political-economic contexts in the United States and their countries of origin?

As I read the interview transcripts, analyze media accounts of military recruitment, and hear more about how many working-class youth struggle with their future plans after high school and college, I understand, once again, the need for careful ethnography of Latina/o youth, their families, and their communities. For students in Bellow Academy's JROTC program, their decision to participate in JROTC is inextricably linked to their families' economic circumstance. Contemplating a career in the military after high school is also deeply informed by their understanding of what kinds of jobs are available to them, a concern with how they will finance a college education, and the dream of gaining particular skills and experiences that will translate into economic security. All these dreams are increasingly circumscribed by a local political economy in which they are often not only superfluous but also regarded as a threat and a danger. Dominant perceptions of them as (undocumented) immigrants, "hoodlums," and "at risk" youth justify the rise of punitive governance in the form of surveillance, discipline, and, most recently, a 700-mile-long wall along the US-Mexican border.

Latina/o youth and their families therefore find themselves at an uncertain crossroads in this neoliberal moment. As one of the youngest and fastest-growing groups in the country, they fill American public schools, seek to go to college, and face diminishing government support in the form of Pell Grants and other financial aid at a time when college education is increasingly unaffordable, even in public institutions. These changes are concomitant with the federal government's active role in educational policy in the form of No Child Left Behind, which allows military recruiters to have unfettered access to students—in school cafeterias, hallways, and career days throughout the year—and to students' personal information so that recruiters can follow up on conversations and contacts made during school hours. The number of JROTC units has also expanded since the late 1990s, with President Bill Clinton lifting the cap on JROTC units from 2,900 to 3,500.

Thus, many young people, faced with a limited range of choices, turn to the military and JROTC to provide skills, support, and values they believe to be critical for their success. In this way, Latina/o youth access precious federal resources, but they do so by participating in militarized understandings of citizenship, rights, and duties. If, as political theorist Judith Shklar (1991:3) notes, "the struggle for citizenship in America has... been overwhelmingly a demand for inclusion in the polity," Latina/o participation in military service and JROTC may be seen as one way of laying claim to their rights, as well as demanding their complete inclusion in the American nation, especially at a time when their presence is contested and resisted. The problem, however, is that this kind of inclusion is contingent and provisional; it also relies on reinvigorated notions of a citizen-soldier that can be employed to exclude and deny others full citizenship rights. Perhaps one of the saddest consequences of neoliberalism is that it reduces rather than expands the social meaning of citizenship.

Notes

1. All personal names and school names throughout this chapter are pseudonyms.

2. Berlowitz and Long also note powerful attempts by pacifists to challenge the preparedness activists' calls for conscription and the growth of the military. See Lutz 2001:33–36 for how these debates unfolded in Fayetteville, North Carolina.

3. See Berlowitz and Long 2003; Lipman 2003; Lutz and Bartlett 1995, 1998; Mariscal 2004; Saltman 2003.

4. Sections of the following analysis draw from Pérez 2006:56–58.

5. *New York Times*, "Chicago Reverses 50 Years of Declining Population," March 15, 2001; *Chicago Tribune*, "Hispanics Increase City's Population," March 15, 2001.

6. According to the 2000 census, Latinas/os are a majority in eleven of the city's seventy-seven community areas. See *Chicago Tribune*, "Hispanics Increase City's Population," March 15, 2001.

7. Latino Institute 1995.

8. John Betancur, Cordova, and Torres (1993) point out that despite Cubans' and South Americans' economic success, their wages according to the 1980 census still approximated those of Puerto Ricans and Mexicans rather than that of whites. The 1990 census, however, paints a very different picture, emphasizing the growing gap between Puerto Ricans and other Latino groups in terms of average incomes, employment rates, and poverty levels.

9. See Chicago Urban League, Latino Institute, and Northern Illinois University 1994, 1995a, 1995b.

10. Ranney and Cecil argue that economic restructuring has had an adverse

effect on women, Latinos, and blacks in the Chicago metropolitan area who were largely located in assembly work, electronics, and machine operation. The loss of employment in the manufacturing sector as a result of economic restructuring, for example, "imposes serious costs on a segment of the population which requires specific government remedies" (Ranney and Cecil 1993:13).

11. Cordova 1991:37. For more on Puerto Ricans, Latinas/os, gentrification, and housing, see Pérez 2004:135–141.

12. Latinos United's lawsuit against the CHA and the US Department of Housing and Urban Development ushered in important changes in CHA housing policies in 1996. CHA housing offices were opened on the north and south sides of the city; CHA implemented an aggressive $1.6 million campaign to inform Latinos of housing services available to them; CHA advertised in the Spanish news media the opening of a Section 8 waiting list; and CHA agreed to set aside 20 percent of its yearly vouchers for Latino families.

13. Chicago Public Schools, "CPS at a Glance," February 2005, http://www.cps.k12.il.us/AtAGlance.html, accessed March 2005. The following analysis draws from Pérez 2006. The three full-time military academies, Chicago Military Academy, Carver Area High School, and Austin Community Academy, all opened since 1999.

14. Ana Beatriz Cholo, "Military Marches into Middle Schools," *Chicago Tribune*, July 26, 2002; Chicago Public Schools, JROTC Program Book, n.d.; Education to Careers (ETC) FY2003-2004, http://www.cps.k12.il.us/AboutCPS/Financial_Information/FY2004_Final/CPS_Unit/Education/Education_to_Careers.pdf, accessed March 2005.

15. David Goodman, "Recruiting the Class of 2005," *Mother Jones*, January-February 2002.

16. CPS budget, FY2002 and FY2003. One news report cites that Lt. Rick Mill's goal is fifteen thousand by 2007. Claire Schaeffer-Duffy, "Feeding the Military Machine," *National Catholic Reporter*, March 28, 2003.

17. Elsewhere (Pérez 2002), I have documented how Latina/o youth, especially those in rapidly gentrifying neighborhoods, are implicated in the policing of urban space aimed at curbing, for example, gang activity. Although Chicago's anti-loitering ordinance was declared unconstitutional in 1999, some scholars and activists have highlighted the "ongoing attempts to legalize harassment and street sweeps of youth," and particularly youth of color, who are regarded as dangerous and allegedly "need to be locked up or removed from public space" (Lipman 2003:95).

18. Lipman notes, for example, how Chicago's 1995 school reform law not only gave Mayor Richard Daley control of the schools but also allowed Chicago Public

School CEO Paul Vallas (and eventually Gery Chico) to establish "a corporatist regime focused on accountability, high-stakes testing, standards, and centralized regulation of schools," which has resulted in the retention of thousands of Latino and black youths, as well as their being sent "to mandatory remedial programs and basic education transition high schools" (Lipman 2003:81). The result has been a deepening stratification of academic programs and stronger centralized control over local school districts.

19. Saltman (2003:21) notes, for example, that attempts to address the militarization of education "must go beyond challenging militarized schooling so as to challenge the many ways that militarism as a cultural logic enforces the expansion of corporate power and decimates public democratic power."

20. The students I interviewed were heterogeneous in language ability (ranging from fully bilingual in English and Spanish to predominantly monolingual in either language) and in length of stay in the United States; it did not appear that either of these factors accounted for differences in experiences and attitudes regarding JROTC and military service. Students specified country of birth, but I did not ask them to identify their citizenship or legal status. None referred to their legal status in explaining their decisions to participate in JROTC or to consider military careers in the future.

7

The Specter of Slavery

*Workfare and the Economic Citizenship
of Poor Women*

Jane L. Collins

Rachel Fernandez was born in Puerto Rico, but her parents moved to Milwaukee when she was still a baby.[1] At the time I interviewed her, she had four children, three of whom were living with her. She was on parole from a minor drug conviction. Rachel was feeling very grateful to have her children back and was working hard to reestablish a stable place for them. She had turned to the state of Wisconsin's new workfare program, hoping that the caseworkers there would help her get her GED and find an office job. But the requirements of the Wisconsin Works (W-2) program left her frustrated:

> I do what they want me to do. Things I don't want to do....Like right now, they gave me an activity to work at a pantry shop [food pantry] that I'm not interested in whatsoever. My interest was computer and office assistant classes, and they don't want to put me in that. But they force us to do it just to get our little paycheck. Sometimes I feel like saying, "Screw W-2." You know? But I can't, because I can't afford my rent or my bills, so I have to do the things they want me to do.

Serena Clark grew up in a house full of drug addicts. She started selling drugs when she was eleven. But when she was about sixteen, a religious organization took her in and helped her overcome her addiction. For a while, she traveled around the country, giving testimony about her experiences. Returning to Milwaukee, Serena married and gave birth to a son in 2001. In 2003 she turned to Wisconsin's workfare program to see whether she could get support while training as an AODA (alcohol and drug abuse) counselor. She was participating in a minority training program at a reputable drug and alcohol treatment center and believed that she had found her calling. But her "employment counselor" felt that this was not in keeping with the work-first philosophy of the state program. Serena was critical of what she perceived as the shortsightedness of this approach:

> She says I shouldn't be wasting my time at the [counseling training], that I need to make more time to do my job logs, or I need to find a full-time job, you know, like working as a waitress, rather than having a part-time job and doing what I want to do for my future. She wants me to give up my hopes, my dreams. What the hell am I gonna do that for? Give up all this I accomplished just to be a waitress?

Building on accounts such as these, in this chapter I seek to understand the temporally and geographically specific labor market of southeastern Wisconsin from 1999 to 2004. I explore the way in which Wisconsin's reformed welfare practices—as implemented by private agencies contracted by the state—have shaped the labor market experiences of low-wage workers. Many evaluations of the historic welfare reform of 1996 —named, without shame or irony, the Personal Responsibility and Work Opportunity Reconciliation Act (PRWORA)—have concluded that its expulsion of impoverished mothers to the bottom of the labor market did not much improve their circumstances. But I make a stronger claim: the policies of welfare reform that force poor mothers to work long hours outside the home have undermined the economic citizenship of these women.

LABOR MARKETS AND WELFARE

Debates over the impact of welfare on labor markets date back to Elizabethan poor laws. Claims that any aid makes those who receive it dependent and weak have accompanied every new initiative to provide relief. Hirschman (1991) and Somers and Block (2005) call this response a "rhetoric of perversity," which asserts that aid to the poor creates perverse incentives, breeding dependency and undermining the will to work. Based in Malthusian metaphors of natural law that interpret scarcity as a "spur to labor," this rhetoric warns against the dangers of state intervention in the labor market.

In contrast, those who have advocated public aid have understood it as softening the harshest impacts of market rationality. One of the most explicit formulations of this perspective can be found in Karl Polanyi's (2001) *The Great Transformation*. Polanyi argued that, when eras of market fundamentalism push labor to the breaking point, social groups demand what he called a "double movement" (Polyani 2001:79): a network of policies designed to temper the treatment of labor as a simple commodity.

In a similar way, Frances Piven and Richard Cloward have seen welfare policies as responses to the destructive effects of unregulated labor markets. In *Regulating the Poor* (1993), they present the history of the welfare state in the United States not as a progressive liberalization but rather as characterized by periodic expansion and contraction. They argue that government provided social supports only when threatened with civil disorder and that when disorder waned, government withdrew support in ways that reinforced work discipline. Tracing the history of the two major relief expansions of the past century—the New Deal and the War on Poverty—Piven and Cloward link them to the social uprisings of their periods. After these movements were palliated and order restored, federal agencies returned control of social programs to localities and instituted new rules that channeled workers back into the low-wage labor market (Piven and Cloward 1993). Although a number of authors have criticized Piven and Cloward for their functionalism (Kincaid 1990; Shaver 1989) and for neglecting gender and domestic labor (Gordon 1988), their work remains a compelling account of how welfare programs articulate with struggles over labor rights and regulation.

Recent work by Jamie Peck has brought these debates into the post-PRWORA, workfare era. Peck (2001:6) claims that workfare "is not about creating jobs for people who don't have them" but about creating "workers for jobs that nobody wants." He sees welfare as establishing a floor under the labor market, setting the conditions under which certain groups, at certain times, have access to means of subsistence outside the market. He decries the rhetoric that frames workfare as overcoming the motivational deficiencies of the poor; instead, he argues that it is designed to counteract the weak pull of contingent and undesirable work at poverty wages (Peck 2001:185). In Peck's analysis of local workfare regimes, he focuses on what he calls the "boundary institutions" of the labor market: these include welfare offices, but also schools, hospitals, and prisons. Peck (2001:52) argues that these institutions adjust the flow of workers into and out of the labor market and also remake the workers themselves, shaping their attitudes toward work and wages, their expectations about employment continuity and promotion, and their identities.

Building on these accounts, I explore the way in which Wisconsin's reformed welfare practices, as implemented by private agencies contracted by the state, adjusted the flow of workers in and out of the labor market and remade workers in the context of the labor market of southeastern Wisconsin from 1998 to 2004.

GENDER, RACE, AND ECONOMIC CITIZENSHIP

Kessler-Harris (2001:17) has written about the changing rights that "accrue to men and women as part of the obligation to engage in wage work." Like others who study the American welfare system, she notes that the US state has attached its most valuable benefits first to property and later to wage work. In particular, it has distributed rights to income security—programs such as social security and unemployment insurance—through work, rather than residence or citizenship. For this reason, Kessler-Harris finds T. H. Marshall's (1950) classic list of citizenship forms (civil, political, and social) incomplete. Because key rights have been tied to earning in the United States, she proposes the additional category of economic citizenship—which interacts with, but is distinct from, other forms (Kessler-Harris 2001).

Judith Shklar traces the rise of work as a marker of citizenship to the Jacksonian period. Jacksonian democrats asserted that to work and to receive an earned reward was a right; they held that we are citizens only if we earn. They developed the idea of the worker-citizen—who was, of course, white and male—by contrasting him to the slave, on one hand, and the idle aristocrat, on the other. For them, the emblem of the proper citizen was the white male craft worker (Shklar 1991). As Fraser and Gordon have shown, the language of dependency marked this boundary. Those on one side were autonomous, independent workingmen who supported their families, and those on the other were considered psychologically or morally unfit for citizenship (Fraser and Gordon 1994:318).[2]

Many scholars have pointed out that, theoretically, respect and resources in the public sphere could have been tied to family roles and that caregiving could have been a route to democratic participation. In the early twentieth century, protective labor legislation and mothers' pensions began to solidify a new role for "mother-citizens" (Lister 1997). But each step toward enhancing the social rights of motherhood closed paths to economic citizenship for women by requiring them to stand back from the labor market. Thus, welfare programs in the United States "created a...pattern of rewards and discouragement that effectively regulated the family lives and labor market behavior of mothers in line with patriarchal expectations," at least until the passage of the 1996 welfare reform act (Kessler-Harris 2001:13–17).

The rights and benefits of economic citizenship forged during the New Deal—social security, unemployment insurance, access to credit, lower mortgage rates—accrued mainly to men by virtue of their status as workers. But the policies of this period configured citizenship along lines of race as well. Seeking support from southern politicians, Roosevelt excluded from New Deal programs the categories of work in which blacks predominated (such as agricultural and domestic labor). Workers in these sectors had no access to social security, workers' compensation, or unemployment insurance. Because these jobs were rarely unionized, their workers gained no protections under the new National Labor Relations Board; they were also exempt from the wage and hours protections of the Fair Labor Standards Act (Mettler 1998; Quadagno 1994). As Dorothy Roberts (1996: 1563) has argued, "racism structured the political choices that led to the current system of welfare," and America's stratified and unequal welfare programs and labor laws reflected, and perpetuate, a "racial definition of citizenship."

Over the second half of the twentieth century, with growing labor force participation, some women moved into economic citizenship. Since the 1970s and particularly in the 1990s, a new balance of power between workers and employers eroded key benefits of economic citizenship for all workers: decreasing job security, loss of benefits. More temporary and casual work resulted. Welfare reform in 1996 intersected with these two trends. The reforms, which required poor women to work for benefits rather than claim these as mothers, placed them on the threshold of economic citizenship at the moment that our social contract vis-à-vis work was changing.

DATA AND METHODS

Working with a research team, I conducted the interviews in this chapter between April and July 2004 as part of a project at the Institute for Research on Poverty at the University of Wisconsin.[3] Using a sampling frame that ensured proportional coverage of differences in race and other important factors, we randomly selected potential participants who had recently been enrolled in a "lower tier" of the Wisconsin Works (W-2) program from the state welfare system's administrative records. Wisconsin Works, the Wisconsin version of welfare reform, has an especially heavy focus on work.[4] Sixty-nine percent of the women we contacted in Milwaukee and Racine counties agreed to be interviewed.

Our interviews covered household composition, work and income, work–family balance, livelihood problems and solutions, social networks and support, and social program participation. We collected work histories for each woman, focusing on her last five jobs. Because we had access to state data on W-2 participation, food stamp receipt, and supplemental security income (SSI), as well as to unemployment insurance data on jobs, we verified each woman's personal account with state records. In all instances, women's responses to our interview questions were consistent with the official data.

THE LABOR MARKETS OF MILWAUKEE AND RACINE

Milwaukee and Racine share a past as industrial centers and a present characterized by struggles to move to a service-based economy. Milwaukee has made more headway toward this goal than Racine, having invested heavily in tourism and downtown entertainment facilities in the 1990s, but both counties have a much higher share of their workforce in manufacturing than the nation as a whole (20 percent and 30 percent, respectively, as opposed to 11 percent [COWS 2000, 2002]).

Both counties also have experienced deindustrialization. Analysts have described Milwaukee as "devastated by the rust belt recession of the 1980s" (Bernhardt, Dresser, and Rogers 2004:233). Since the 1970s, the city has lost almost 60 percent of its manufacturing jobs. Some have referred to this pattern of job loss as a "stealth depression," evolving slowly as unemployment rates have crept up and discouraged workers have left the labor market (Levine 2003a). Not only have manufacturing jobs disappeared, but also overall job growth has been anemic, up only 0.4 percent between 1991 and 2000. In addition, all net job growth in the metro area since 1995 has occurred in the suburbs, leading economists to talk about a "structural spatial mismatch" between the high unemployment in the inner city and job growth in the suburban "greenfields" (Levine 2003a:3, 12).

Deindustrialization did not affect white and black families equally. Zeidenberg notes:

> During the post-war economic boom, large numbers of blacks migrated to Milwaukee, Racine and other northern manufacturing cities. Many were able to move out of poverty and into the working class. In fact, by the 1970s, black workers in Wisconsin earned median wages well above their national counterparts.

> However, the loss of manufacturing jobs in the 1980s has led to
> increasing concentrations of poverty in black communities....
> These high poverty neighborhoods grew continuously in size
> between 1969 and 1989, with most of the expansion occurring in
> the 1980s. [Zeidenberg 2004:4–5]

In 2003, the unemployment rate for the city of Milwaukee was 9.3 percent, at a time when the average for the fifty largest US cities was 6.9 percent (Levine 2003a:7). But even this very high number hid massive disparities. Unemployment for white workers was 3.3 percent in 2000; for black workers, it was 16 percent (Levine 2003b). In 2002 nearly 60 percent of working-age black men in the city were jobless, by far the highest rate of any city surveyed by the Bureau of Labor Statistics (Levine 2004:3). In 1990 the city ranked last among major US metropolitan areas in the proportion of blacks holding managerial jobs, and in 1992, last in the number of black-owned firms (Levine 2003b).

The large number of African American men whom Levine found to be "outside" the labor market is connected to rates of black imprisonment in the state. The disparity in black:white imprisonment rates in Wisconsin at the end of the 1990s was 20:1, the third highest in the nation. The black:white ratio of new prison sentences for drug offenses rose from 22:1 in 1990 to 67:1 in 1999. Nearly half these new sentences were for the ambiguous category of "intent to deliver." Researchers attribute much of this disparity to "back end" criminal justice processing, such as sentencing decisions, but also to law enforcement practices such as "sweeps," where police clear out "high crime" neighborhoods by arresting everyone possible on any charge possible (Oliver 2001; Oliver and Yocum 2002). Men with a criminal record, and especially felony convictions, have difficulty re-entering the labor market.

Not unexpectedly, these trends affect income and poverty. African American household income in Milwaukee was 50 percent of white household income; Milwaukee ranked forty-ninth among the fifty largest urban areas on this measure. The black poverty rate in metro Milwaukee in 2000 was 32.5 percent, six times the white rate. White residents of Milwaukee were twice as likely as black residents to own their homes. Pervasive patterns of residential segregation led some inner-city neighborhoods to be 95 percent black (Levine 2003b).

Like Milwaukee, Racine County has experienced deindustrialization, although manufacturing remains a more important part of its employment base. It experienced modest job growth over most of the 1990s, with the majority of new jobs concentrated in construction (COWS 2000:6). The per capita income and educational attainment of Racine's inhabitants are slightly higher than those for Milwaukee, and its proportion of African American and Latino residents is somewhat smaller. But like Milwaukee, Racine is a divided city. A report on concentrated poverty notes that in 2000 Racine had one center-city census tract with a poverty rate of more than 45 percent. This tract was 75 percent black (Zeidenberg 2004:18).

WOMEN'S LABOR MARKET HISTORIES

It is common in American political culture to portray women who turn to the welfare system as dependent and unwilling to work. Aid is said to create perverse incentives that lead poor women to withdraw their labor from the market and to focus on raising children. As Roberts (1999), Solinger (1999), and others have shown, lifestyles that society encouraged for middle-class white women in earlier decades were pathologized by public discourse when chosen by poor women. The corollary to the dominant view of welfare dependency is that, with proper incentives and pressures, poor women can get and keep jobs and that work will eventually lead to a living wage and to self-sufficiency.

In a review of empirical studies of welfare reform and work, Mary Corcoran and her co-authors show that both assumptions are untrue. They found that poor women can and do get jobs but that there is considerable volatility to their work trajectories linked to physical and mental health problems, substance abuse, family stresses, employer discrimination, and partner violence (Corcoran et al. 2000:249). In a similar way, we found that roughly half of the women with whom we spoke were working at the time of the interview. Of those who were not, half were looking for work, and the other half had a serious health or mental health problem or an ill or disabled child. All the women had held a variety of jobs in the past, some as many as twenty-five. More than 60 percent had worked at a job for more than a year. Some had held responsible managerial positions. Still, the work trajectories for many women were disrupted by personal or family crises.

The volatility of women's employment was not just a product of their personal dilemmas, however, but was inextricably linked to the kinds of employment they found. Many of these jobs (15 percent) were seasonal or temporary in nature. Few offered sick leave, personal days, or maternity leave. When the women we interviewed were ill, had a sick child, or were about to give birth, they had few alternatives. They talked about quitting jobs when they had to care for children who were hospitalized or injured, when they had to take in relatives' children, when their kids were in the court system, and when they needed to care for dying parents. They also quit jobs when their cars died and they could not get to work, when their bosses asked them to lift or climb when pregnant or injured, or to take second or third shifts when they could not find child care for those hours. One woman told us, "I ended up suffering from severe depression. I was put on medication, so my doctor suggested I take a leave. And after my leave was up, when I came back, they terminated me." Another said, "They fired me from there because my son got sick and I needed to take off several days in a row because he has chronic ear infections...he had to have surgery to get tubes in his ears."

The majority of the women we interviewed worked in retail or fast food establishments, followed closely by work as nursing assistants or home health care aides. A few worked in factories, for cleaning services, and in telemarketing. One-third had acquired their jobs through a temporary staffing agency. Women's wages in these jobs ranged from $5.75 to $13.75 an hour and averaged $8.63. A Wisconsin legislative audit found that the average annual income of workfare participants who entered work in 2003 was $9,291; the poverty threshold for a family of three was $14,494. Less than 22 percent of those entering work earned more than poverty-level wages (Wisconsin Legislative Audit Bureau 2005:50–52). The audit acknowledged that this was an overestimate because it was based on employer-reported wages and did not include 2,672 women who left welfare but could not find jobs. Only three of the women we interviewed received health insurance through their employers.

The jobs these women held not only were insecure and poorly paid but also had some of the economy's strictest work rules, which helped explain volatility in women's employment. One woman noted, "I ended up getting fired for taking my break fifteen minutes early because I had to go to the restroom. And I was pregnant, mind you!" Another, who had back problems, was fired for allowing a customer to move forty-pound bags of water softener salt onto the conveyor belt in her retail job.

Women felt the effects of the stealth depression that beset the local economy. One said, "Factories you can't do, because they are packing up and moving overseas." Another said, "A lot of businesses are closing, and people are losing their jobs....There's so many people here that look for jobs every day, and all you can find is fast food restaurants, and that's not gonna pay the bills." Another simply said, "Jobs right now are an endangered species!" In a more personal vein, one woman explained, "People are expected to have more skills...so having your GED or high school diploma isn't good enough anymore....Yes, I could go to McDonald's or Burger King and flip burgers, or whatever, but, realistically, how am I going to send my children—my three children—to college off of $6.75 or $7 an hour pay?"

Women also spoke of the job market difficulties of black men—putting a human face on a 60 percent jobless rate. One said bluntly:

> Stop putting all these men in a penitentiary! You got everybody's daddy, brother, and uncle locked up in the Wisconsin prison system. These men come home after ten and twelve years, and they still can't get a job to provide for their kids, which makes them become repeat offenders. You know, how can you live your life if you've done your time but you can't get a job! McDonald's won't even hire convicted felons!

As these women suggest, poor families faced a labor market that was not only weakened by deindustrialization and job flight but also distorted by deep racial disparities.

WORKFARE ERODING ECONOMIC CITIZENSHIP

Although all low-wage workers in Milwaukee experienced a deindustrialized labor market with insecure jobs and few benefits, women whose lives touched the welfare system were in a unique position. As heads of household responsible for families, they used the system as a safety net to replace benefits they would have had from employers in good jobs—or from most jobs in earlier decades. The system's strict work requirements sent them back to work the moment their crises had abated. Through its community service jobs program, the system placed them in some of the economy's least skilled and least desirable jobs, churning them, to quote Peck (2001:14), "back into the bottom of the labor market." Working twenty to forty hours a week, often for private sector employers, these women were still considered to be receiving "assistance" and therefore could not access many of the benefits that normally accompany paid work.

Benefits "Wal-Mart Style"

Beginning around 2003, labor movements began to note that many families receiving food stamps and medical assistance were working full-time at low-wage jobs, suggesting that taxpayers were subsidizing corporations too stingy to provide wages above poverty level or benefits to their workers. In 2005 a few states and municipalities began framing laws to force such firms to pay higher wages and cover more benefits. The most visible of these bills passed in Maryland in April 2005 and was reaffirmed in January 2006 when the legislature overturned the veto of Governor Robert Ehrlich Jr. (*Washington Post* 2006a). The bill required companies with more than ten thousand employees to spend 8 percent of their payroll on health benefits or to pay the balance into a state health insurance fund for low-income workers. The legislation, which was quickly dubbed the "Wal-Mart Bill," was struck down by a federal judge on July 19, 2006 (*Washington Post* 2006b). Chicago passed an ordinance requiring a $10-an-hour wage and $3 per hour of benefit expenditures for big box retailers on July 26, 2006 (*New York Times* 2006), which Mayor Richard Daley vetoed on September 11 of that same year.

As wages and working conditions erode, the rules of the "new economy" force workers to rely on state agencies for basic benefits and for subsidies, such as food stamps, that bring their income to subsistence levels. If a decent wage and health insurance were formerly rights of economic citizens, earned in return for hard work, then that route is now closed to poor women, no matter how many hours a week they labor. Instead, the benefits and subsidies that make survival possible are doled out as state aid.

This shift became clear to me when I heard Della May Collins, one of the women we interviewed, refer to her W-2 check as her "unemployment." She had stopped working in 2004 when doctors diagnosed a pituitary tumor, and she received benefits through the Wisconsin Works Transitions program (W-2T) during her surgery and recovery. She did not receive unemployment compensation or disability pay, because the fast food job she had held for three years was part-time and had irregular hours, although she often worked forty-hour weeks. These kinds of casualized work relations (no long-term contracts, part-time schedules, fluctuating hours, temporary placements) denied women access to programs, such as unemployment compensation, that have been key elements of economic security for workers since the Depression. Without access to these entitlements, they turned to the state for "aid."

Several women told us that when they became pregnant, their bosses suggested that they stop work and apply to the state's Caretaker of Newborn program, which provides benefits for twelve weeks after a birth, promising their jobs back when they return. The employers in question ranged from factories, to large retailers, to small service franchises. Some women also said that their firms offered health insurance for a high monthly payment and that personnel officers told them "off the record" that, with their salary, they would still be eligible for state medical assistance and "that might be a better value." A Wisconsin legislative audit in 2005 noted a large increase in women who received Caretaker of Newborn support between 1998 and 2004: "The reason may be that some of these individuals were already employed before they entered W-2 and were using the program as a form of paid maternity leave" (Wisconsin Legislative Audit Bureau 2005:55). As this trend was covered in the Wisconsin papers in 2004, the danger was that public outrage would lead to program cuts rather than hold corporations' feet to the fire, leaving low-wage workers bereft not only of the benefits that used to come with a job but also of the means-tested "handouts" that now substitute for them.

Workfare as Downward-Mobility Machine

The second way workfare erodes economic citizenship is by fostering downward job mobility. To grasp how this downward pressure works, it is necessary to understand the job programs in place under Wisconsin's welfare reform. As figure 7.1 shows, the state reserves transitional placements for women who "because of severe barriers are unable to perform independent, self-sustaining work," whereas community service jobs (CSJs) aim to move women into the labor market (Wisconsin DWD 1999b). In Milwaukee County, caseworkers assigned about 60 percent of W-2 participants to CSJs in 2002. They sent 63 percent of black women and 58 percent of Latinas to these placements, compared with 52 percent of white women (Wisconsin DWD 2004:7). The state targeted these jobs at individuals "who lack the basic skills and work habits needed in a job environment and who could benefit from positions offering real work opportunities with added supervision and support" and "an opportunity to practice work habits and skills" (Wisconsin DWD 1999b). Most CSJ assignments included twenty hours of work, ten hours of educational activity, and ten hours of job search, or twenty hours of work and twenty hours of job search per week, and the jobs involved office work, light industrial/housekeeping, and thrift store and care work (Robles, Doolittle, and Gooden 2003:21, 50).

As part of welfare reform, Wisconsin hired five private agencies to manage its welfare caseload. The staff of these agencies determined whether workers were ready for employment and assigned them to activities, including job placements with non-profit, for-profit, or public organizations. In practice, most of the larger job sites in Milwaukee belonged to the administrator agencies themselves (Goodwill, the YWCA, United Migrant Opportunity Services, the Opportunities Industrial Center, as well as for-profit Maximus). Privatization of services gave caseworkers tremendous discretion. Some listened to participants' needs and tried to make appropriate

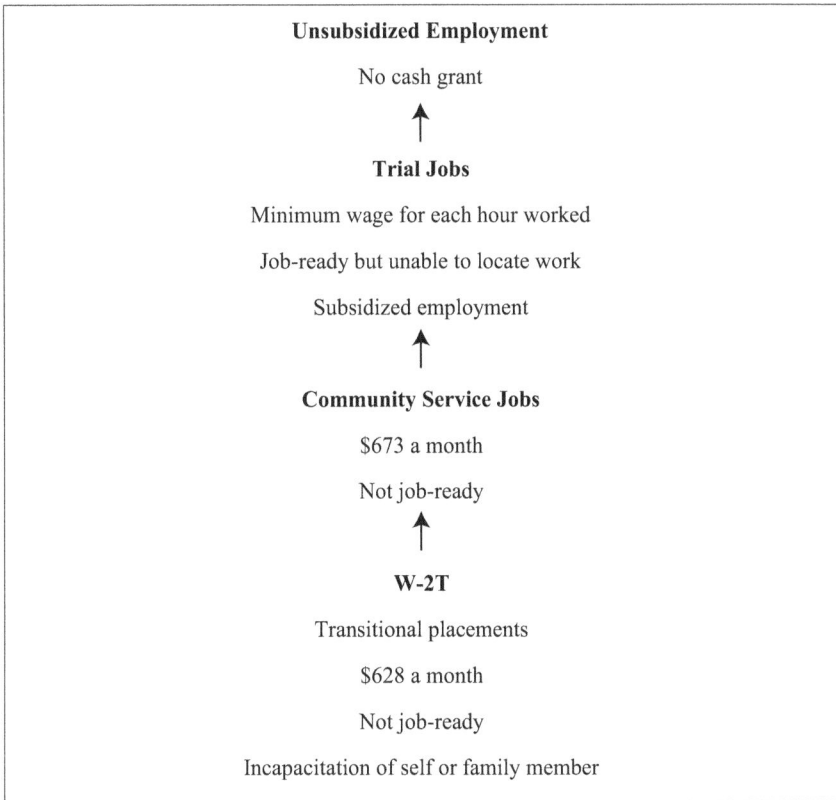

Unsubsidized Employment

No cash grant

↑

Trial Jobs

Minimum wage for each hour worked

Job-ready but unable to locate work

Subsidized employment

↑

Community Service Jobs

$673 a month

Not job-ready

↑

W-2T

Transitional placements

$628 a month

Not job-ready

Incapacitation of self or family member

FIGURE 7.1.
The W-2 Employment Ladder (Wisconsin DWD 1999a).

matches, but others offered no opportunities to express preferences or make choices. Program evaluations suggested that caseworkers based assignments more on the availability of work slots at sites than on the background, skills, or goals of the participants (Robles, Doolittle, and Gooden 2003:33).

Participation in CSJs was associated, in a disturbing number of cases, with downward job mobility for the women we interviewed. This pattern was shaped by changes in the job market, as well as changes in social programs. Women who left or lost a good job in the late 1990s could not always find an equivalent job a year or two later, because the labor market was weaker and the quality of jobs was declining (COWS 2004; Dresser and Rogers 2004; Tilly 1997). In addition, available training opportunities narrowed during this period because two agencies lost their contracts with the state because of corruption or mismanagement (DeParle 2004:chapter 14).

Several women told of leaving clerical or managerial positions and then moving through a series of less responsible jobs. When they turned to W-2 in a crisis, they were placed in CSJs that involved unskilled manual work.

One woman, Rowena Watson, had worked for three years as a manager of a group home for adults with developmental disabilities. She supervised staff members, was salaried, and had benefits, including health and life insurance. She described this period of employment as the best time in her life:

> Me and my kids were doing well. I didn't have to ask nobody for nothing. I didn't have to kiss nobody's ass. I could do things with my daughter that we have not done in so long....I worked a lot, but she was always taken care of by my grandmother. We had a car. We went out to eat every Friday. You know, I even took my daughter to work with me, and she would sit at the kitchen table and do her homework...just like a family.

Although Rowena enjoyed this job, she quit after several experiences of what she interpreted as racism.

> Well, I was a young black supervisor in a very big company with a bunch of Caucasians....They started doing little things to me. They would come and get my time sheets, and they wanted to see receipts...like they were just trying to find something to fire me about. I got really tired of it. And I know me, and I think they knew that eventually I was going to say something, so I resigned from my position so that I could keep my supervisory title. Because I thought, "I can go anywhere and become a supervisor," you know, especially as a caregiver.

From 2001 to 2003, Rowena worked as a certified nursing assistant. Then, during a pregnancy in 2003, her doctor told her that she would have to take medical leave. Because her employer offered no leave, she turned to W-2. When we interviewed her, her baby daughter was seven months old, and she had been assigned to a community service job.

> They send me places to work. One of them is on the north side—you help them cut down their rubbish and their trees. Another one, they send me down to the City of Milwaukee Department of Public Works, and you help them fix the streets. Or that island out there, you know, they have people from W-2 go out there and

water the grass and plant the flowers. What am I going to do cutting down bushes? Am I going to put that on my resume?

Ebony Jackson provides another example of downward mobility. Ebony was a mother of five children—two were grown and three still lived at home. She had finished high school and taken some college courses. In 1996 she worked as an office manager for a community development organization in Milwaukee. She loved the job, which required considerable administrative and clerical skill.

> We helped the senior citizens clean their houses and make repairs, picking them up, taking food to them…that was very fulfilling. I started out as a clerical aid and worked my way up to executive secretary. I already had the secretarial skills, but I didn't have computer literacy yet and I learned a lot there. I learned to do payroll, calculating percentages, helped with audits, learned how to do inventory. And my boss trusted me to handle money, so I went to the bank for the company.

Ebony lost this job when the organization's funding was discontinued, six months after she had started there.

When she turned to the welfare office for help in finding a new job, Ebony was assigned to a trial job with another community organization.

> It started off that they were trying to use me as a joke [because she was a workfare placement]. But they didn't understand that I'm a hard worker. I worked my way up to executive secretary for a skilled trade apprenticeship program. I did job recruiting, secretarial work, document production, ran errands…I did a lot of things in that office. I enjoyed that job because I could see that the community was receiving help that they needed.

Nevertheless, she was never hired for a permanent position.

> I had that job for over a year. As a W-2 participant, you are supposed to be hired after six months, legally. I didn't know any of that. I just kept working because I liked working. But the company took advantage of me because the label "welfare recipient" was tagged to my head, so they refused to hire me, regardless of all the skills and talent that I had. I had a stigma once I got on the program.

When the state found that Ebony's boss was embezzling large amounts of money, it shut down the agency, and Ebony lost her job. Unable to pay her rent, she ended up in a homeless shelter. There, the periodic depression she had been battling became worse. She had experienced numerous episodes of domestic violence in her life. At that time, she said, she was "having nervous spells" and did not know why: "I take medicine to keep me from shaking because I had that much fear in me. I had nightmares. My children were affected, and I wound up having to get on welfare."

Ebony was placed in a Transitions program for a while but then was assigned to a CSJ that required job search and employment activity. She said, "They [the CSJ program] stuck us all in factories and had us doing jobs nobody wanted to do. And that's the honest-to-god truth—from picking up trash on the street, like the people at the county jail have to do, to working in the Goodwill with the disabled people."

In both these cases, women with significant skills and experience left the labor market for a brief period and re-entered through W-2 programs. Their experience was shared by 39 percent of the women we interviewed and 68 percent of those assigned to CSJs, providing a vivid illustration of what Peck calls "churning workers back into the bottom of the labor market," "creating workers for jobs nobody wants," and the construction of "a new category of forced labor, compelled to accept low wage work" (Peck 2001:14, 6, 188, respectively).

When Work Is Charity: Return to the Poorhouse

The third way workfare erodes economic citizenship is by forcing women to work but labeling the wages they receive as aid. When a woman holds a community service job, she is considered to be receiving welfare. The "time clock" that limits her lifetime benefits to five years is ticking. The state's contract agencies monitor her attendance at work and sanction her by reducing her check if she misses a day. This ambiguous status—eerily reminiscent of workhouses in the nineteenth century and earlier—denies women the independence and autonomy associated with wage earning since the Jacksonian period.

Ebony alluded to this problem when she said, "The label 'welfare recipient' was tagged to my head." She expressed the sense that she was not viewed as a "real worker" because she had been sent by the welfare agency ("It started off that they were trying to use me as a joke"). Because she had been assigned to the job by the state, Ebony could not transform her hard work into economic citizenship. She could not forge a direct contract with her employer, who preferred to continue hiring her on an indirect and subsidized basis. At the time of our last interview with her, Ebony had been engaged in a job search as part of her W-2 assignment.

> I had been offered a position as an executive secretary, which is what I used to be. I let one of my caseworkers know that I had the job but that I had to go in for my second and third interviews. She called the temp service that I had signed up with and told them, "Well, she's on welfare, so we want to monitor her for a year and a half, and let me give you the $1,500 [subsidy]." I had-n't told them that I was a welfare recipient, and because they found out, I couldn't get the job for $15 an hour. They decided to give it to someone else and started offering me jobs for $6 an hour, which was not enough for me to actually get off welfare and stay off. You know, I know what I'm worth and I'm capable of doing, and $6 an hour was like a slap in the face. I tried to go for some of the jobs, but they were so far across town to where I couldn't commute on the bus. So I got depressed again and was ready to give it up, till I looked at my children and said, "Well, I've got to feed my babies."

She added, "There ought to be a law passed that you can't check a person's socioeconomic status. If they come and you find out they are ready to do the job, let them work. They shouldn't have to know that you are on wel-fare."

Delia Carter told a similar story. She had been assigned to job search and had called a number of companies that seemed promising. Then she found that her caseworker was calling them to verify her log entries. Delia said, "She was calling the places that I had written on my job logs. That's like lowering me. How is the W-2 gonna call the place? Then they're only gonna think I'm qualified for getting $5.15 an hour.... If they see that I'm getting a W-2 check, you think they're gonna give me a job? No, they're gonna look at me as a statistic!"

There are several issues of grave concern here. One is the way in which moving thousands of poor women into the bottom of the labor market drives down wages and undermines public employee unions. Both Piven (1999) and Boris (1999) report examples of public and private agencies fail-ing to renew contracts with workers at a market wage to take advantage of subsidized workfare participants. The second issue is whether women who participate in workfare are protected by labor laws. The initial PRWORA legislation did not provide for minimal employment standards. Subsequent administrative rulings by federal agencies have clarified the circumstances under which federal employment law applies to workfare participants, and the 105th Congress established that they were covered under minimum-wage laws and entitled to health, safety, and fair labor protections (NELP 2002).

Nevertheless, the National Employment Law Project (NELP) suggests that the law and administrative rulings are not as clear-cut as they may seem. For example, women placed in "work training" programs like community service jobs are not covered by unemployment insurance. NELP lawyers express concern that "many workers continue to suffer terms and conditions of work which are vastly inferior to those of the paid employees with whom they often work side by side." They note that a lack of Title VII (anti-discrimination) enforcement creates opportunities for sexual harassment and that the lack of explicit provision for workers' compensation results in a failure to recompense workers injured on the job. Finally, they point out that workers who complain—whether of unsafe conditions or harassment—are especially vulnerable to losing their benefits and have no access to an appeals process in most states (NELP 2002; US Department of Labor 2005).

A third issue concerns the Fourteenth Amendment rights of women in workfare assignments. The Fourteenth Amendment states that "included in the right of personal liberty and the right of private property...is the right to make contracts.... Chief among such contracts is that of personal employment, by which labor and other services are exchanged for money or other forms of property." As historians have pointed out, freedom of contract has never been absolute, and many labor struggles (over the minimum wage, maximum hours, and health safety regulations, for example) have given government the power to regulate the terms under which individuals can make a deal. Still, as Kessler-Harris notes, historically our legal system has "treated workers as individuals, each capable of negotiating and each protected by the Fourteenth Amendment's prohibitions on deprivation of property...[labor's] right to freely contract to sell itself...commonly known as freedom of contract" (Kessler-Harris 1991:38). For political theorist T. H. Marshall (1950:10), the ability to follow the occupation of one's choice in the place of one's choice was a key aspect of citizenship. Therefore, it is disturbing that, under Wisconsin's welfare reform, signing an employability plan appears to cancel an individual's right to choose when, where, and under what conditions she will work.

Lack of access to this fundamental right was troubling to many women on workfare in Milwaukee. As one told Robles, Doolittle, and Gooden

(2003:60), "You love your research…what you're doing. What if your boss came to you and said, 'Now your CSJ assignment is to pick up garbage.' You wouldn't like that. If you put people in a CSJ that they don't care about, they won't learn….It won't work."

Another woman I interviewed said, "You can't decide where you want to go. You have no opinion on any of this….It's like you're a child and your parents are running your life for you, because you don't have no choice." These women were convinced that there was something wrong about the state's ability to dictate the kinds of work they would do and the conditions under which they would do it. In the words of one analyst, "welfare recipients who are told they must work at whatever job is available see the specter of slavery and indentured servitude come to haunt them again, returned from a not so distant past. And the persistence of racism makes that fear plausible" (Shklar 1991:97).

CONCLUSIONS

I have examined workfare not as a project to change individual behavior but as a design for changing the rules that govern the lower tiers of the labor market. I follow Peck in suggesting that, as jobs become less desirable—as they come to pay only a fraction of a living wage, cease to offer benefits, require night and weekend shifts, and become, in many cases, increasingly dangerous—it becomes necessary to force people into them. In the case of workfare, women who once had an option to stay home to raise children—if they were willing to do it on $600 a month—are now being forced into these degraded jobs.

These trends are about regulating gender, as well as about regulating the labor market. The women who are being forced into work are mothers raising children. Because of their poverty (which brings with it things like inferior health care and lack of access to transportation) and because of the demands of raising children (with chicken pox, teacher's meetings, ear infections), these women need flexible jobs more than most of us. But as we have seen, the jobs they are able to get in fast food, retail, care work, and housekeeping are among the least flexible in the economy. These also have the most punitive work rules.

For women who have to quit their jobs in order to get time off to care for their kids, or to recover from an illness, or to have a baby, the welfare system still provides a safety net. It may have narrow eligibility requirements and time limits and may be extremely punitive in its own right, but it provides these women with "benefits" they do not get from their jobs. In this way, it allows employers to continue offering employment under conditions that do not provide a living and cannot reproduce the labor force.

Women who accept this aid enter into a Faustian bargain, for they must give up their claim to economic citizenship in order to receive help. They must agree to be treated as dependents and must give up their right to choose when, where, and under what conditions they will work, to sue for fair treatment, and to receive many of the benefits that have traditionally come to workers through their jobs. Participating in these programs propels them into the labor market with the racialized label of "welfare recipient" tagged to their heads. No matter how many jobs they have held, how many years they have worked, or what skills they have, they are marked as deficient workers.

This bargain traps women at the lower end of the labor market, making upward mobility into jobs that pay a wage that can support a family all but impossible. The way out, of course, is to get a job independently. But unless that job provides benefits and flexibility, a woman will be forced to return to workfare programs as soon as she needs time off to care for family. This bargain pathologizes the need for flexible work hours in ways that reverberate beyond workfare. It treats such needs as unacceptable deviations from the "ideal [male] worker norm" (J. Williams 2001:chapters 3 and 4)—the idea that the worker will work long hours with only scheduled vacations and without interruptions for family responsibilities throughout their entire adult life, a model made possible because they have access to a "flow of family labor" from their wives (J. Williams 2001; see also Roberts 2004b). In doing so, it ties universal questions about how our children will be cared for when mothers work and who will provide medical insurance to the "failures" of poor women. The question shifts from why employers are not providing benefits or why the state is not regulating work, to why poor women are not able to solve these problems the way the "rest" of society does. And if the rest of society is struggling with the same issues, they invite the stigma of being associated with the "disorganized poor." This is a new form of labor market discipline *and* a new form of gender discipline.

In prescient work, completed in the early 1990s (before PRWORA), Shklar (1991:98) wrote, "Workfare has nothing to do with economics. It is about citizenship." At the time, she wrote that the issue was "whether able-bodied adults who do not earn anything can be regarded as full citizens" and "if they are not, may...they be treated with that mixture of paternalism and contempt that has always been reserved for the dependent classes?" (Shklar 1991:98). Today, the issue has shifted, for most of the women Shklar wrote about have already been forced into work. The question now is whether, in turning to the state for subsidies to their less-than-living wage, for medical care, or for the time off they need during illness, they will be so marked. If so, the link between wages and economic citizenship forged in the Jacksonian period has been broken, and a new class of "dependent workers," laboring outside the social contract, has been created.

Notes

1. All names used are pseudonyms.

2. Fraser and Gordon (1994) trace the evolution of the idea of dependency from the preindustrial period, when wage earners were seen as shamefully dependent on property owners, to the industrialized period's view of waged employment as a new form of property. This new perspective obscured workers' dependence on their employers and their status as subordinates in that relationship, while masking the productive labor of those labeled dependent (housewives, slaves).

3. The project was the W-2 Child Support Demonstration Evaluation, Phase III, led by Maria Cancian and Daniel Meyer and funded by the Wisconsin Department of Workforce Development (DWD). The research team included three graduate students at the University of Wisconsin: Victoria Mayer, Nicole Breazeale, and Angela Cunningham. Patricia Brown and Steve Cook helped draw the sample. The project covered three counties: Milwaukee (twenty interviews), Racine (ten interviews), and Dane (ten interviews). Because the labor market of Dane County is very different, this chapter focuses only on Milwaukee and Racine.

4. "Since 1997, no cash assistance has been available to families unless they participate in work or work-like activities...or have a child less than 13 weeks old....Cash benefits are available only after a period of program participation" (Cancian et al. 2002:2). Wisconsin began work-based welfare reforms in the late 1980s, well ahead of the rest of the nation (Cancian et al. 2002). "Lower tier" programs include Community Service Jobs, Caretaker of Newborn benefits (available to mothers of children up to thirteen weeks), and W-2 Transitions (a program for women with obstacles to immediate employment, including health or mental health problems and substance abuse).

8

The Racial Geography of State Child Protection

Dorothy Roberts

The US child welfare system has always been an instrument for regulating the poor. State child "protection" is rooted in the philosophy of child saving—rescuing children from the ills of poverty, typically by taking them away from their parents (Gordon 1999; Lindsey 1994). Most cases of child maltreatment involve parental neglect, which is usually difficult to disentangle from the conditions of poverty. The child welfare system hides the systemic reasons for poor families' hardships by attributing them to parental deficits and pathologies that require therapeutic remedies instead of social change. Child welfare practice overly relies on coercive intervention and child removal rather than supports families to avoid child abuse and neglect.

Although black children were virtually excluded from openly segregated child welfare services until the end of World War II, the system has since evolved into one of the state's chief means of supervising poor black families (Billingsley and Giovannoni 1972; Roberts 2002). As the child welfare system began to serve fewer white children and more black children, state and federal governments spent much more money on foster care and less on in-home services to families (US DHHS 1997). Today, black children are grossly overrepresented in the US child welfare system: they make up about one-third of the nation's foster care population yet represent only

15 percent of the nation's children (Perez, O'Neil, and Gesiriech 2003; US DHHS 2006). A black child is four times as likely as a white child to be in foster care (Child Welfare League of America 2000).

Although alarming, these statistics do not reveal the spatial dynamics of the child welfare system's racial disparities. State custody of children has a *racial geography*. In the nation's cities, child protection cases are concentrated in communities of color. Many poor black neighborhoods, in particular, have extremely high rates of involvement by public child welfare agencies, especially placement in foster care. For example, in 1997 one out of ten children in central Harlem had been placed in foster care (Katz 2000). In Chicago, most child protection cases are clustered in a few zip code areas, which are almost exclusively African American (CFRC 2006; Testa and Furstenberg 2002). The overrepresentation of black children in the foster care population, then, represents massive state supervision and dissolution of families concentrated in black neighborhoods.

What is the sociopolitical impact of this on poor black neighborhoods? Although researchers are investigating the reasons for racial disparities in the child welfare system, the *community* impact of these disparities remains obscure (Courtney et al. 1998; Goerge and Bong 2001; Lane et al. 2002). I began to explore this question in 2005 in a small case study of Woodlawn, a black neighborhood in Chicago with high rates of foster care placement (Roberts 2006). By conducting and analyzing in-depth interviews of twenty-five black women who lived in Woodlawn, the study aimed at better understanding how child welfare agency involvement affects community and civic life and shapes residents' attitudes about government and self-governance. I use *neighborhood* to signify the geographical site of study and *community* to signify the social relations that neighbors engage in with one another, such as pooling resources or joining together for civic projects. In short, my study focused on the impact of concentrated state child protection in the geographical space of a neighborhood on the community relationships within that neighborhood.

At first, what I discovered surprised me. The women I interviewed identified numerous ways in which the intense agency involvement in Woodlawn damaged both family and community relationships. Yet, contrary to what I expected, most did not believe that the agency was overly involved in their neighborhood. Rather, they called for greater state supervision of financially motivated foster parents, as well as greater financial assistance for needy caregivers. I came to realize that this apparent paradox reflects the consequences of neoliberal social reforms. As these neighborhoods are stripped of social programs in the government's shift to market solutions for poverty, residents must increasingly rely on more punitive state institutions to meet their needs. The racial geography of state child protection also illustrates the critical role that institutional racism plays in the neoliberal state's new forms of punitive governance.

THE GEOGRAPHY OF CHILD WELFARE, NEOLIBERALISM, AND RACIAL INJUSTICE

In *Shattered Bonds: The Color of Child Welfare* (2002), I hypothesized that intense levels of state supervision of children and their families have negative consequences for family and community networks, which are supposed to prepare children for civic life and self-governance. By fostering citizens' moral development free from state control, families play a vital role in a democratic political system (McClain 2006). Placing large numbers of children in state custody—even if some are ultimately reunited with their families or transferred to adoptive homes—interferes with a group's ability to form healthy connections among its members and to participate fully in the democratic process. The child welfare system's racial disparity also reinforces the quintessential racist stereotype: that black people are incapable of governing themselves and need state supervision. The intense involvement of these state agencies in black neighborhoods can therefore be viewed as a means by which the public child welfare system helps to maintain the subordinated status of black people in the United States.

The concentration of child welfare agency supervision in inner-city neighborhoods also plays a significant role in the intensifying shift toward neoliberal governance. Federal child welfare policy looks to a private remedy for family poverty—adoption—instead of curtailing the flow of poor, minority children into foster care by providing needed resources to their families (Roberts 2002). In the past decade, federal and state policies have shifted away from preserving families and toward "freeing" children in foster care for adoption by terminating parental rights. Most notably, the Adoption and Safe Families Act (ASFA), passed by Congress in 1997, promotes adoption through a set of mandates and incentives to state child welfare departments. As a result of ASFA, most state agencies shortened time frames for achieving permanency, increased emphasis on adoption, and implemented concurrent planning that prepares adoptive homes for foster children while providing the children's parents with services aimed at family reunification (US DHHS 2005b). ASFA also imposed arbitrary timelines that shorten the time within which agencies should petition for termination of parental rights.

The overlap of ASFA and the 1996 federal welfare adjustment law marked the first time in US history the federal government mandated that states protect children from abuse and neglect without a corresponding mandate to provide basic economic support to poor families (Courtney 1998). Like welfare policy's promotion of marriage, the reliance on adoption furthers the neoliberal agenda to replace state support for families with private remedies for social and economic inequality.

At the same time that government has reduced support for families, there has been a parallel increase in state intervention in poor people's lives. Over the past two decades, the welfare, prison, and foster care systems have clamped down on poor minority communities, especially inner-city black neighborhoods, increasing many families' experiences of insecurity and surveillance. Welfare reform is no longer a system of aid. Rather, it is a system of behavior modification that attempts to regulate the sexual, marital, and childbearing decisions of poor unmarried mothers by placing conditions on the receipt of state assistance (Mink 2001; A. M. Smith 2007).

The contraction of the US welfare state paralleled the expansion of prisons that stigmatizes inner-city communities and isolates them further from the privileges of mainstream society (Davis 2003). Social scientists have used sociological theories about neighborhoods to study the community-level impact of high incarceration rates in African American neighborhoods (Braman 2004; Clear et al. 2003; Fagan, West, and Holland 2003). Poor African American communities have suffered the brunt of the staggering buildup of the prison population over the past thirty years. Research in several cities reveals that the exit and reentry of inmates, like that of children in foster care, is geographically concentrated in the poorest, minority neighborhoods. A host of empirical studies conducted in the past decade has found that incarceration has become a systematic aspect of neighborhood residents' family affairs, economic prospects, political engagement, social norms, and childhood expectations for the future (Roberts 2004a). The mounting evidence of neighborhood-wide devastation caused by mass imprisonment suggests that the concentration of child welfare agency involvement in the same African American neighborhoods also has widespread repercussions.

THE COMMUNITY-LEVEL EFFECTS OF CHILD WELFARE SUPERVISION

In the past decade, there has been an explosion of social science research on how neighborhood characteristics such as poverty, joblessness, and residential stability, as well as community-level social dynamics, affect children and families (Sampson 2002; Sampson, Morenoff, and Gannon-

Rowley 2002). William Julius Wilson pioneered this type of research in his 1987 book, *The Truly Disadvantaged*, in which he argued that the deindustrialization of central cities resulted in the extreme concentration of poverty and unemployment in African American neighborhoods. Residents of these neighborhoods, he claimed, experienced "concentration effects" that imposed burdens on them above and beyond those caused by their individual and family characteristics.

Since then, numerous researchers have theorized and measured how the concentration of social and economic disadvantage in urban neighborhoods affects residents. The ecological context of neighborhoods became as important a focus of investigation as the demographic features of the people who live in them. Noting that child-related problems "tend to come bundled together at the neighborhood level" (Sampson 2001:6), a significant segment of these studies examine how neighborhood social composition and processes influence the well-being of children and adolescents (Brooks-Gunn et al. 1993). These neighborhood-oriented approaches to child welfare, however, overlook the role of state institutions in mediating the effects of concentrated poverty on the well-being of children and other residents. I am interested in the impact on neighborhoods of the concentration of both disadvantage and intense involvement by state child welfare agencies.

I began to investigate the community impact of child protection services in one of the black neighborhoods on Chicago's south side that Wilson wrote about in *The Truly Disadvantaged*. Bordered on the north by the University of Chicago, Woodlawn has been a frequent site of sociological research and battles over encroachment by university buildings. The 2000 census shows that more than 95 percent of the neighborhood's twenty-seven thousand residents were African American (Northeastern Illinois Planning Commission 2002). Woodlawn is also one of Chicago's poorest neighborhoods. The median annual family income was $24,500, with one-quarter of families earning less than $10,000. Half of the female-headed households with children in Woodlawn lived in poverty.

In 1937, when Chicago businessman Carl Hansberry, the father of playwright Lorraine Hansberry, purchased a home in Woodlawn, a white signatory to a restrictive covenant on the property challenged him in court. The US Supreme Court eventually ruled in favor of Hansberry on a legal technicality (*Hansberry v. Lee*, 311 US 32 [1940]). Racial covenants had effectively kept Woodlawn a white area: in 1940 African Americans made up only 17 percent of the population (Chicago Fact Book Consortium 1995). The US Supreme Court's 1948 landmark decision in *Shelley v. Kraemer* declared racially restrictive covenants unconstitutional, officially opening the gates of Chicago neighborhoods to thousands of blacks migrating from the South in search of employment.

In the following decades, Woodlawn saw a massive demographic transformation in both the size and the complexion of its population. "Between 1930 and 1960, Woodlawn's population increased 23 percent to an all-time high of more than 81,000" (Chicago Fact Book Consortium 1995:138). As blacks moved into the neighborhood, Woodlawn's housing stock became grossly overextended, and whites fled to better and more homogenous housing. By 1960, 90 percent of the neighborhood's residents were black and crowded almost exclusively into renter-occupied apartment buildings. Woodlawn experienced a steady decline in subsequent decades as deindustrialization brought staggering unemployment, depopulation, and disinvestment.

Woodlawn has one of the highest rates of foster care placement in Chicago. At the end of 2005, almost two hundred of approximately nine thousand children in the neighborhood were in state-supervised substitute care, living either with relatives or with strangers (CFRC 2006). The vast majority of Chicago neighborhoods experience less than half of Woodlawn's placement rate of twenty-one per one thousand children. A few other poor African American neighborhoods, such as Grand Boulevard and the Near West Side, have double Woodlawn's rate. In no white neighborhood in Chicago are children placed in foster care at a level even approaching that of these black neighborhoods. Figures for any given year provide only a fraction of all the neighborhood children who were in foster care in prior years; they do not reveal the number of residents who spent some part of their lives in foster care. Thus, the total number of Woodlawn families who have experienced state supervision is even greater than the available statistics show.

During the summer of 2005, with the help of a research assistant, I interviewed twenty-five black women who lived in Woodlawn. Many of the women, ages twenty-four to fifty-six, were residents of a housing project in Woodlawn, and half the interviews took place at a community center located in the housing project. Most of the women had some personal involvement with child welfare agencies: as foster children and foster parents and as siblings or cousins of those placed in foster care. None of the respondents reported being investigated by child protective services or having their own children placed in foster care.

The women interviewed were aware of intense involvement by the Illinois Department of Children and Family Services (DCFS) with families in their neighborhood. Indeed, most estimated the number of Woodlawn families under DCFS supervision to be at least half:

> Over half of the community, I would say. Yeah, it's a lot.

> My God, probably thousands.

> I'm gonna say 90 percent.

> It's common because people always getting their children taken away. So, yeah, it's common.

> From 60th to 67th, State to Stoney Island, even with it being 150 cases just in that little vicinity, 150 apartments or families or whatever, or everybody in the whole three-flat.

> I think everyone in Woodlawn knows someone in the system.

Most of the women understood the function of DCFS to center on removing children from their homes and placing them in foster care. Tiara, a twenty-four-year-old whose friend was investigated by DCFS, stated, "I try not to know what the initials stand for, but I do know that in this neighborhood, to me, DCFS is the people that take your kids if you are not taking care of them correctly." Christina, also twenty-four years old, with a friend involved with DCFS, agreed: "It just seems like they're all about taking the child out of the home. You know, I've never really known of a situation where if someone told on the family and they let the child stay and deal with the problem."

The women identified significant effects of agency involvement in Woodlawn on both family and neighborhood social relationships. They reported that DCFS supervision of parents interfered with parental authority and caused family conflicts over agency placement of children in the care of relatives. Many felt that placing children in foster care damaged the children's ability to form social relationships and that the agency's constant surveillance created distrust among neighbors. Not only did DCFS cause children to disrespect their parents, the women reported, but also the agency bullied parents into relinquishing their authority over their own children. Some felt that parents who do not have the fortitude to withstand DCFS regulation simply give up. Twenty-four-year-old Aisha, whose cousins had been placed in foster care, told me, "That's what I say about DCFS. They will come right in and snatch your children....Some people fight for their children. That's why they end up getting the children back. But if you don't know much about DCFS and you don't know how to go about doing this thing, you'll probably lose your children to the system."

Pearl, a counselor who provided services for DCFS but also had relatives and neighbors involved with the agency, explained:

> I believe when DCFS is involved in the situation, I believe that a sense of disconnection returns. But when you have to have supervised visits to see the natural family, not to mention, you know, aunts, grandparents, and relatives, supervised visits, I mean, the family has now become even more disconnected with the fact that maybe a grandparent could have came over and took the kids for a week or two weeks but now they have to have permission from the state....I believe it's another form of slavery.

Tiara elaborated how the multiple requirements imposed on mothers by DCFS caseworkers can break down their will to regain custody of their children:

> So if you drop dirty [fail a drug test] because you been hanging with your buddy, you gotta go through the whole procedure. Now this could be a twelve-month case. Now if you one of those people that ain't strong enough and now time's gone past, you don't even want your kids back. Now adoption papers coming up in like ten months because the court wanna know why you ain't doing your service plans right, so to speak.

Some women believed that the psychological injuries caused by foster care placement hamper children's ability to form healthy social relationships later in life. Aisha stated:

> The child's gotta go through all this ridicule, being tossed about, your mother is nothing, your family is nothing, you been taken away. And it kinda makes the child feel like unwanted. And that why we have a lot of men and women growing up today very rebellious and very hurt and doing a lot of things out of their hurt because of the suffering and ridicule that they dealt with as a child.

Because so many Woodlawn residents have been involved with the foster care system, it is likely that the social disabilities the women described have a considerable impact on neighborhood relationships.

Another effect on neighborhood relationships that the women discussed is the distrust among neighbors created by pervasive DCFS surveillance of families. As one resident put it, "[DCFS] disrupts the community …I would say it's a trust thing." Many observed that it is common for residents to call DCFS to report their neighbors for child maltreatment, destroying a sense of trust among them. Residents must look over their shoulders for fear that a neighbor is noting a parental misstep or that an observant stranger is a DCFS caseworker. Twenty-seven-year-old Cassie observed:

> I mean, [DCFS] shouldn't cause a problem, but if somebody calling DCFS on you and they come knocking at your door and you wondering why they at your door and you wondering who called them, then that's a problem. That's a big problem.…That's why you got to watch what you do and what you say and all this, 'cause you don't know who you could be talking to. Out on the street you don't know who you could be talking to. She could be DCFS, writing down stuff, taking notes, all of that, and you don't know who she is. So you have to be careful. You have to be very careful. Because, like I say, you don't know. You don't know.

Heightening the sense of suspicion among neighbors is the perception that DCFS is commonly used as a means of retribution. Some respondents believed that frequently residents falsely accused others of child abuse in order to seek retribution against them. "I think, personally, that people are using DCFS as revenge now. They're revenging," Tiara stated. "You can argue with somebody. They call DCFS on you." The use of DCFS as a common means of problem solving and recrimination is a compelling sign of the agency's entrenchment in neighborhood culture. It suggests that intensive state supervision damages neighborhood relationships not only by creating distrust among neighbors but also by encouraging a destructive alternative to productive mechanisms for resolving neighborhood conflict.

Like Pearl, quoted above, several women described DCFS as a form of slavery or prison and placed it in a broader system of coercive neighborhood regulation. Early in the interview, Whitney, a twenty-three-year-old who was in foster care as a child, described DCFS as "jail for kids, basically." Later, she characterized the housing project where she lived in the same terms: "This is a hazard to people's lives. I'm serious. They have a camera now, a police camera, and it's just like I'm in jail, girl. I am." Aisha described the impact of family disruption on the neighborhood's civic life in especially powerful terms. She believed that people who are separated from their families by state child welfare workers have difficulty joining with other residents on neighborhood projects:

When you are taken away from your family, that is a form of separation, and they learn from that, growing up to be separated. You know, like to be separate. I can't really explain it, but it's not really set in them to be united, or to be one, or to come together to do anything. Because they've been separated, I guess. Yeah, like we can never come together to do anything over here....It definitely has an effect on the community because bringing separation like that, I don't know what it does, but we cannot as a people and as a community come together. No, we have not came together on anything. That's why nothing is accomplished here.

TYING ECONOMIC SUPPORT TO CHILD REMOVAL

One of the most powerful discoveries I made in Woodlawn is the tension created by the child welfare agency's role as both investigator of and provider for neighborhood families. The child welfare system is staffed by social workers who are supposed to provide services to families. Yet, these same service providers investigate parents alleged to have maltreated their children and coerce parents to comply with rehabilitative measures by threatening to take away their children permanently. Social work professor Leroy Pelton emphasizes the threat to family integrity created by the child welfare system's dual function:

> The investigative/coercive/child-removal role diminishes, hampers, and overwhelms the helping role within the dual-role structure of public child-welfare agencies as huge and increasingly larger portions of their budgets are devoted to investigation and foster care, with little money left over for preventive and supportive services to combat the impermanency of children's living arrangements. [Pelton 1993:271]

Although the women I interviewed criticized the agency's damage to neighborhood relationships, most nevertheless expressed a desire for continued or greater DCFS involvement in Woodlawn to meet the material needs of its struggling families. The child welfare system exacts an onerous price: it requires poor mothers to relinquish custody of their children in exchange for state support needed to care for them (Roberts 2001). If social disruption is the price residents must pay for needed financial support, then most respondents were willing to pay it. They made it clear, however, that they preferred more financial support with less disruption of family relationships and criticized the necessary linkage of family financial assistance with investigation and child removal.

The women saw a need for more DCFS involvement in their neighborhood for two reasons: to supply additional financial resources to families and to monitor foster homes better, mainly because of the negative effects of financial incentives for taking in foster children. Many respondents understood the agency's role as a chief financial resource for families. Positive comments about DCFS often concerned its financial support for mothers, foster parents, or foster children but not its protection of children from abuse and neglect. Twenty-seven-year-old Angela, who had been in foster care, explained:

> They're doing a good job [in Woodlawn]....Because it does help them out with their, you know, financial-wise, pay bills and stuff like that. They help them out. They do give them money for keeping the kids too....Because I know the caseworkers are so nice because, like I said, my husband, his mom had adoptive kids, and she get $2,500 for the kids, a month alone.

Whitney pointed to DCFS's financial role in less positive terms:

> I would say the only people that's probably benefiting the most out of DCFS is the foster parents. That's it. And that's only because they getting a little financials that they do get, because they don't get anything.

Most of the children DCFS removes from parents are placed with relatives. Kinship foster care is a significant source of financial support for relatives' care giving, because foster care stipends are much larger than Temporary Assistance to Needy Families (TANF) benefits. As Wanda observed, "The only [positive impact of DCFS] that I can think about is the resources that they do provide children or grandparents or other family members who take in their family members." The level of state support for kinship caregivers, however, directly correlates with the level of state intrusion into their families. Most states, including Illinois, require that relatives meet the same licensing requirements as nonrelative foster parents to receive foster care payments. The extended family must exchange its autonomy over child rearing for financial support and services needed to raise its children.

Despite their gratitude for caseworkers' financial assistance for their families, many of the women in Woodlawn also commented on the negative impact of financial incentives to become a foster parent. A common criticism of foster care was that foster parents often took poor care of children because they were in the business "just for the money." Forty-five-year-old child care worker Estelle complained:

> I know people who...just used the children, you know, just 'cause they get paid, you know. I mean, you know, if you want a child, you take care of the child, and you should want it from the heart instead of just because you get the money. I know it's a lot of people who are just using the children.

Aisha similarly observed:

> A lot of people do it just for the money. A lot of people are taking these people's children for the money, not that they care anything about the child. I know from my grandmother that sometimes that people do not care about the child. As long as that check is rolling in every month, they will let the child stay there.

Francis, forty-eight, whose daughter was the subject of a DCFS investigation, also questioned foster parents' motives:

> Because foster people, they don't give a care about them kids. All they want is the money, you know. And then a lot of times you see foster kids with foster parents and the kids look like some thrift store reject, you know. And you get money for these kids. Ain't no way they should look like they look, you know.

Paradoxically, some women believed that DCFS should be more involved in foster homes because some foster parents were interested only in the money and because the agency did not support foster parents enough. Beverly, who was involved with DCFS as a foster child and as the adoptive mother of her niece, expressed both sentiments about the agency:

> I don't think they're involved enough. Why? Because I believe that what they need to do before they even put children in other people's homes, relative or whoever, my thing is, I think they need to observe the person's house, the person whose house they're going to put the children in, at least a month before. Why I say that, because a lot of people get these kids, they start this, for the money. The kids are still being neglected, and I don't think DCFS is going out checking on them enough....
> There's another lady over here, she got her nephew, and she

was complaining about how they weren't sending her no money, like eighty dollars she got. First, she had one baby. She wasn't getting nothing for that baby.…You need money to take care of these kids. I'm not asking for a million dollars, but give me something to work with. And that kind of thing people have problems with, with the DCFS. The money thing.

Perhaps the tension women expressed involves distrusting other foster parents' motives while wanting greater remuneration for their own foster parenting. It also reflects the perverse trade-off created when foster care constitutes one of the neighborhood's few remaining means for addressing parental poverty. The state's reliance on substitute care of children creates financial incentives for bad caregivers and insufficient support for good ones.

The women's concerns also stem from the child welfare system's preference for paying foster parents to care for children over providing adequate supports directly to poor mothers. Although Congress restructured welfare in 1996 by abolishing the federal entitlement to public assistance for children, foster care remains a well-funded entitlement program. The stipends paid to foster parents far exceed welfare benefits, the only public assistance available to poor mothers outside the child welfare system (Urbina 2006). Moreover, the monthly foster care payment is multiplied by the number of children in the foster parent's care, instead of the marginal increase per child under TANF.

Although most of the women wanted greater DCFS presence in Woodlawn, they did not uncritically accept the terms of its current involvement. Many condemned the agency's narrow role rooted in investigating families rather than helping them. Michelle, thirty-four, who helped to raise her nephew when her sister was investigated by DCFS, poignantly observed that the agency responded only to allegations of child abuse rather than to family need:

> The way I see it is that [people in Woodlawn] don't look like DCFS can really help them. Like I said, the advertisement, it just says abuse. If you being abused, this is the number you call. This is the only way you gonna get help. It doesn't say if I'm in need of counseling, or if I'm in need of my children don't have shoes, if I just can't provide groceries even though I may have seven kids but I only get a hundred-something dollars food stamps and my work check only goes to bills. I can't feed eight of us all off a hundred-something-dollar food stamps. So I'm saying, they

> don't know that DCFS can help them in a positive way. They only
> do negative things. They only take my children away. I think that
> is the big issue. I don't want to lose my children, so I'm not going
> to call DCFS for help because I only see them take away children.

Having stripped Woodlawn, like other inner-city neighborhoods, of social programs, low-income housing, and guaranteed public assistance, the state uses the punitive system of foster care to deal with struggling mothers who lack the resources they need to care for their children. Poor families are left in the bind of resenting child welfare agencies' surveillance and interference yet wanting the agencies' continued presence as one of the few remaining sources of public aid. The child welfare system's racial geography shows that neoliberalism's harshest effects will be felt in poor communities of color. Woodlawn is a site of this tension not only because it is a poor neighborhood, but also because it is predominantly black. The disproportionate involvement of African American children in the nation's foster care population stems, in part, from their high rates of poverty. But it is also caused by a racist model of the ideal family and stereotypes about black family dysfunction, as well as the political choice to treat black families' problems in an especially punitive way. The punitive governance that accompanies the neoliberal shrinking of public programs is inextricably tied to racial subordination that makes this trend seem desirable.

CONCLUSION

The women's accounts of child welfare agency involvement in Woodlawn were marked by a striking tension. The women reported that intensive state supervision had damaging consequences for family and community relationships but that they relied on this same state involvement for needed financial support. Most respondents viewed DCFS as both a chief threat to families and a chief family resource. I expected the concerns expressed by most of the women about DCFS's disruptive social impact to support calls to evict the agency from the neighborhood. Most of the women, however, saw a need for *greater* DCFS involvement in Woodlawn.

This finding is perhaps the most telling evidence of the powerful community impact of intense child welfare agency involvement in neighborhoods. Although the residents recognized the corrosive effects of DCFS on their community, most recognized their community's reliance on the agency to meet its needs. Many also criticized, however, the link between state investigation and support of families. Neoliberalism's distinctive union of privatization with punitive governance is reflected in the disruptive formula of "child protection" that makes family assistance hinge on state custody of children.

Acknowledgments

I am grateful to Courtney Bell, Nayna Gupta, Aisha Khan, and Yondi Morris for assistance with this study and to the other participants in the March 2006 New Landscapes of Inequality advanced seminar at the School for Advanced Research for their helpful comments on an earlier draft of this chapter. The Searle Fund and Kirkland & Ellis Research Fund provided generous financial support.

9

Withered Memories

Naming and Fighting Environmental Racism in Georgia

Melissa Checker

Mentioning the term *environment* to adults in the Hyde Park neighborhood of Augusta, Georgia, prompted them to tell of the dust that covered their walls and reappeared as fast as they could wipe it off.[1] They spoke about the toxic release sirens blaring from the industrial ceramics plant on one edge of the neighborhood, sometimes for eight hours, forcing them to go to the mall or the movies to escape the noise (let alone the toxic release). They told of how they had permanent tickles in their throats and how their children were never far from their inhalers. They described how their children could not dig in the dirt around their houses or play in the ditches that lined the streets of their neighborhood. For the African American residents of Hyde Park, the environment was not something to be protected from human intervention and conserved for the preservation of wildlife. Rather, their environment was poisonous, and they needed to be protected from it. Moreover, their "environment" represented discrimination and the thwarting of their American dream.

Hyde Park, home to approximately 250 mostly low-income African American families, was at one time surrounded by roughly seven polluting facilities, including a ceramics factory, the Southern Wood Piedmont (SWP) wood preserving factory, a brickyard, a Georgia Power plant, a scrap metal yard that stretched 10.8 acres, and two auto repair shops. A highway curved

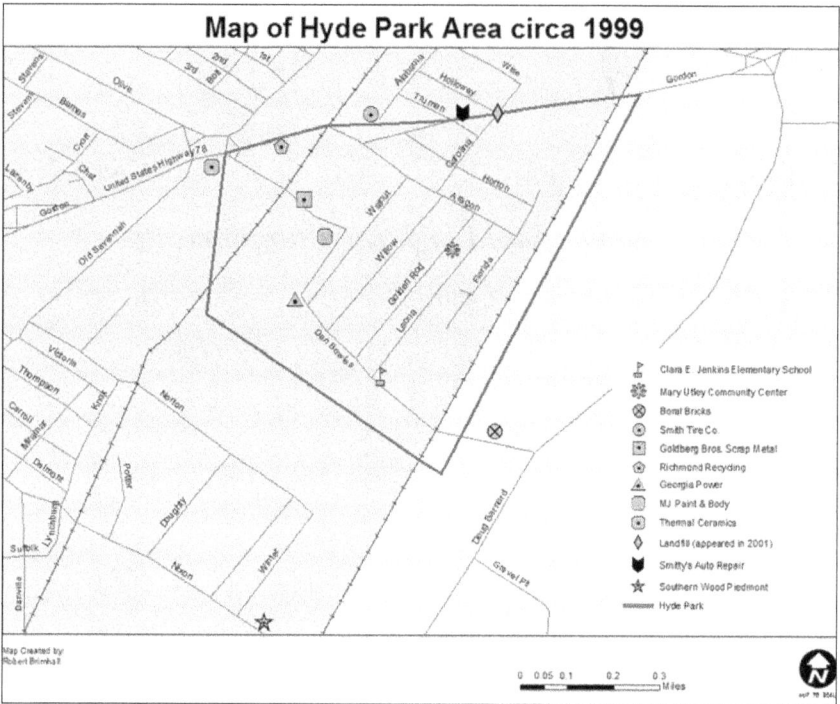

Map of Hyde Park Area circa 1999

Legend:
- Clara E. Jenkins Elementary School
- Mary Utley Community Center
- Boral Bricks
- Smith Tire Co.
- Goldberg Bros. Scrap Metal
- Richmond Recycling
- Georgia Power
- MJ Paint & Body
- Thermal Ceramics
- Landfill (appeared in 2001)
- Smitty's Auto Repair
- Southern Wood Piedmont
- Hyde Park

Map Created by: Robert Brimhall

0 0.05 0.1   0.2   0.3 Miles

FIGURE 9.1.

Map of Hyde Park area, Augusta, Georgia, circa 1999. Drawn by Robert Brimhall and reprinted by permission of NYU Press from Polluted Promises *(Checker 2005b).*

along the southwestern edge of the neighborhood, and entering it required crossing one of two sets of railroad tracks (figure 9.1). At its inception in the 1950s, the neighborhood's industries and easy transportation access prom-ised its African American residents employment and economic stability. However, as industries strove to expand their profits through technological advances and global outsourcing, the people of Hyde Park lost out. Globalization and neoliberalism combined to diminish both factory work and environmental regulations, deteriorating the local environment and the health and well-being of local residents.

By the time I came to Augusta in 1998, Hyde Park, which sat on the edge of the city only six miles from the center of its downtown, amalgamated the best and worst of urban and rural life. Homes were surrounded by wide yards with leafy trees, and people often sat on porches, chatting with their neighbors. At the same time, Hyde Park was also typical of urban neighborhoods plagued by disinvestment—its unemployment rate was

18 percent, and median household income in the neighborhood was $8,983 (Sociology Research Methods Students et al. 1998). Many residents worked two or three jobs to make ends meet. Because railroad tracks and the highway physically isolated the neighborhood, drug trafficking had become a major local industry.

"Toxic donuts" such as Hyde Park exemplify how spatial landscapes reflect the neoliberal pursuit of profit without regard for social costs: we find them across the globe as local governments and elites, as well as multinational corporations, dispossess local communities of their clean air, water, and soil in the name of capital accumulation. Development projects in southern Africa, Pakistan, India, and Colombia, for example, benefit landholding elites and local governments while harming poor people, ethnic minorities, and women (Agarwal 1992; Derman and Ferguson 2004; Dove 2001; Escobar and Paulson 2004). In the upper Amazon basins of Ecuador, the petroleum industry has depleted the ecological and economic resources of indigenous people (Alston and Brown 1993:183; Dorsey 2002). Coca-Cola workers in Colombia, Peru, Nicaragua, Russia, Pakistan, and Chile charge that the company is destroying community water resources. In India, farmers say that Coca-Cola gave them toxic waste material to use as fertilizer, drained water supplies through excessive pumping, and polluted groundwater by the indiscriminate release of wastewater (Gill and Romero 2006).

The future portends to be more of the same—as global warming (stemming, in large part, from unchecked capital growth and consumerism) intensifies, poor people and people of color will increasingly bear the brunt of its effects. To combat such circumstances, grassroots activists across the globe are combining environmentalism and social justice to fuel a worldwide movement known as environmental justice.

By exploring the pursuit of environmental justice in one small community, this chapter concretizes the ways in which neoliberal policies and ideologies affect people's everyday life. First, the deregulation of industries to promote capital growth has allowed lenient environmental standards, resulting in a proliferation of contaminated sites. Second, the premise behind state deregulation is that "freeing," and thus "growing," the market inevitably benefits society as a whole (see di Leonardo, chapter 10, this volume). Upholding this premise, especially in the face of highly visible economic and social inequality, requires investing in a repertoire of discourses that bolster and maintain it. This chapter explores several of those as they relate to the case of Hyde Park, namely, the belief that industrial siting decisions are race-neutral, that the legal system is color-blind, and that environmental science is unbiased and value-free. Because they paradoxically underlie the very institutions designed to protect humans from an uncontrolled market, these ideologies facilitate and justify environmental disparities.

Importantly, this chapter also shows that, for the people whose neighborhoods are continuously slated for polluting industries and who overwhelmingly happen to be people of color, no justification can suffice. In other words, activists and advocates for environmental justice are well familiar with the sometimes subtle (and sometimes blatant) ways in which racial biases continue to structure (and undermine) American institutions. This chapter, then, demonstrates how everyday people like the residents of Hyde Park resist neoliberalism, in part, by asserting their own experiences of institutionalized racism. At the same time, I argue that even as Hyde Park residents challenged neoliberalism, neoliberal ideologies also shaped the residents' environmental justice battles. I thus demonstrate how contemporary environmental justice activists strategically navigate discourses of race neutrality by alternately adopting and resisting them.

Globalization, as the first chapter of this volume explains, is a multivalenced term that signals an increase in global flows of materials, as well as in trade and migration. Neoliberalism, for the purposes of this chapter, is an ideology that facilitates globalization. By presuming that the less the state regulates businesses (particularly, environmental regulations), the more the market will grow and society in general will benefit, neoliberal ideology promotes the idea that a healthy market inevitably provides for all citizens. Inherent in this view is a valorization of individualism—individual businesses must be allowed to maximize their profitability so that individual citizens can prosper. Conveniently, this perspective also renders issues such as racism matters of private acts of prejudice, masking the fact that systemic racial discrimination continues to structure social relations (Lipsitz 1995, 2006; also see Brown et al. 2003; Brown and Wellman 2005).

The research presented here demonstrates the disjuncture between race-neutral ideologies and the consequences of systemic discrimination by grounding them in everyday human experience. As I follow Hyde Park residents' attempts to remedy their environmental situation, I track how the institutions that were supposed to provide objective mechanisms for recourse were actually premised on bias and inequality. My findings here are based on fourteen months of intensive fieldwork in Hyde Park between 1998 and 1999 and less intensive field research that has continued since that time. My primary research methods include participant observation, quantitative surveys, archival research, and interviews. Of the estimated

250 adults in Hyde Park, I have interviewed approximately 26 (10 percent) at least once and have met and spoken with at least 75 percent of the neighborhood's adults.

Weaving ethnographic information throughout my chapter, I first explain how racial discrimination and economics are inextricably intertwined and mutually constitutive—together they produce uneven geographies and environmental racism. Second, I show how the residents of Hyde Park resisted the idea that their environmental situation was the "natural" result of a free market and instead viewed it as part of a long history of discrimination. This assertion counters fundamental American discourses about fairness and neutrality, which support neoliberal ideas and hamstring the success of race-based claims for justice. The third part of this chapter argues that biases hidden but inherent in legal and scientific institutions, which are supposed to protect people from uncontrolled market forces, preclude environmental justice communities from ever finding the "proof" that would win them the expensive settlements or cleanups they need to remedy their situations. Fourth and finally, I conclude by describing how environmental justice activists in Hyde Park and across the United States challenge neoliberalism and the environmental disparities it creates.

ENVIRONMENTAL INEQUITY AND THE FALLACY OF MARKET DYNAMICS

Time and again, I am asked to explain how it is that the siting of hazardous waste is based on anything but market principles. This quest grows out of prevalent neoliberal ideology, which characterizes urban landscapes and environmental hazards as arranged according to a pragmatic, reasonable, economic logic. Why would a corporation put a factory in the middle of a white middle-class neighborhood when there is less expensive and more easily procured land over in the Hispanic or African American neighborhood?

Certainly, I agree that industries choose to locate where land is cheapest; however, there are many reasons that land is cheap—and most of them have to do with institutional forms of racism. Indeed, numerous studies show that race, *not* income, is the most potent variable in predicting where hazardous waste facilities are located—more powerful than poverty, land values, and home ownership. More specifically, a 2007 study by the United Church of Christ reported that the proportion of people of color in neighborhoods hosting toxic sites is almost twice that of the proportion of those living in nonhost neighborhoods. Where facilities are clustered, people of color make up more than a two-thirds majority. Ninety percent of states with facilities have disproportionately high percentages of people of color living in host neighborhoods. The enforcement of environmental regulations also depends significantly on an area's socioeconomic makeup. For example, penalties imposed on hazardous waste generators are five hundred times higher in places with white populations than in those with minority populations (Bullard et al. 2007). Clearly, simple market dynamics cannot explain these statistics. Neither can what scholars refer to as "traditional racism," in which discrimination happens through individual bias or legal segregation.

Rather, the "structural" racism that has prevailed in the post–civil rights era is cumulative and insidious: deeply held values about individualism, hard work, opportunity, and self-reliance obscure its existence. In other words, white Americans tend to define racism as deliberate, intentional, individual acts—a view that cannot accommodate structural racism (see Lipsitz 1995, 2006). As a result, skeptics argue that siting decisions are not motivated by racial biases. However, the factors leading to disproportionate pollution and contamination include a host of racist practices and procedures embedded in seemingly race-neutral institutions that structure everyday life.

Even if corporations *do* use race-neutral criteria when they locate hazardous waste sites, other kinds of institutional discrimination collectively contribute to siting decisions and make it almost impossible for residents to leave and escape contamination. First, the generally white racial makeup of local zoning and planning boards gives African Americans little say in factory or incinerator siting decisions. Minority neighborhoods are also more likely than white neighborhoods to be rezoned (again, by often all-white planning boards) from residential to commercial or light industrial uses. Second, federal policies and tacit sanctioning of discriminatory practices have made the accumulation of equity extremely difficult for people of color—in 2000, white median net worth was ten times that of blacks (Brown and Wellman 2005:201). Much of this disparity stems from housing discrimination. For example, because the Federal Housing Administration historically favored investment in segregated suburbs over inner-city areas, current generations are left with a legacy of little-to-no equity to pass on to their offspring (Lipsitz 1995:370–373). In more recent years, numerous studies have shown how, despite the Fair Housing Act and other civil rights reforms, realtors continue to steer African Americans toward existing "ghettos" and how mortgages and home improvement loans are still allocated most often to white neighborhoods. Minorities with the same resources and credit cards as whites are denied mortgages twice as often (Massey and Denton 1993). In sum, constraints in residential choice make African Americans less able to accumulate wealth (Brown and Wellman 2005).

Segregated housing markets also lead to inequality in schools, which are financed through property taxes. Poorer educations give African Americans less access to the kinds of jobs that would enable them to move out of a contaminated neighborhood. Moreover, employment discrimination against African Americans continues to prevail in our society. As well as lack of access to jobs, lower wages limit the opportunities of African Americans to leave a contaminated neighborhood—and even if they did leave, they would likely have little choice but to move to another contaminated neighborhood. Finally, many of those who can choose to move to a white neighborhood are reluctant to do so because of experiences of racism and persistent white antipathy toward integration (Cole and Foster 2001; see also Bullard 2000). Completing this vicious cycle, growing up with lead, dioxin, or mercury poisoning makes children miss or perform more poorly in school, further curtailing their educational and job opportunities and therefore limiting where they can live. Environmental racism is thus emblematic of the cumulative discrimination set in place decades ago. Despite civil rights reforms, public policies that promote growth and limit government intervention work together with the remnants of private prejudice. Specious ideologies about race neutrality then hide the ways in which race shapes contemporary landscapes, leaving poor people and people of color to bear the burden of living with our nation's toxic waste.

HOW TO PREPARE A TOXIC DONUT

On a warm October evening in 1999, Reverend Charles Utley, a fifty-four-year-old high school guidance counselor and minister, described the Hyde Park of his childhood: "Well, Babcock [Industrial Ceramics Factory] was there. The power plant was there, but it wasn't as large as it is. The rest of it was just beautiful landscape. Just land, trees, and sage fields. Where the junkyard is, that was the area that we could plant. Nothing there." Like many of Hyde Park's original settlers, Reverend Utley's parents left a life of sharecropping and moved their young family to Hyde Park from Waynesboro, Georgia, in the mid-1950s in search of the better job opportunities that the growing city of Augusta offered. For its original settlers, Hyde Park combined the best of two worlds—surrounded by trees and fields, it appeared bucolic, but only six miles from downtown Augusta, it was also close to the many job opportunities that the city's growing economy promised. Relocating to Hyde Park, then, gave former sharecroppers the chance to take a giant step toward a prosperous future while keeping a toehold in their rural pasts.

Not only was land in Hyde Park affordable—and available—to African

American farmers, but also it was close to the kinds of jobs obtainable under the Jim Crow system. When the Utley family moved to the neighborhood in the 1950s, they shared it with Southern Wood Piedmont (SWP), a thermal ceramics factory, a brickyard, and a new power plant. Of course, those industries, and the fact that the land was swampy and flooded often, explained why it was set aside for African Americans in the first place.

Even so, for $50 the African American farm laborers of Waynesboro and other nearby rural areas could finally acquire their own piece of property. Charles Utley explained: "A lot of families moved in that were [from] the rural areas [where] you couldn't own the land—you were crop sharers.... And that was the reason my family moved here, because otherwise they would never have the opportunity to purchase the land. They had to sharecrop it. And they had saved up money to move to this area." Land ownership thus provided an enduring sense of security denied to African Americans during years of enslavement and exploitation. Moreover, it enabled former sharecroppers to build real equity to pass down to future generations. Long-term resident Bernice Jones, who moved from Waynesboro to Hyde Park in 1954, explained: "This is a neighborhood where people who were basically farmers and other people who had probably done sharecropping and who had never owned property came together buying property with the idea that they were going to buy something and build homes to have for their children to be raised in."

Not only does real estate provide equity, but it also acts as a linchpin for economic and social opportunity, opening doors to better education, employment, safety, insurance rates, services, and wealth. Home ownership also shores up status for future generations—another critical part of the American Dream (Perin 1977; see also Edelstein 2003:62; Gregory 1998; Harrison 1995a:39; Hochschild 1996:42, 47; Stack 1996). For Hyde Park residents, owning homes and land represented a chance to join the American mainstream during a time when blacks were still not given full citizenship rights.

But as the neighborhood grew, so did the industries surrounding it. Between the 1930s and the 1950s, at least four other waste-producing businesses joined SWP, Boral Bricks, and Babcock and Wilcox Ceramics Factory. Although the number of industries expanded throughout the 1970s and '80s, technological advances meant that the number of jobs diminished. As a result, as local incomes deteriorated, Hyde Park's unemployment and crime rates (especially drug selling) increased. In 1998, 47 percent of Hyde Park residents earned less than $10,000 per year, with 67.4 percent of residents living below the poverty level (Sociology Research

Methods Students et al. 1998). Day-to-day struggles to make ends meet took precedence over other concerns, particularly environmental.

Hyde Park's case shows how industry often begets industry—rather than recognize that neighborhoods like Hyde Park already have a number of toxic burdens, policymakers see such areas as tainted, so they turn these into literal dumping grounds. Then, as globalization and mechanization make it easier for companies to downsize and/or move operations overseas, neighborhood residents are usually among the first to be fired. Unemployment contributes to the impoverishment of such areas, and community members' primary focus becomes putting food on the table and paying light bills, leaving little time to challenge a proliferation of toxic hazards. For example, for many years Hyde Park residents resigned themselves to the conditions that their factory neighbors imposed on them as a part of neighborhood life. They grew used to the residue that covered their cars, the oil that often appeared on the top of ditch water, and the tap water that sometimes "had an odor to it."

But in 1988 Southern Wood Piedmont closed, and things began to change. Five years earlier, groundwater wells at the factory had revealed onsite contamination from wood-preserving chemicals (including creosote, arsenic, chromium, and PCBs).[2] Subsequent investigations established two plumes of contamination. SWP decided to close its Augusta plant, partly because the soil and groundwater contamination could not be adequately remediated as long as the plant remained in operation.[3] The next section describes how, after Hyde Park residents learned about the factory's closing, many of their memories became tainted with fear. I also demonstrate how residents connected the history of discrimination described above to the contamination of their neighborhood. Through this process of understanding and explaining their environmental situation in racial terms, residents resisted the notion that urban landscapes are the "natural" result of free market forces. Yet, as I also show in ensuing sections of this chapter, despite the experiences of people like those living in Hyde Park, dominant ideas continue to deny institutional discrimination. Thus, explaining and fighting it is an exceedingly complicated matter.

TAINTED MEMORIES AND EXPLAINING THE DIFFERENCE BETWEEN BLACK AND WHITE

A half mile from Hyde Park, residents of the Virginia Subdivision neighborhood were unsurprised at the plant's closing. At the time, the subdivision was a mostly white, low-income neighborhood right on the border of SWP and across a field from Hyde Park. Several long ditches ran from

SWP property through Virginia Subdivision and into Hyde Park. As early as the 1970s, Virginia Subdivision residents had begun filing complaints with the Georgia Environmental Protection Division about a foul odor emanating from their drinking water and their backyard wells. They also documented the number of residents with cancer and were alarmed by the results.[4] In response, the US Agency for Toxic Disease Registry (ATSDR) conducted a health consultation in 1987. Its report discouraged residents from using well water and suggested that certain ditches were potentially contaminated (Governor's Task Force 1996). Residents of Virginia Subdivision, joined by several local companies that owned property around SWP, filed a class action suit seeking damages for trespass, nuisance, and neglect. In mid-1990 SWP's parent company settled the lawsuit for approximately $8.6 million.

Around the time the factory closed, a large flood swept over Hyde Park and left in its wake a foul smelling, bluish-white mud and houses full of corroded furniture. Johnnie Mae Brown remembered the "high water" of 1990: "Most people in the neighborhood didn't even think about [the environment] until we had that flood. After the flood, we knew that something was wrong because that water, everything that the floodwater touched, it was no good no more."

Hyde Park community leaders heard about the subdivision lawsuit just after the flood, and they began connecting the two events. Although the subdivision was adjacent to SWP, whereas Hyde Park was located across a field from the factory, the neighborhoods were connected by a series of ditches that lined both sides of Hyde Park's streets. Moreover, the same chemicals found in Virginia Subdivision were discovered within 15 feet of an elementary school within Hyde Park's borders (Hewell 1989:1A).[5] Some residents alleged that they had seen SWP trucks dumping waste into nearby fields at night.[6] Although they had not filed any legal actions against SWP, Hyde Park residents believed that for SWP to offer them a settlement and/or to have been included in the lawsuit would have been "the moral thing to do."[7]

Soon, local leaders contacted the University of Georgia's (UGA) Extension Office for Richmond County. Extension agents tested produce and soil from Hyde Park gardens and found elevated levels of arsenic and chromium. The director of the Extension Office later went on record stating that he would not eat anything from a Hyde Park garden. Subsequent analyses of the test results varied. UGA scientists advised against eating from gardens, but the Richmond County Health Department contended that the levels were safe for ingestion. The results alarmed residents, and almost all decided to let their gardens die (see Huth 1991a, 1991b). News of contamination also meant that homes were now unsellable. The soil imbued with Hyde Park residents' American dreams became the very source of their dreams' destruction.

Now, residents' memories of their neighborhood were tainted with fear and danger. For instance, before 1970, residents did not receive city water or gas. Instead, they used outdoor pumps connected to underground wells and heated their homes from wood-burning stoves, on which they also cooked. After some reports concluded that Hyde Park's groundwater and soil were contaminated, however, residents feared that the water they had pumped was filled with toxic chemicals. In addition, a common chore for neighborhood children was to go into Southern Wood Piedmont's (SWP) field, gather leftover creosote-treated wood chips, and then take these home to burn in their stoves.[8] Charles Utley remembered: "We would get the firewood from the chips that they would use to make the wood, and it was easy to burn, so we would take that and we would put it in the heaters and we would heat with that." However, as Robert Striggles explained, "You see, when we was burning that wood, we didn't know that it was harmful to us. We was burning creosote. We didn't know that creosote was a cancer-causing agent." Residents also worried about having attended family barbecues on the SWP site. Wives of SWP workers wondered not only about their husbands' health but also about having washed their husbands' work clothes by boiling them.

Residents had always connected the fact that their neighborhood lacked urban resources such as adequate police protection, litter control, and refuse disposal to racial discrimination. In 1968 they formed the Hyde and Aragon Park Improvement Committee (HAPIC) as a civil rights association to demand city water, sewage, streetlights, and paved roads.[9] In 1991 they definitively linked the contamination of their land to that history of racial struggle.

Hyde Park residents had faced the double whammy of being black *and* poor, but overwhelmingly they agreed that racism, not classism, was the primary reason for their neighborhood's contamination. Totsie Walker, who had lived in the neighborhood for roughly forty-one years, said, "[Being black is] the biggest part. If we was in a mixed-up neighborhood, they would've done something. But you see, it wasn't. Now you see, that's the way I feel about it...they just don't care, you see." Ollie Jones, who had lived in Hyde Park for forty-two years, agreed:

> You want me to be frank with you? If this was a white neighbor-
> hood, now I'm being honest, government would've stepped in

here and wouldn't have been about two or three words said. Another thing is if this had been a rich neighborhood, it wouldn't have been nobody in here. They would have moved them out of here. But most of the people are poor, black people.... If you look at [Virginia Subdivision] the majority of the peoples over there is white people, right? And Piedmont is connected to this place too, but they were complaining over there. They didn't hesitate. They bought them out.

Like many residents I interviewed, Jones tacks back and forth between race- and class-based reasons for Hyde Park's contamination. However, when he compares his neighborhood to Virginia Subdivision, where income levels are similar to those in Hyde Park, he clearly concludes that "they never bought them out" because "the majority of people there [were] white."[10] Similarly, Johnnie Mae Brown pointed to both race and class as factors in Hyde Park's contamination but admitted that race played a more significant role:

> Yeah, I think we're black, low-income people in the neighbor-hood. And not everyone is on the poverty line, you know, but we're still in the neighborhood. And I think it's because we're black first of all. That's the most important. We're black, poor people. And they just build anything they want around us, and we don't have no say-so.

Brown's statement "we're black first of all" highlights her perception of the powerlessness of blacks in Augusta, regardless of income level, profession, or home ownership.

Nearly all Hyde Park residents I spoke with agreed that their situation (as Charles Utley once said) "had 95 percent to do with race."[11] Some recalled that Jim Crow–era housing restrictions were why they had to live in the midst of factories in the first place. Others, like activist Arthur Smith, pointed to racial stereotypes: "I think, with Hyde Park and Aragon Park, it was the arrogance again of big companies saying, 'Those people are not educated. Those people do not vote.'" Some Hyde Park leaders cited more systematic practices of racism, referring to their situation as "environmental apartheid" or "residential holocaust." Charles Utley called it "a form of genocide" stemming from a deliberate, planned, and systemized racism made up of both corporate greed and discriminatory political institutions. Notably, most residents referred to "they" when describing their environmental problems, citing some kind of collective racism, which ranged from traditional to more subtle forms. Hyde Park residents clearly understood that their neighborhood became a prime location for toxic industries *not* as the natural result of a free market, but rather as part of a legacy of discriminatory and disempowering practices.

Once they understood their contamination as an issue of racial discrimination, residents launched their battle for environmental justice. However, in the two decades since HAPIC's formation, race-based activism in the United States has changed significantly. Although legal institutions are supposed to counterbalance profit seeking at human expense, remedies to environmental racism are hindered by discourses of neutrality, just as the racial discrimination that leads to uneven urban geographies works under the guise of neutral market forces.

For example, many grassroots environmental justice groups initially turned to the courts, filing race-based lawsuits under the Equal Protection clause of the Fourteenth Amendment. Yet, almost none of these have prevailed. Since 1976, the US Supreme Court has defined "race discrimination" as "intentional or purposeful conduct on the basis of race, or at least some consciousness of race as a factor motivating conduct." To prove that a community is contaminated because of its racial or ethnic makeup, a plaintiff must provide evidence that a specific person or group of people deliberately caused the contamination as a race-conscious act. Because most contaminations happen over long periods of time and result from the cumulative racism described earlier, it is almost impossible to prove intent (Cole and Foster 2001:63). Intent must also be attached to individual actors. The intent clause encapsulates what George Lipsitz refers to as "the language of liberal individualism," which makes any discussion of non-individual-based racism nearly impossible (see Lipsitz 1995, 2006). Thus, in reflecting neoliberal thought, notions of legal neutrality facilitate rather than check capital growth.

When HAPIC did file a lawsuit against ITT/Rayonier, it charged the corporation with trespassing, lowering residents' property values, and diminishing their quality of life through contamination, not racism. The reason is that even if residents could demonstrate the racial dynamics behind their situation, they would need to prove scientifically that their health was at risk. Here, we find another seemingly value-free institution— environmental science. In the following section, I argue that environmental assessments and the science upon which they are based, instead of being "neutral," contain inherent biases that preclude most environmental justice communities from proving that their health is in danger and from finding remedies for their situations.

MELISSA CHECKER

NOT NECESSARILY NEUTRAL: ENVIRONMENTAL
SCIENCE AND POTENTIAL BIAS

In the first few years after filing its 1991 lawsuit, Hyde Park underwent a battery of tests on its air, water, and soil. Not only did one study advise residents to stop growing their own vegetables, but also a 1991 mortality survey found death rates in the SWP area to be five times higher than in comparable communities. In 1992 a dermatologist observed a high number of SWP-area residents with arsenical keratosis.[12] That same year, a neuropsychologist found a high degree of neurological abnormalities among Hyde Park residents, which he believed could be attributed to exposure to toxic chemicals. For every study that found evidence of contamination and linked it to endangered health, however, another found the opposite. In particular, studies conducted by the US Environmental Protection Agency (EPA) and the US Agency for Toxic Substances and Disease Registry (ATSDR) concluded that, despite elevated levels of arsenic, chromium, and other heavy metals, there was no clear or significant relationship between contaminants and poor health.[13]

Yet, in 1998 more than one-third of Hyde Park residents reported having family members with circulatory problems, respiratory conditions, skin disease, or cancer, and time and again, they enumerated their experiences of poor community health (Sociology Research Methods Students et al. 1998). David Kimbrough, whose father and brother worked at SWP and died at an early age, said that his own daughters suffered from hyperventilation, dizziness, and fainting spells until he and his wife stopped allowing them to play outdoors. Many other residents reported unusual and untimely deaths of family members. To name a few, Johnnie Mae Brown's sister died of cancer at the age of thirty-two, Totsie Walker's adopted son (who also worked at SWP) died of a heart attack before he reached forty, Robert Striggles' brother died of cancer in his fifties, and Ollie Jones died of a heart attack at the age of fifty-five.

With all the studies conducted on Hyde Park, why is there no definitive answer about whether chemical contamination is linked to poor health? Communities across the country are in a similar predicament. For environmental justice communities to achieve any kind of remedy to their situation, they must prove conclusively that chemicals in their air, water, and/or soil cause their health problems. Most often, we look to seemingly objective science for such proof. However, as scholars from an array of disciplines have demonstrated, scientific knowledge, far from being value-free, is imbricated with capital interests. University scientists often sit on advisory boards for corporate and governmental entities, and many act as standing consultants.

One study found that one-third of the Massachusetts Institute of Technology's biology department had formal ties to biotech companies (Hubbard and Wald 1993). Prevailing ideas about scientific objectivity obscure such biases and, in so doing, facilitate corporate evasion of responsibility for environmentally related illnesses. Yet again, one of the very institutions designated to regulate the human costs of a free market does no such thing.

The hidden values underlying science and scientific decisions are clearly exemplified in the environmental risk assessment process, each phase of which excludes many of the experiences of environmental justice communities. For instance, the initial stage in environmental risk assessment determines whether a particular substance causes a disease or other adverse health effect by focusing on one effect at a time, called an "endpoint." Endpoints can include cancer, reproductive and developmental disorders, central nervous system symptoms, trauma, infections, and rashes (Israel 1995:483). Scientists themselves must prioritize which endpoints they study, according to various factors. For example, cancer is frequently chosen as an endpoint because it is particularly sensitive, easy to identify, and a prominent public concern (Israel 1995; see also Anglin 1998).

The second stage of the risk assessment process studies dose response, or how much of a particular substance will cause an adverse health effect. These experiments are primarily based on animals, despite the fact that animals and humans can react to chemicals very differently. The tests are also performed at high doses and then extrapolated to low-dose situations; this process, too, is uncertain. For example, because the costs of such tests are high, researchers use only a few hundred animals. Individual chemical sensitivities also vary widely in both animals and humans (Tesh 2000:27–28; see also Dark 1998). The smaller the pool of animals, the more difficult it is to spot adverse health effects. Also, many lab rodents are bred to be genetically similar. This uniformity makes them even less comparable to genetically and geographically diverse people (Schettler, Barrett, and Raffensperger 2002; see also Douglas and Wildavsky 1982).

Most studies quantify the adverse affects of toxins by using a "typical person," usually defined as "a hypothetical adult, 'Caucasian' male, 10–30 years old, 154 pounds, five feet seven inches tall, and 'Western European or North American in habitat and custom'" (Shipak 2007:7). In other words, standard comparison techniques fail to provide information on the range of ways in which women, children, elderly, or already sick people—far more susceptible groups of people—might react to a chemical. Scientific standards also do not account for cultural diversity. The ATSDR study on Hyde Park, for example, analyzed fish samples from a nearby fishing pond. The researchers then estimated the likelihood that a 70-kilogram adult who consumed 18 grams of fish a day for more than one year would get sick. Based on that estimate, they found that the fish posed no danger (US ATSDR 1994). However, it is well known that people of color (including children, the elderly, and sick people) consume closer to 20–24 grams of fish per day (West et al. 1992).

Institutionally, high-dose studies are mandated to concentrate on immediate responses to exposures, but numerous diseases have long latency periods and their link to harmful chemicals may not become evident for many years. For example, birth defects have especially delayed onsets, and many cancers do not show up for twenty to forty years. Studying immediate responses to a chemical gives only a partial picture of its potential harm (see Fitchen 1988). Because environmental hazards are studied in laboratories rather than in natural settings, studies also do not account for how the chemicals in various compounds might interact with other kinds of air, water, or soil pollution. In sum, although scientists might be able to establish cause-and-effect relationships between one chemical and one disease under controlled conditions, the chances of establishing definitive cause-and-effect relationships in the real world are slim (see Fitchen 1988; Montague 2003; Novotny 1998:141).

As difficult as it is for scientists to resolve the precise level at which a chemical will pose a risk to humans, an even more difficult problem with risk assessment comes in its third phase—exposure assessment. Here again, environmental scientists are constrained by funding issues and institutional protocols that call for isolating data and focusing on one chemical at one time (Wigley and Shrader-Frechette 1996; see also Anglin 1998; Bryant 1995; Kriebel et al. 2001; Novotny 1998; US EPA 2003). Yet, many communities are exposed to dozens of chemicals from extant and abandoned factories, not to mention particles emitted from cars, trucks, and trains. For instance, a number of Hyde Park residents spent years working at various chemical-producing plants in the neighborhood, and many were exposed to chemicals throughout their lives by burning creosote-coated wood in their stoves and drinking well water. Furthermore, the neighborhood is located between two sets of railroad tracks and adjacent to a highway. All these factors add up to multiple exposures over long periods of time. Yet, risk assessments typically overlook such compound exposures, and even more troubling, scientists are only beginning to learn about the cumulative effects of toxins. The EPA has begun to develop methodologies for including cumulative risk in the assessment process, but these methods are only in their nascent stages (US EPA 2003).

Finally, many of the illnesses that communities like Hyde Park complain of, such as developmental disorders, asthma, and circulatory and respiratory problems, generally result from a range of genetic, environmental, and social factors. Indeed, in some cases, an illness may not be directly related to a particular chemical but may be exacerbated by, or exacerbate, toxic exposure. For example, two common health problems in low-income African American communities are diabetes and hypertension. Not only can toxic agents provoke Type I diabetes, but having diabetes also creates metabolic impairments, which makes a person susceptible to toxic-related illness (Hubbard and Wald 1993:78). Moreover, a recent study published by the American Diabetes Association found strong correlations between concentrations of persistent organic pollutants and the prevalence of diabetes (Lee et al. 2006). Similarly, hypertension can lead to kidney disease, which inhibits the body's ability to process toxic exposures (Israel 1995:506).

Health officials and other governmental agencies frequently blame the health problems prevalent in communities like Hyde Park on "lifestyles" (that is, smoking, eating the wrong foods, and not exercising) rather than on environmental toxins (see Cole and Foster 2001; Shipak 2007). We know that there are correlations between income levels and smoking, diet, and exercise, but these factors provide too easy an "out" for health officials. "Lifestyle" implies free choice; however, families in environmentally contaminated communities are told not to grow produce, and their local grocery stores do not carry affordable, quality fruits and vegetables (Kilman 2005; see also Hubbard and Wald 1993). Blaming the victim in these ways circumvents questions of toxic contamination that would place responsibility for community members' poor health squarely on the shoulders of polluters and local governments.

Environmental cleanups and community relocations are enormously expensive. If environmental science becomes less biased and focuses more on cumulative risk in poor communities and communities of color, the parties that provide remedies to environmental injustice—corporations or governments—have much to lose. In its guise of neutrality, environmental science enables evasion of responsibility and ensures that the likelihood of pinpointing a direct connection between chemicals and illness will remain extremely rare.

CHALLENGING RACISM IN A RACE-NEUTRAL ERA

The insidiousness of institutional racial biases in a neoliberal period presented new challenges for HAPIC activists. Unlike their civil rights battles of the 1960s and 1970s, they found that fighting for environmental justice required tailoring their activism to contemporary political and social climates. Rather than emphasize their racial identities, in many of their public presentations activists represented themselves as homeowners whose quality of life had been ruined by local polluters. As part of that strategy, HAPIC initially joined forces with residents from Virginia Subdivision (many subdivision residents claimed that they had not received enough money from their settlement to move yet its conditions required them to refrain from any more lawsuits). The two groups expanded their strategies to include extralegal remedies such as lobbying the government by contacting city council people and state and congressional representatives (Charles Walker and Cynthia McKinney) and petitioning the state Environmental Protection Division and the US Environmental Protection Agency.

In their rhetorical strategies especially, HAPIC activists adapted to post–civil rights era contexts. For instance, Charles Utley frequently emphasized publicly that the environment affected everyone and was "not about black or white, but all colors." Utley admitted that he did not always mention the part about racism: "You have to get a feel for your audience." In other words, certain audiences preferred to hear only the first part of his message—interracial harmony. HAPIC leaders were well aware of multiculturalism's political currency, and by emphasizing diversity they increased their chances of winning political favor. Moreover, by casting the environment as color-blind and by de-emphasizing racial concerns, HAPIC appeared attractive to professional environmental groups that wanted to diversify their memberships but may not have wanted to work with separatist or threatening African American groups.

A coalitional and multicultural strategy reflects post–civil rights era changes. As the contributors to this volume have noted, over the past several decades "diversity" and "multiculturalism" have neatly fit into neoliberal ideologies that recognize multiple identities, as long as they are divorced from economic and social justice (di Leonardo 2004). Although coalition building is certainly a worthwhile endeavor, social scientists caution that the use of purely celebratory multiracial or multicultural rhetoric can mask, or neutralize, the continued existence of racial hierarchies (Appadurai 1996; Goldschmidt 2004; Harvey 1989; Jameson 1991; Lowe 1996; Turner 1993).[14]

At the same time, more privately or in the company of other activists of color, HAPIC activists maintained a racialized view of their situation, continuing to assert that their problems "had 95 percent to do with race." They strategically alternated between race-neutral and race-specific discourses, developing a complex environmental narrative that, at times, stressed their racial victimization and, at other times, emphasized the environment's potential to threaten all races alike. This deliberate tacking back and forth underscores how political actors, even though they might use prevailing discourses, do not necessarily embrace these. Rather, naming and challenging racism, given neoliberal logics of neutrality, require complicated negotiations of discourse and language, as well as expansions of traditional strategies and narratives.

REBALANCING ENVIRONMENTAL BIASES

Another important strategy for HAPIC activists was their development of extensive networks with those in the national and international environmental justice movement. These activists work to oppose neoliberal practices that privilege capital accumulation over human health, and they challenge the race-neutral discourses that facilitate environmental injustice. In a clear example of trends toward race neutrality, the second Bush administration changed the federal definition of environmental justice to emphasize the concept of environmental justice for everyone and de-emphasize minority and low-income populations (see Checker 2005a). National activists have raised concerns about such language—certainly, they are in favor of environmental justice for all people, but they also recognize the need to acknowledge that certain communities are drastically overburdened with toxins. National activists also consistently lobby for cumulative environmental risk assessments and more relevant health analyses.[15]

In addition, activists advocate alternatives that would reduce reliance on the science of risk assessment and would instead emphasize more participatory and citizen-centered conceptions of justice. Some promote the implementation of the Precautionary Principle, that precautionary measures should be taken when an activity raises threats of harm to human health or the environment, even if scientific cause-and-effect relationships are not fully established. Importantly, the initiator of such an activity would bear the burden of proving that a given activity was safe, reversing the current standard, where the public bears the burden of proving that a particular activity is risky (Montague 2003).

Finally, environmental justice activists have pushed hard for waste reduction, especially considering the global ramifications of environmental justice and climate change. Already, much of the United States' toxic waste winds up in indigenous and marginalized areas in developing nations, exacerbating their extant pollution problems. In China, for example, particularly rapid economic growth has been accompanied by the rapid deterioration of natural resources, as well as a proliferation of pollution problems. In 2005 there were nearly fifty thousand uprisings related to pollution in rural areas (McLaughlin 2006). Accordingly, US environmental justice activists are working to build cross-border coalitions with other groups. For example, activists in the US South have allied with activists in South Africa, activists in the Southwest have formed partnerships with counterparts in Mexico, and victims of radiation in Russia tour the globe to share their stories (even meeting with Hyde Park activists in 1999). A crucial front in the global environmental justice battle, therefore, is to fight for the worldwide reduction of energy expenditures and, consequently, the need for toxic waste sites.

CONCLUSIONS

By tracking the experiences of one community, this chapter aims to demonstrate how discursive analysis is not just an academic exercise. It also has concrete, practical implications for the everyday life of people. Not only does cumulative racism underlie decisions about where to site toxic waste–producing facilities, but also the seemingly neutral legal and scientific institutions that should protect communities from injustice actually perpetuate it. In other words, neoliberal discourses of race neutrality rationalize the political, economic, and cultural systems that propagate global environmental disparities. But enumerating the various structures that create such inequalities is only one step toward dismantling them—it is equally important not to lose sight of their very real consequences. For example, Hyde Park residents were well aware that ideas about the natural effects of a free market led to a proliferation of toxic sites around them and hobbled their ability to fight environmental racism. Yet HAPIC activists strategically navigated race-neutral discourses by alternately harnessing and resisting them.

Finally, Hyde Park activists are not alone. Indeed, across the globe a small number of determined activists are exposing environmental discrimination for what it is. Through concerted and consistent actions, as well as perseverance learned in the course of lifelong struggles, they are chipping away at the facade of market-based logic, ultimately to declare that the jig is up.

Notes

1. Some of the information presented in this chapter also appears in Checker 2005b and 2007.

2. Until the institution of federal environmental regulations in the 1970s, SWP discharged its residual water into Rocky Creek and Phinizy Swamp and burned treated wood waste, producing smoke and fly ash. By 1979, in compliance with new federal regulations (such as the Clean Water Act), SWP had redirected its waste disposal and installed monitoring wells on the plant's property.

3. From the "Southern Wood Piedmont Augusta Plant History," a document prepared by SWP's attorney.

4. These illnesses, however, were never proven to correlate with the toxic chemicals found in residents' groundwater.

5. SWP's attorney pointed out that they instituted an extensive remediation program, constructing a slurry wall around the site that is impervious to water, excavating the most contaminated parts of the soil, and flushing hundreds of thousands of gallons of groundwater into the county's sewage system.

6. Virginia Subdivision residents made similar allegations, and some said that they had photographed such activities. However, I never saw such photographs or any other documentation of illegal dumping, and SWP denies that it ever took place.

7. The settlement is highly contested. Virginia Subdivision residents claim that after paying legal fees, they did not have enough money left over to move, and African American residents of Virginia Subdivision charge that they did not receive as much compensation as white families. SWP spokespersons maintain that settlement amounts were distributed according to whether a particular property was found to be contaminated by wood-treating chemicals.

8. It should be noted that SWP did not sanction such activities. Furthermore, the ATSDR has stated that none of these activities could cause adverse health effects. See US ATSDR 1995.

9. Aragon Park is a small neighborhood that was adjoined with Hyde Park until 1954, when the city ran its new Gordon Highway through the two neighborhoods. Hyde Park continued to include the smaller neighborhood in its organizing activities.

10. That Virginia Subdivision residents actually received very little money did not mitigate Hyde Park residents' sense that racism had much to do with their being left out of the lawsuit.

11. See Gwaltney 1993, Prince 2002, White 1999, and Williams 1974, who document similar findings about viewing certain issues through a race-identified lens.

12. This skin condition results from long-term arsenic ingestion that causes multiple lesions, commonly on the palms and soles but also on the fingers and proximal portions of the extremities.

13. As summarized in Governor's Task Force 1996.

14. See also Balibar 1991; Gregory 1994; Harrison 1995b:49; McLaren 1994; Shankar 2004; Takaki 2002.

15. In the late 1990s, after several commissioned reports and sustained pressure from grassroots environmental justice groups, the Clinton administration began exploring cumulative risk assessments. In 1997 the EPA Science Policy Council issued preliminary guidelines for scoping cumulative risk assessments. Those pursuits continued under the Bush II administration. In addition, under Bush II, the National Environmental Justice Advisory Council designated a Working Group to concentrate on cumulative risk assessments. Another Working Group worked on recommendations for more effective, integrated, community-based health assessments, intervention, and prevention efforts that consider socioeconomic and cultural factors in community health assessments. See US EPA 2003.

10

The Neoliberalization of Minds, Space, and Bodies

Rising Global Inequality and the Shifting American Public Sphere

Micaela di Leonardo

The parlous state of global and American affairs examined in this volume gives rise to the obvious question: why are these shifts toward higher and higher levels of inequality and increasing constraints on democracy not being transparently represented in the US public sphere? This is an old question, a question addressed by multiple scholarly literatures, a fragile progressive public sphere, and a furious contemporary blogosphere. Although we must base our answer in the present, on bedrock political-economic analyses of the deregulation of private media and the defunding and censorship of public media in the United States, the strengthening state-aided corporate stranglehold is only part of the story. As well, increasingly authoritarian US rule added to increasingly blurred lines of accountability, enabled by swift capital movement and endemic outsourcing, and even our heightened national culture of fear do not conclusively provide the entire answer.

We need, as well, to consider neoliberalism's pull, not just push, factors in assessing changing mentalités in the United States. The celebratory vision of globalization provides us with one window onto these "pulls": the allure of an ever growing and newly affordable cornucopia of globally produced commodities, the charming prospect of "revitalized urban life" as global gentrification transforms vast tracts of the world's cities, in part through sweeping impoverished populations to their hinterlands, and the seeming racial democratization signaled by widespread celebration of indigenous and hybridized identities. In the American urban context, Matthew Ruben has written compellingly of neoliberal urbanization as having encouraged a suburban optic: "the necessary point of observation and enunciation for urban diagnosis, providing a vantage point from which the city may be apprehended precisely as a site of national otherness" (Ruben 2001:443).

This suburban optic is one element of what I label the neoliberalization of consciousness—the profound and largely unrecognized ways in which all of us have shifted our understandings of our own and others' lives over the past few decades. To explore the process of neoliberalization of consciousness, I use two long-term research case studies. The first examines the changing lives and urban imaginaries of the residents of New Haven, Connecticut, over the past two decades of economic bust and boom, and the second examines the Tom Joyner radio show, its monumental national commercial success, its critical progressive politics, and yet nearly total invisibility in the larger American public sphere. The first case helps to flesh out our understanding of how on-the-ground perceptions of American urban space have altered with neoliberal shifts.[1] The second engages with the many differences that race does and does not make in our neoliberalized American public sphere—how racialized political dissent can be hidden in plain sight and thus not enter the public transcript.

AMERICAN URBAN IMAGINARIES: THE NEW HAVEN CASE

Oh, many changes! Now is 100 percent safe! [South Asian cabdriver commenting on downtown New Haven, August 8, 2005]

So forget what you heard about New Haven 15 years ago from your aunt's hairdresser's best friend. Like a classic American musical, New Haven is undergoing a dramatic and spectacular revival—a revival befitting such a venerable theater town. [*The Guide to Downtown New Haven*, a booklet presented by New Haven Savings Bank, 2005]

It's the new New York. [Realtor John Cuozzo, quoted in "Curb Appeal: New Haven Leads Region in Housing Price Gains," *New Haven Register*, August 14, 2005]

I think that all that we hear about New Haven not being a place for poor people, that's what we've gotta believe...we're creating more poor people, and we're ushering them out of town! [Black woman attorney, New Haven native, 2005]

New Haven has had a complicated presence in the American imaginary over the course of the twentieth century and into the twenty-first. It is, first of all, an Ivy League company town. The site of Yale University since the eighteenth century, its center is defined by a still existing village green surrounded by old churches and a commercial area. The Yale campus itself helps to maintain the Anglophiliac fiction of dreaming spires; its main buildings, including the library, law school, gymnasium, and many "colleges" (residence halls), are built in the style sardonically labeled "1930s Gothic." That is, their stone pediments, bas-reliefs, and gargoyles are the work of impoverished Italian stoneworkers hired by the university for a pittance during the Depression.

These workers are at the center of the second image of New Haven, as a fundamentally white-ethnic, blue-collar town—a gritty, red-brick industrial center since the nineteenth century, former home of the Winchester armaments company and dozens of other light and heavy manufacturing concerns. Like most eastern seaboard and industrial Midwestern cities, New Haven experienced landslide migrations, first from Ireland in the mid-nineteenth century and later from southern and eastern Europe, until the passage of restrictive federal immigration legislation in 1924. New Haven's white ethnics were overwhelmingly Italian and Irish. The city also boasts a long tradition of militant white-ethnic unionism. The spillover from this can be seen in Yale's repeated failures to rein in its custodial and maintenance staff, Local 35, in 35's comradely assistance to its sister union, Local 34, during the notoriously successful strike by clerical workers in 1985, as well as the two unions' deep involvement in the always struggling graduate students' union, GESO (Ladd-Taylor 1985; Oberdeck 1991).

The third, lesser-known layer of this *pentimento* urban portrait is the town's black population, always present but greatly swelled by Northern migration from the Carolina South for Connecticut Valley tobacco cultivation, by wartime industrial employment opportunities in the 1910s and 1940s, and by ongoing flight from the Jim Crow South through the 1950s. There are also black migrants from other Northern locations, those who arrived originally from the Cape Verdes Islands, a small number of professional-class in-migrants from all over the United States, and, a more recent addition to demographic complexity, migrants from the Francophone and Anglophone Caribbean and a significant newer population of Puertorriqueños, some of whom identify as black. Mexicanos, largely undocumented, began arriving in the summer of 2000 in concert with their post-NAFTA influx across the South and up the eastern seaboard.

New Haven's black population intersected with its Yale and white ethnic identity in the 1960s in the course of civil rights organizing and urban unrest and, most particularly, during the infamous 1970 trial of Black Panther Bobby Seale (Bass and Rae 2006). Just before the excursions and alarums of campus Vietnam-era politics, however, Yale political scientist Robert Dahl in 1961 published the book that was to etch New Haven's portrait in stone—to provide the most enduring image of the city to an American audience. *Who Governs?* established New Haven as *the* exemplar of political pluralism, new-style post-war urban democracy, and inclusive win/win politics. *Who Governs?* rapidly became a standard social science college textbook and established New Haven as the political scientists' Holy Grail for "democratic pluralism." The pluralist process that Dahl celebrated in particular was then mayor Richard Lee's town-gown coalition of the 1950s and early 1960s, which cleverly gained access to more than $180 million in federal urban renewal dollars—a grotesquely disproportionate amount of federal money expended in all American cities during that period—and transformed the New Haven urbanscape. Demographically speaking, Dahl was also celebrating the working together of professional-class WASPs and the working-class-origin white ethnics in this process, as well as the growth politics candidates who followed Lee into the mayoralty. Dahl did not deal at all with black New Haven's exclusion from this "democratic," this successful "pluralist" process, except in one asterisked, bottom-of-the-page admission.

A group of "community power studies" scholars in the 1970s and 1980s challenged Dahl's pluralist model in general and his New Haven case study in particular. William Domhoff (1978) demonstrated the "interlocking directorate" of government and corporate capital involved in the Lee enterprise and its siphoning of federal money into private profits. Stone and Sanders (1987) documented Lee's ultimate failure as a politician despite his success as mayor. Fred Powledge (1970) has noted the grandiose benefits to Yale University and St. Raphael's Hospital but losses for the populace as a whole. Both institutions gained vast tracts of land formerly housing the poor and working classes. Low-income housing was destroyed and not replaced—what we would now label accumulation by dispossession. Fully one in five of New Haven residents—disproportionately black—were displaced. Functioning industry and small business were discouraged, white flight and suburbanization exacerbated, and even the civic centerpieces of Lee's plan—the coliseum, the parking garage, the shopping mall—deteriorated into shabbiness and disuse. And 1960s black and white radical organizers were defeated through the carrot of cooptation—a handful of public administration jobs and some short-term federal antipoverty money—and the stick of police harassment, including physical violence and widespread illegal wiretapping.

Under Nixon's administration, urban renewal and War on Poverty federal funding was converted into Community Development Block Grants, which were structured to provide even fewer benefits to working-class and poor urban dwellers, irrespective of the intentions of individual urban regimes. Nixon, Ford, and Carter each further cut federal money flowing to cities, and Reagan shut off the spigot altogether in the early 1980s. National federal enforcement of civil rights laws slowed to near stoppage. Under Reagan and then Bush the First, the United States experienced significant upward income redistribution, and a variety of indices indicating improvement in minority economic lives began to move in reverse. The muckraking political-economic analysis of the community power scholars failed to enter the public transcript, but a resurgent "blame the victim" structure of feeling—the urban underclass—captured the American imaginary (di Leonardo 1998:114–127).

New Haven, a city of about 124,000, is in many ways a vest-pocket New York, absent the tradition of rent control and with the addition of a tax-avoiding major industry (Yale University) and a more regressive tax structure (state income tax was not enacted until 1991). During the 1980s, the city experienced the same real-estate speculation spiral and then collapse; the same cycles of stalled gentrification, with extraordinary proliferation of scandalous city tax abatements for friends in high places, slumlords, and bank and owner abandonment; the same emptying out of middle-income occupations and therefore residents; and the same increase in minority residents. In 1980 New Haven was nearly 60 percent white; by 1990 the majority of the population was black or Latino. By 2000 that minority percentage had jumped 11 points, to 61 percent. The number of residents speaking Spanish in the home doubled between 1990 and 2000, and the poverty level increased slightly. But during the same period, echoing the increased wealth and gentrifying fever of urban, upper-income Americans during the Clinton economic boom years, the level of home ownership rose 9 percent (US Census).

Similarly, both cities in this period elected their first black mayor; each mayor had little appetite for mobilizing radical political change; and each inherited the combination of inflated expectations and fiscal crisis. Inevitably, each was forced to administer austerity, lost popularity, and was voted out of office. In 1991 alone, New Haven's John Daniels laid off hundreds of city workers, cut recreation programs, and partially shut down the public libraries. This boom-to-bust era—with its concomitant skyrocketing minority immiseration, the associated burgeoning of a youth-run drug industry (with an estimated turnover of $1 million a day), and white anxieties over the real estate bust and street crime—was a perfect fit for journalist William Finnegan's much noted, two-part *New Yorker* series. He limned the city as dirty, desperate, and dangerous, lyrically skimmed over the political-economic production of poverty, and managed to blame poor mothers for poverty and associated crime (Finnegan 1990; Rierden 1991).

The neighborhood in which I lived in New Haven—from 1985 to 1991, with frequent stays in the years since—never quite became a ghetto but has remained a historically working-class area on the margins of immiseration. It lies due west of the Yale campus. Between the two sites is a residential/commercial area, Dwight/Edgewood, which became a prime drug-selling site during the late 1980s because of its rundown character and key location near the exit ramps of both freeways. Directly north of the neighborhood is a mixed middle-class/affluent area, Beaver Hills, which has become the major professional-class, black residential neighborhood. Perhaps not coincidentally, abutting this integrated neighborhood is Dixwell, one of the three main, named New Haven ghettos. Directly south of my neighborhood is The Hill, the second ghetto, originally Italian and Jewish and recently heavily settled by Puerto Ricans. A wooded park provides the natural boundary on the west of the neighborhood. Past the park is Westville, one of the most affluent and whitest residential areas in the city, one of two neighborhoods historically inhabited by those Yale faculty who do not commute from the wealthy, white, shoreline suburbs. But, unnoticed by politicians and many residents, that boundary eroded in the go-go 1990s as unemployment dropped precipitously, open prostitution and drug trafficking disappeared, and the city brightened up with infusions of Yale University cash. By 2000 the Dwight/Edgewood and Westville populations were equally racially integrated.

In 1986 the major arterial street bounding the north of the neighborhood boasted a kosher butcher, a Hadassah thrift store, and other Jewish-owned and patronized small businesses, the leftover commercial scaffolding of a heavy Jewish settlement now largely suburbanized. By 1991 only Hadassah remained, despite the new settling of a significant group of Hasidim in both my neighborhood and in Westville, which now boasted three *mikvahs* (ritual baths). The arterial's character altered, ethnicized in a different direction, as several stores and restaurants catering to

Caribbean blacks opened. It altered further in 1988 when a local entrepreneur, a "hip capitalist," moved what had been a small, crowded health food grocery in the Edgewood area into a rehabilitated former nightclub, giving the city its first health food supermarket. By 2005 the small businesses fronting the arterial were entirely black owned and run, with the health food supermarket almost the sole exception.

The neighborhood's housing stock is largely composed of three-story, wooden, single-family houses built in the 1920s and 1930s, a smaller number of Victorian-era structures, and a few apartment houses of various periods, with small, grassed front yards and mature deciduous trees. Throughout the neighborhood are clusters of homes still inhabited by single owners; others have been cut up into three-flat rentals. The block in 1986 was all white with the exception of one house, owned since the 1960s by a then elderly black woman who lived on the third floor and rented the two flats beneath to working-class black couples. By the time I moved out in 1991, most of the houses on the block had some working-class black tenants. The house next door had shifted from all white to all black in the period of a year. My landlord, then divorced from my landlady, moved into my apartment, and a black family moved in downstairs. My landlady had only black responses to her rental ad and tried to put the house on the market only to be told that it was currently unsalable.

Throughout the 1980s and late into the 1990s, all New Haveners, across race, class, gender, and age, spoke to me about the city in terms of poverty, drugs, and crime. They varied in their interpretations of those urban realities, but most, across all identity categories, made use of the readily available, victim-blaming terms of underclass ideology (see di Leonardo 1998: 319–332). Working-class black American Patti Hendry, for example, happily greeted me as a new neighbor because, she said, she wanted to get away from black people. Despite Patti's rigid gentility, though, her white, professional-class neighbor Paul automatically suspected Patti and her husband, James, of driving their car over his snowy lawn (the culprit was actually the white newspaper carrier).

By 2005 New Haven was experiencing the same housing bubble as the rest of the nation, and my old landlord told me happily—as did every other home-owning New Havener with whom I spoke during that period—how much money he could get for his house on my old block, should he choose to sell. Despite the Bush Jr. economic downturn, New Haveners, across race and class, like Americans as a whole, were filled with housing-bubble economic optimism. Most of them also noticed and approved the recent infusion of Yale money into downtown development—part of a Yale

Corporation plan to create a *cordon sanitaire* around the campus, to gentrify the area in order to induce wealthy parents not to send their offspring to campuses lodged in cleaner and wealthier surroundings. Yale even "bought" and closed off an entire street from the city. Many echoed the boosterism of the local real estate industry: New Haven was the "new New York," undergoing a revival. More politically attentive residents, like the black woman lawyer quoted at the beginning of this section, noted that the housing bubble was pricing long-term working-class and impoverished residents right out of town.

The attentive ethnographer, as well, could perceive the traces of neoliberal shift—a Potemkin Village private surface with all the most basic public services removed beneath—in even the most gentrified downtown sections of the city. (Harvey [2005] and Zukin [1995] note that the "revived" New York, as well, is privatized and delimited.) Early every weekday morning around the Green, Broadway and Chapel streets are filled with young men of color wearing private corporate uniforms who sweep the sidewalks and clean the gutters outside the museums and the high-end boutiques and restaurants. One block over, the streets remain filthy for weeks at a time. The failed Chapel Square Mall of the urban renewal period, with new infusions of capital, was transformed in 2005 into a "postmodern" apartment building—but the free local weekly newspaper immediately began carrying letters from renters complaining about slipshod construction.

The gracious nineteenth-century marble public library on the Green is closed every weekend. On Mondays at noon, within ten minutes of its opening, a line of at least a dozen eager New Haveners, most of them of color, is waiting to check out books, and every computer terminal is immediately taken, with hardly a white face to be seen. The visitor, looking down, would realize that this public space, like the streets outside the highly gentrified, privatized core, is rarely cleaned. The bathroom floors are thick with dead flies, flies that will remain for weeks because the city's budget no longer can stretch to public janitorial services.

Matthew Ruben's suburban optic applies almost frighteningly well here—we see New Haveners, absent progressive critics like the black woman lawyer, taking on a fundamentally neoliberal, top-down and outside-in, touristified means of apprehending their city, its residents, and its workings. We could take New Haven's dead flies on the public library floors as a metonym for the worlds unimagined by the suburban optic, by neoliberal consciousness.

THE PROBLEM OF THE MEDIA, THE PROBLEM OF MEDIA ANALYSTS

(February 1, 2005) *The Tom Joyner Morning Show* (*TJMS*).[2] Tom Joyner talks about a woman who lost both her husband and son in the Iraq war and about Bush's recent advocacy of an increased death benefit and extending troops' stay:

> J. ANTHONY BROWN: Now, I went to trade school, and this is not hard to figure out.
>
> JOYNER: Yeah.
>
> J. ANTHONY BROWN: Bring 'em home!
>
> SYBIL WILKES: You'll save more money that way.

(March 30, 2005) Tom Joyner reports that the US military is having trouble recruiting blacks into the military:

> MS. DUPRE (sardonically): Wha-a-t?
>
> SYBIL (up and down the intonational contour): Oh, really?
>
> JOYNER: Yeah, that's what I said. [pause, then falsetto voice] "Is you *crazy*?" [laughter]

(September 14, 2005) Black female radio caller to *TJMS*: "Ms. Dupre, can you tell me what the difference is between them shoving us in the Superdome and them shoving us on the boat back in Africa?"

(September 15, 2005) Black woman caller to *TJMS*: "What's on my mind is, President Bush says he cares about the people hurt by Katrina, but he's awarding contracts to his cronies like Halliburton and says he won't make them pay the prevailing wage!"[3]

(February 10, 2006)

> JOYNER: So the top story this morning is that President Bush, while trying to get people behind the Patriot Act, announced that he stopped a terrorist attack in 2002!?
>
> J. ANTHONY BROWN: White people need a word that's equivalent to *NP* [nigger, *please*]. [studio crew laughter]
>
> MELVIN: They really need that! No one calls him on anything!
>
> SYBIL: And here's the thing. The polls are going up in support of secret wiretapping!…

TOM: And they're controlling the media! I didn't hear one artist say anything at all at the Grammys…

SYBIL: And everyone needs to see George Clooney's film *Good Night and Good Luck*—it stinks of the McCarthy period, which is what we're experiencing again.

The crew of *The Tom Joyner Morning Show* may not be documenting New Haven's local dead flies, but they do have a lock on the black New Haven listening audience and they have been contemporaneously alive to a significant amount of national dirt ignored by the mainstream American media until stories are deemed "safe" to print or broadcast. As we can see from the transcripts, these black radio entertainers are, in concert with their call-in listeners, articulating an emphatic antiwar politics, a dissent from the Bush White House's punitive governance on the basis of fear, and clear analyses of both the corporate cronyism inherent in the White House's outsourcing of the war and the Katrina cleanup to friends in high places and the self-censorship of the mainstream media.

Radical political-economic analysts of changes in American media have focused, understandably, on recent negative neoliberal shifts: the defunding of public media and deregulating of private media; waves of mergers and acquisitions resulting in a few megacorporations controlling most print, video, and audio news sources; the deterioration of news into "infotainment" (Herman and Chomsky 1988; McChesney 2004). But, ironically, these and other radical analysts, as well as mainstream media and even black cultural studies scholars, have almost entirely missed the rapid decade-long growth, wild success, and unusually progressive politics of *TJMS*, a genuine black elephant in the national living room. Both the *TJMS* phenomenon and its mainstream invisibility, as I will demonstrate, illustrate the raced and gendered contours of contemporary American neoliberal process.

Tom Joyner, a North Carolina–born, Dallas-based disk jockey, earned the sobriquet "Fly Jock" in the early 1990s, when he managed to work as a DJ in both Chicago and Dallas simultaneously by flying between the two cities three days a week (Williams 1998:133). He syndicated his eponymous show in 1994 as a weekday, drive-time show presenting "music, news and information, guests from politics and entertainment, and an assortment of entertainment segments that include open telephone lines, humorous advice, and commentaries by Tavis Smiley" (Brooks and Daniels 2002:9). The show grew extraordinarily rapidly, to an audience of five million by 1998, topping seven million by 2001, jumping to eight million by 2004–2005 (Anderson Forest 2004; Smith 1998, Themba 2001).

NEOLIBERALIZATION OF MINDS, SPACE, AND BODIES

This audience is more than double Don Imus's (before his firing in 2007), comparable to Howard Stern's (before his satellite radio launch), and more than half Rush Limbaugh's (Kiley 2005; Moloney 2005). Yet, it barely has registered with the mainstream media that have so compulsively covered these three disk jockeys, as well as many others with even smaller audiences. Since its founding, for example, *TJMS* has garnered only twelve mentions in the *New York Times*, most of them en passant, none at all in 2005, and only one by September 2006. In contrast, Howard Stern, with the same size audience, over the same time period, was deemed worthy of 501 *New York Times* stories, most of them full-length.

TJMS is now syndicated in 115 markets and represented most strongly in the US black belt: across the South, the black-settled Southwest, the Southeast, the Midwest, and the eastern seaboard (Conan 2005). Political scientist Melissa Harris-Lacewell (2004:237) has declared it "the single most recognizable forum of black talk in black America today."

(WVAZ-Chicago commercial, late 1990s) Older black man with Delta-inflected voice states matter-of-factly: "I don't like...that rap."

Like the hundreds of black stations on which it appears, the Joyner show appeals to adult, working-class audiences and features "old-school" music, that is, 1960s–1980s soul, combined with contemporary black pop, neosoul, some gospel, and hip hop, but rarely rap. Aside from Joyner, the cast includes a half-dozen middle-aged comics with particular shticks. Among them are Sybil Wilkes, as we have seen, who plays both straight woman and "the schoolmarm" (my term, not theirs)—the most well-informed and politically progressive member of the crew. Then there are Myra J, who has a regular feature, "Tips for the Single Mom," and plays a saucy, heterosexually active but simultaneously respectable and hard-working single mother; Ms. Dupre, the older New Orleans–bred psychic who offers up "your lucky numbers" once a week; J. Anthony Brown, who plays a working-class clown with a taste for white women; and Melvin, who plays a very "queeny," older gay Southern man and has a regular call-in feature, "Melvin's Love Line."

Insofar as a small handful of scholars and journalists have noted *TJMS* and its politics, they have tended to define those politics as black nationalist (see Brooks and Daniels 2002; Burroughs 2001:215; Curtis 2005:3; Harris-Lacewell 2004:241–243). Certainly, the show is designed for an exclusively black audience and includes community self-help elements, but "nationalist" is a catchall political label for historically specific formations that can shade left or right (Robinson 2001). And certainly, contemporary

US politics since the social-movement 1970s are also more complex than the left/right binary. In particular, New Rightists newly defined a constellation of issues in terms of "family values," which have taken on key salience in American politics.

Sociologist Stephen Steinberg, in *Turning Back* (1995), has traced the key ideological shift that allowed our modern American family values rhetoric to blossom, to a Lyndon Johnson speech at Howard University in 1965. The speech, partly written by Daniel Patrick Moynihan, simultaneously called for affirmative action to remedy past discrimination and made subtle use of Moynihan's now notorious report on "the breakdown of Negro family structure" to blame black Americans for their own oppression (Steinberg 1995:107–136).

Thus began the long march, through both the public sphere and the academy, of the association of American racial minority status with "faulty" female-headed families and with the neat substitution of family structure for endemic structural discrimination as the cause of black and brown poverty—part of late anthropologist Oscar Lewis's "culture of poverty." That core counter-empirical claim was joined, from the Jimmy Carter era forward, by a rising political critique of "big government" and a tendency to look to families to perform basic public functions in the wake of state abrogation of responsibility (di Leonardo 1998:112–127).

With the neoconservative triumph of Reagan's 1980 election, racist backlash against civil rights and misogynist backlash against the second wave of the women's movement found welcome in the White House. Reagan's synergistic and delusional claims that black "welfare queens" were draining the public purse through massive fraud actually became reflexive "common sense" for millions of Americans. The huge social program cutbacks of the Reagan years, particularly in social support and public housing, produced skyrocketing minority poverty rates, which were then explained through use of newly refurbished "culture of poverty" ideology. Reagan even had the audacity to claim that the rising homeless population of the 1980s was engaged in a "lifestyle choice" (di Leonardo 1998: 269–271).

Thus, the stage was set for Vice President Dan Quayle's 1992 election-year attack on the network television show *Murphy Brown*, whose eponymous white, professional-class heroine became pregnant and gave birth to a baby out of wedlock. The airwaves and the centrist-to-neoconservative press were filled with assertions that black American women had "contaminated" white women. The modern usage of *family values* was set. Although Clinton won the election, as sociologist Judith Stacey has shown, he soon capitulated to communitarian elements in the Democratic Party on both women's rights and gay rights, and as an avatar of neoliberalism, he had never stood strongly for minority economic justice (as opposed to nominal civil rights) in the first place. In 1996 Clinton moved to "end welfare as we know it" (Stacey 1997).

For the full contemporary flavor of the term *family values* to be developed, it was only necessary for the religious right, over the course of the 1990s, to respond hysterically to the efforts of some gay Americans to marry and to adopt children. *Family values* now refers most generally to the belief that only white heterosexual married couples in which the woman does not work outside the home during their children's minority years are capable of rearing children properly. It functions secondarily as an implicit slur against all Americans not living in such households (Stacey 1997). As we can see from the evolutionary trajectory of the term, it simultaneously indexes our neoliberal era with its associated evacuation of all nonmilitary governmental responsibilities and its fetishization of the family as the institution responsible for care of those made vulnerable by youth, age, disability, illness, or unemployment. In the most recent transmogrification of the term, some pollsters claimed that Bush won the 2004 presidential election because of "moral values" voters—which translates as family values plus overt rightist religiosity (Seelye 2004).

The Joyner crew, beyond their black civil rights and anti-Bush, antiwar stance, articulate widely shared black American *dissent* from family values ideology, most particularly by the broad liberal working class that is both the show's audience base—the modal listener is a clerical or service worker—and the majority of the nation's black population.[4] The crew's politics are seamlessly woven into their comedy, laden with frequent references to celebrity culture, particularly black celebrities.

(January 24, 2005) Myra J, in "Tips for the Single Mom," says that she wants to celebrate *American Idol* winner Fantasia's new popular song, "Here's to All My Baby Mamas," and has some suggestions for new songs for her. Fantasia, by the way, is widely known to be a single mother.

> "I Can Do Anything, Includin' Forget about You"
>
> "All My Designer Bags Are Filled with Diapers"
>
> "He Bought Groceries, I Think I'm in Love"
>
> "I'm Goin' to Get My Tubes Tied"
>
> "The Babysitter Only Stays til Midnite, What We Gon' Do?"
>
> "The Only Thing You're Getting out of This House Is Your Kids"

Myra J's version of infotainment is simultaneously hilarious and laden with pragmatic, pro-single-mother politics. This vision of hard-working, responsible, but sassy single mothers is worlds removed from Reagan's welfare queens.

TJMS not only normalizes single motherhood with a regular feature, "The Thursday Morning Mom," but also honors "Real Fathers, Real Men" —male devotion to and sacrifice for children who are not always biologically theirs (which may also be true of the Thursday Morning Moms). In all these endeavors, the show works from the premise of women's and gay equality—but this stance is played out through comic interaction rather than as political manifesto.

(February 25, 2005) "Melvin's Love Line":

> ANONYMOUS (female caller): I'm Anonymous, from Milwaukee.
>
> JOYNER CREW: Okay, Anonymous. [laughter]
>
> ANONYMOUS: And I got a problem. My girlfriend goes off and won't tell me where she's goin'.
>
> JOYNER: Same sex, same problem. It never changes.
>
> MELVIN: That's it!
>
> J. ANTHONY BROWN: And people say they don't like gays, but it's all the same.

(February 25, 2005) After an airing of the latest segment of *TJMS*'s mock soap opera, "It's Your World," in which a woman character tells her male lover that she is "seeing other people" and refuses to tell him how many, declaring at the closing, "A woman needs a little mystery":

> J. ANTHONY BROWN: She's seein' other people? They're writin' him soft!
>
> MYRA J (to J. ANTHONY BROWN): Oh, get a tissue out, you little man-person!
>
> SYBIL (falsetto): Ninny, ninny, ninny!

(April 1, 2005) During a discussion of the rumor that *American Idol* contestant Anwar, "the one with the dreads," has a "male-friend" website:

> JOYNER: Well, let me ask you this, Melvin? Does your meter go off? With Anwar?
>
> MELVIN: BWOOP, BWOOP, BWOOP, BWOOP. Like a truck in reverse!

(July 28, 2005) Tom Joyner says that Boy Scouts waited for President Bush three hours in the hot sun and that many "fell out" (fainted)—even adults:

> JOYNER: I hate to admit this, Sybil, but women are smarter. You would not find Girl Scouts waiting for the president three hours in the hot sun. No, uh uh."
>
> SYBIL: *Hot*-la!

TJMS's progressive take on gender and sexuality is fundamentally counter to the mainstream press's vision of a black-majority world full of misogynist rappers and homophobic preachers, as well as to radio scholar Susan Douglas's vision of the new talk radio phenomenon as fundamentally encoding male ressentiment of post-feminist, female social power (Douglas 2004). Such stances are of a piece with its larger social democratic politics and working-class minority optic on domestic and international issues.

(May 20, 2005) Referring to the short-lived tempest about the Mexican stamp with a racist caricature:

> JOYNER: You know Bush is in the White House on the phone to Fox...saying, "Go ahead. Keep the mess goin' on. I can use it. The last thing I need is blacks and Latinos gettin' together."
>
> MELVIN: Can you spell *diversion*?

The show's combination of pragmatic, anti-neoliberal left liberalism incorporating antiwar dissent and its matter-of-fact support for single-parent households, big-government social programs, broad religious and sexual tolerance, and heavy civil rights focus mirrors the politics of the bulk of the black electorate and gives the lie to widespread misrepresentations by mainstream press and many scholars. With respect to the overt religiosity of contemporary "moral values" rhetoric, the crew broadly identifies as Christian but also sends up black Christian hypocrisy and extreme evangelicalism.

(May 3, 2005) A Sunday schoolteacher caller announces that she's now teaching children that the Second Coming is "close":

> J. ANTHONY BROWN: How close? I heard that fifty-three years ago. Is it any closer now?

TJMS's middle-aged, somewhat coarse but still respectable, working-class pragmatism (of course, all the show's comics are now wealthy, but they *invoke and celebrate* working-classness on a daily basis) lacks the sex appeal, the aura, of the rap world. The youth, misogyny, overt indecency, and claims to wealthy criminality of that world attract and repel different white American populations—and have provided grist for the hard-working mills of hundreds of cultural studies dissertations and books. *TJMS*, however, flies under the radar of the white American "love and theft" of black American culture so well analyzed by Eric Lott (1993): the comics are neither young nor hip, nor nasty enough to garner widespread white fascination. And they are so boringly politically progressive, exactly like most black Americans. The impetus in the mainstream—and even progressive—press since the Reagan years has been instead to find and highlight "man bites dog" stories about black American politics: pieces on individual black conservatives or rightist black ministers (see, for example, Banerjee 2005, 2006a).

DEAD FLIES AND BLACK ELEPHANTS

The *TJMS* phenomenon, however, illustrates more than the ongoing Jim Crow/love and theft nature of American society, the political possibilities even within the genre of infotainment, and the progressive, outlier political status of the majority of black Americans. With the New Haven case study, it also documents the overarching process of the neoliberalization of minds in our era. That is, as a commercial show in an era in which public media have been defunded and cowed by rightist political pressure, *TJMS* relies on corporate sponsorship for its very existence. As we have seen, the *TJMS* crew and its listening audience can and do criticize corporations such as Halliburton and the oil behemoths that are unlikely ever to underwrite the show. But they do not bite the corporate hands that feed them, and those hands are many and powerful: McDonald's, Southwest Airlines, Home Depot, Budget Rent-a-Car, Kraft, Tyson, and (the horror) Wal-Mart. On one hand, despite black Americans' disproportionate membership and activism in US unions, the show will broadcast public employment labor news (the government is not a sponsor!), but rarely do we hear news about the unionized private sector. On the other hand, the show will criticize many airlines' treatment of their employees, because *TJMS*'s airline sponsor, Southwest, is unionized. And the show certainly fails to criticize individualizing consumerist ideology. Given that it offers a wildly popular and largely left-liberal alternative to most mainstream US media, we might say that this is As Good as It Gets in the commercial, for-profit, American public sphere.

There is a further and final insight we might glean from these case studies. Reading Tom Joyner's early, self-published autobiography (1995),

I discovered to my profound shock that not only did he start out as a Reagan Republican who approved of Rush Limbaugh but also that he literally benefited from neoliberal process: What enabled him to begin buying up small radio stations and jump-start his career was his friendship with Mark Fowler, Reagan's chair of the FCC (Federal Communications Commission), who oversaw the first wave of media deregulation. Although other crew members' influence and the general liberal turn (on social issues) in the Clinton years may help explain Joyner's significant political shift, a pragmatic assimilation to the politics of the show's natural audience cannot be discounted. In general, it is the case that media respond to citizens' political organizing and activism, rather than the reverse.

At the same time, we can see in both cases the multiple ways in which neoliberalism tends to evacuate civic space. In New Haven, on one hand, this process is directly inscribed in the urbanscape as privately owned, run, and even cleaned public space expands and as public institutions increasingly fall into neglect and disrepair, even as residents' need for them reaches crisis proportions. *TJMS*, on the other hand, represents the ways in which a commercial institution may end up substituting for defunded and enervated local and national civic activism and organizations. As we have seen, though, that substitution comes with strings attached: imagine how useful a resolutely pro-union, anti-Wal-Mart *TJMS* could be to the American labor movement and thus to the majority of black Americans, as well as Americans in general.

The neoliberalization of American consciousness, then, is both insidious—operating at many levels, some much more difficult to discern than others—and, thankfully, partial. The black New Haven lawyer's statement and *TJMS*'s very existence demonstrate this. Reversing the process demands analyses like those offered in this volume, as well as informed activism on local, national, and global levels.

Acknowledgments

Thanks to all my fellow advanced seminar participants, especially Jane Collins, for comments on earlier versions of this chapter.

Notes

1. Some of this analysis is an updated version of my treatment in *Exotics at Home* (di Leonardo 1998:319–332).

2. Please see also my "Neoliberalism, Nostalgia, Race Politics, and the American Public Sphere: The Case of *The Tom Joyner Morning Show*" (*Cultural Studies*, published electronically March 8, 2007) and "Whose Homeland? The New Imperialism, Neoliberalism, and the American Public Sphere" in Jeff Maskovsky and Ida Susser, eds., *Rethinking America: The Imperial Homeland in the 21st Century* (Paradigm Press, in press).

3. All transcriptions are by the author, done contemporaneously with broadcasts. Ellipses indicate gaps in transcription. *TJMS* does archive a small portion of each show on its website, blackamerica.com, but rarely the spontaneous political conversations that constitute the bulk of the broadcast material in this study.

4. Regarding majority, black, working-classness, see Zweig 2000:32–33. My evaluation of the class status of the *TJMS* audience is based both on Arbitron's 2005 study of varying black radio audiences and on my own decade-long observation of *TJMS* callers. Regarding black American political orientation, see CNN's (2004) exit polling after the Bush/Kerry presidential race. Black American status determined a reported vote for Kerry by a greater margin than any other identity category—including gender, income, education, union membership, and ideology—except Democratic Party affiliation.

11

The Neoliberalization of Compassion

Darfur and the Mediation of American Faith, Fear, and Terror

Amal Hassan Fadlalla

> We are the world, we are the children
>
> We are the ones who make a brighter day
>
> We're all a part of God's great big family
>
> And the truth, you know, love is all we need
>
> — *"We Are the World"*

The current Darfur conflict is one in a long genealogy of modern African crises that have captured the world's attention. Declared by the UN as one of the worst humanitarian disasters in the twenty-first century, by late 2006 the conflict had displaced 1.8 million people, with an estimated two hundred thousand killed.[1] The Darfur conflict moved to the center stage of media reportage and international events amidst increasing global economic disparities, threats of sanctions and invasions, and escalating politics of fear. It entered the realms of presidential debates, television dramas and shows, video games, print media articles and reports, website debates and discussions, and religious activists' rallies in more than fifteen US cities.

Although the increased media attention raises awareness about human suffering, the representations of the Darfurian conflict in US popular media and the Save Darfur campaign have produced fragmented knowledge about the region and its long history of poverty and conflict (see Flint and De Waal 2005), packaged in the oversimplified moral categories of "Arab Muslim" aggressors against "black Muslim" victims and of "helpless refugees" vis-à-vis compassionate Western actors, politicians, and leaders.[2] Media images of victimized Darfurian women and children, now staples in

Western news coverage of Africa's harsh realities of war, poverty, and suffering, are used to attest to the decline of morality and the death of humaneness, generating new waves of humanitarian activism and compassion (see Moeller 1999). The Sahel famines of the 1980s received similar coverage as media images of emaciated Ethiopians and Sudanese traversed the globe, shaping various NGOs and celebrity activists' humanitarian discourses and practices regarding the famine. We Are the World and its parent organization, USA for Africa, relied on the efforts of superstar celebrities such as Bob Geldof, Harry Belafonte, and Michael Jackson, who used their social capital and visibility to raise awareness of suffering in "faraway places" and to shift the Western gaze to the essence of humanity and sameness beneath differently colored skins (see Lutz and Collins 1993:283).[3] Using the rhetoric of what I term *familial globality*, these celebrities' efforts—songs and concerts—generated millions of dollars, which were donated to relief organizations committed to ending African poverty. But nearly three decades later, Africa is more entrapped than ever in the expanding neoliberal market and debt economies, plunged deeper into destitution and violent conflicts (see De Waal 1997; Imam 1994; Okome 1997; Schoepf, Schoepf, and Millen 2000).

Today, there are fourteen thousand aid workers providing humanitarian assistance to Darfurians while rich Western governments and accountable institutions fail to provide sufficient funds and to address the root causes of poverty and suffering plaguing poor nations.[4] New efforts by celebrities such as George Clooney and Angelina Jolie and by religious and secular activists stepping in to fill the governance void receive much press, but far less media attention is given to the economic and political histories underlying African calamities. In what follows, I explore the Darfurian conflict and recent American reporting on it against the broader context of US and Western neoliberal economic policies and sanctions, regional conflicts over power and resources, and the related burgeoning privatization of humanitarianism. As well, given post-9/11 realities, I analyze the various ways in which representations of Islam and of Muslims figure in neoconservative/neoliberal humanitarian narratives of faith and compassion. Thus, I attempt to document how global compassion itself has been neoliberalized in the contemporary American context.

MARGINAL CITIZENS: FAMINES, WARS, AND HUMANITARIANISM
Despite the Sudan's economic potential—its abundance of natural resources, including oil—it remains one of the poorest nations in the world, owing to decades of colonial and postcolonial policies that have

deepened ethnic and class divisions and resulted in the destitution of large sections of the Sudanese population. The Sudan's mandatory subscription to IMF (International Monetary Fund) policies and structural adjustment programs, under the pretext of accelerating development through liberalizing local economies, led to the world's worst humanitarian crises during the 1980s and 1990s (Abdel-Ati 1988; De Waal 1989; Deng and Minear 1992; O'Brien 1985; see also Sen 1981). The transformation of vast agricultural land into mechanized farms producing cash crops for the export market—as well as related unfair terms of trade, devaluation of currency, and high inflation rates—created extreme food shortages and laid the foundation for the isolation and displacement of vulnerable populations of peasants, nomads, and the urban poor. Malpractice in the agrarian sector (for example, land erosion and the removal of vast vegetation covers) contributed to the process of desertification and rain failure, culminating in devastating famines, escalating conflict over land and resources in areas such as western and eastern Sudan, and poor people's increasing vulnerability to malnutrition, disease, and death (De Waal 1997; Fadlalla 2005, 2007).

Only a small percentage of the urban population escapes the risks of hunger and famine; the majority of the country's rural population is left to suffer. Images of the displaced, hungry population storming the suburbs of Khartoum from western Sudan and crossing the Kenyan borders from war-ravaged southern Sudan were widely publicized by Western media and reproduced the fixed imagery of "the famished African child" and the "helpless refugee" (see also Malkki 1996). These mediated images revealed both the government's failure to treat all its citizens as equal subjects and the limits of humanitarianism's capacity to analyze and respond to global inequalities and man-made disasters.

The entanglement of poor countries in the intricate web of economic dependencies and their subjection to the policies of international financial institutions (IFIs) and foreign investors have damaged the already torn, ethnic and sectarian sociopolitical fabric of the Sudan. By the end of the 1980s, a military junta supported by the Islamists, whose hegemonic power led to the defeat of secular visions and to the establishment of a Sharia-guided state, shifted its identity politics toward the conservative right. The government support of Iraq during the first Gulf war and its former business deals with Bin Laden culminated in the American bombing of the Al-shifa pharmaceutical factory in Khartoum and Sudan's subjection to American and Western sanctions, worsening the vulnerability and starvation of its most marginal groups.

The 9/11 attacks and the horrifying media images of a nation under threat violated the notion of American integrity, dignity, and honor and reanimated a politics of fear and porosity. The surveillance of immigrants, Muslims, and "unruly others" became a proper strategy and a justifiable tool of governance by an invading empire. Within this regime of fear and "punitive governance" (Lancaster, chapter 3, this volume), the regulation, categorization, and territorialization of dangerous identities increased exponentially (see also Gupta and Ferguson 1997; Mamdani 2004). Countries such as the Sudan, Iraq, Somalia, and Iran were framed as terror-producing territories occupying an "axis of evil" and posing a constant threat to global security, civility, and Western freedom.

In response, the Sudanese government shifted its business deals to the eastern bloc, especially to China and to other Muslim countries, such as Saudi Arabia, Lebanon, and Malaysia. China represents one of the Sudan's major lenders, with an estimated 45 percent share in the country's oil investment. Acting as proxy capitalists, these countries directed the movement of capital through the Sudanese urban landscape and defined economic development in terms of *khaskhasa* (privatization), serving the interests of local-global investors dealing in oil, telecommunications, construction, and fast-food businesses and providing neoliberalization with an eastern Islamic facade.

Yet, as Sudan witnesses a boom in telecommunications, fancy food restaurants, and new upper-class neighborhoods, the poor urban and rural populations bear the brunt of declining public services, especially in health, education, and housing—a trend that one Sudanese friend who travels every summer between Khartoum and Washington describes despairingly as "too many cell phones, too much malaria."

The intricate histories of racial and ethnic conflict in the Sudan can hardly be subsumed under the fixed dichotomies that infuse the representations of Sudanese affairs in the American media. The constructions of "Arabism" are continuously negotiated, debated, and invented among many Muslims groups, including Darfurians. The term *Arab* has historically been associated with Muslim, Arabic-speaking northern Sudanese and their elite, who have ruled the country since its independence in 1956. Recently, however, the ruling elites have also arisen from the non-Arabic-speaking Nubians of northern Sudan. Moreover, many Sudanese nomads identify as Arabs to denote a pastoral lifestyle and a group identity anchored in notions of land and descent (Fadlalla 2007; Mamdani 2007). To many urbanite Sudanese, *Arab* can be used pejoratively to distance a nomadic lifestyle from constructions of modernity and progress.

Being Arab or non-Arab in the Sudan is complexly determined by ethnic and racial categories that take into account regionality and skin tone, as well as other bodily attributes (Fadlalla 2007). An Arab Sudanese is never white, never black—two categories associated with European and Arab colonialisms and with the long history of slavery in the Sudan (see Sakinga 1996). Whereas a dark-skinned Arab Sudanese identifies as brown, green, or blue, a southern or western Sudanese is racialized as black, dark blue, or having a slave ancestry. Ethnic and racial categorization, however, often rely on regional identification, such as *shamali* (northerner), *janobi* (southerner), and *gharabi* (westerner). Afro-Arabism and Africanism are categories constructed by left-wing intellectuals, poets, and politicians since the sixties in an attempt to build bridges of peace between the North and South, adding to the complexity of socially constructed Sudanese ethnicities. Categories of Arab and non-Arab, however, constantly shift according to claims of power and status, political and social alliances, and intermarriages and neighborly relations and may heighten during conflicts over land and resources.

The simplistic representation of the Darfur conflict as a "Lord of the Rings" African morality tale (Flint 2006) in which villains and victims "never trade places" (Mamdani 2007) fails, most particularly, to name the key causes of ethnic and racial divisions, northern hegemony, sectarianism, poverty, famine, and disease, as well as the commodification of weapons and the emergence of resistance groups in the region. Nevertheless, the reluctance of the ruling elite to reconcile these "wars of visions" (Deng 1995) and to establish an inclusive agenda for plural governance has heightened armed conflicts in the south and west and has dispossessed vulnerable groups in the north and east of their land and bodily integrity. Forced development has become the norm for social and political reform.[5]

Julie Flint, revisiting her own journalistic reporting on Darfur (2006), described how Janjawid militia emerged as a homogenous category stigmatizing poor Darfurian Arabs.[6] The approximately three hundred thousand Darfurian Abbala (camel herders), from which about twenty thousand Janjawid militia are recruited, are impoverished nomadic groups in western Sudan whose rights to land have been denied by colonial and postcolonial governments. But most Abbala, Flint writes, "refused to contribute soldiers, well aware that good relations with their non-Arab neighbors are more important than an alliance with an uncaring government hundreds of miles away" (Flint 2006:B01).

The nomads, like their settled counterparts who suffered Janjawid atrocities, are also bearing the brunt of displacement, hunger, and disease that neither the UN nor the African Union (AU) troops nor the Abuja peace negotiators are including in their agendas. According to Flint, "relief workers who voice their concerns to the UN leadership [are met] with blank stares—and silence. 'We'd bring up the Arabs and mention how they might be suffering and a hush would come over the room,' said an aid worker based in El Fasher, the capital of North Darfur state" (Flint 2006:B01).

Such attitudes refute humanitarian claims of neutrality, but they also invoke predominant perceptions about nomads as backward and as a hindrance to modernization efforts of resettlement and development. Ahmed (1980) rightly asserts that colonial and postcolonial planners have perceived nomads and pastoralists in the Sudan as difficult to administer because of their "traditional" lifestyles and their rugged terrain. Consequently, the facile solutions have often been short-term humanitarian relief and relocation of nomads to work as cheap labor in agricultural schemes. Both are part of colonial and postcolonial liberalization policies and agricultural plans to gear mechanized farming toward export production, not to integrate and promote agropastoral economies (Fadlalla 2007).

Given governments' failure to provide for their marginalized citizens, local and global institutions and charitable foundations, neoliberalizing the notion of humanitarianism, have taken upon themselves the task of uplifting the miserable poor through direct interventions during famines, wars, and conflicts. The poor are thus relegated to the margins of development policies. They become "cumulative numbers" and "abbreviated categories" in professionalized development discourses that theorize and manage their problems but fail to resolve them (see also Escobar 1988). The realities of poverty and suffering are often abstracted in easy-to-consume images and moral categories: "a group of perpetrators face a group of victims, but where neither history nor motivation is thinkable because both are outside history and context" (Mamdani 2007). Within this simple moral world, victims must be "sympathetic—usually women and children," and humanitarian workers are neutral players above "partisan politics or self-interest [who] must be available to 'interpret' the ongoing scenarios" (Moeller 1999:100).

Such representations of "third world" poverty and suffering have their logic in modernization and development theories that have long naturalized the problems of poor nations and their people in the name of civilization and progress. Charity becomes a prerogative of a meritocracy guided by neutrality, humanity, and good conscience to save the poor and to help overcome their unfortunate suffering. Liberalizing humanitarianism thus entails NGOs' competition over institutional and private funds to enable their missions, depending on their visibility as "neutrally partial" players in the field (see also De Waal 1997).

But the poor, left with few survival strategies, can be ambivalent about the "neutral" presence of thousands of relief professionals, who are mostly Western and equipped with vehicles, high salaries, and ready-to-implement plans of action that provide short-term medicine, food, and shelter. Their temporary presence, albeit helping to alleviate the misery of thousands, does indeed gloss the root causes of poverty and global inequalities and perpetuates the cycle of dependency and suffering. NGOs have also created new elites, who earn more than their local peers and who serve the interests of their own ethnic groups, a situation that has escalated "tribal" disputes and conflicts over relief distribution. As well, humanitarian aid has reinforced gendered lineage politics and existing power structures (Fadlalla 2005, 2007).

Claims of humanitarian neutrality, therefore, depoliticize the complex situations of relief operations and obscure the agency of the different parties involved. The Islamists' rise to power in the Sudan, the shift of Western "aid politics," and the use of "relief food" as a weapon of war by conflicting parties, for instance, have made substantially more people vulnerable in drought- and conflict-stricken areas (De Waal 1997; Fadlalla 2007). In Darfur, humanitarian aid workers are caught in a tug of war between the government and rebel factions. The government of Sudan accuses certain NGOs of transporting rebels and fabricating data to implicate the government. Rebel factions who rejected the Abuja agreement depict NGOs as aiding the government and its Janjawid militia. The Prophet Muhammad Danish cartoon controversy that fueled the anger of Muslims worldwide was used as a pretext by the Sudanese government to end the work of several Norwegian NGOs in Darfur and to block one of Jan Egeland's (the Norwegian UN relief coordinator) visits to Darfur.

Recently, tensions have been mounting among the Save Darfur advocacy groups and aid workers providing assistance to Darfurians on the ground. Aid workers accuse the campaign of "misstating facts" through its public ads and endorsing plans that include implementation of a no-fly zone and the use of multilateral force, which hinder the work of saving lives (Strom and Polgreen 2007). Humanitarian provision is embedded in broader political agendas, hierarchies, and interests that, from the start, render unattainable the notion of impartiality and compromise the well-being of the poor and displaced.

COMPETING GROUNDS: SEXUAL VIOLENCE AND THE REPORTING ON DARFUR

Media reports on the ongoing Darfurian conflict produced a plethora of conflated images of Darfurian refugees as both "voiceless," "subordinate" victims and key actors mobilized by the different warring factions and other parties involved. Images of displaced refugees variously described a "landscape of inequality" governed by the waving flags of NGOs over camps and Land Cruisers hurrying through the desert-like territory. Television cameras depicted various scenarios of gendered activities: sheiks roamed outside in their white *jalabias* (local attire) and big turbans, an African Union female solider conversed with a group of Darfurian women passing by on donkeys, girls pumped water from a nearby well where rows of jerricans waited to be filled, other girls carried water on their donkeys or walked around with young siblings tied to their backs, boys carried sacks of relief food on their heads or followed young girls around, and still other children waved and smiled despairingly to get the cameras' attention (CNN, Al-Jazeera, *New York Times*).

A powerful image posted on Sudanile (a web journal, http://www.sudanile. com) in May 2006 showed Jan Egeland, surrounded by a group of Dinka female children, reporting on donors' failure to meet their pledges of $764 million worth of food relief for the hungry in the Sudan, half of whom were Darfurians. The UN relief coordinator's call for assistance was supported by another CNN news program, in which he sat on the ground in a Darfurian refugee camp, surrounded by women telling stories of being threatened by the army and the Janjawid and of losing their husbands and loved ones. In the background, other women were cooking and breastfeeding, their raggedly clothed children consuming their meals in an unhealthy atmosphere of dusty air and pesky flies. Such imagery serves as a powerful strategy, convincing donors of the significance of their endowment through the "appropriation of suffering" (Kleinman and Kleinman 1997) and the justification of compassion as helpless refugees tell their stories (see Moeller 1999).

Stories told by camp refugees, however, reveal more about their political agency and struggle. Egeland had gone to investigate Kalma Camp, the largest (130,382) refugee center in southern Darfur, after the Sudanese government complained that the camp was under the nonsignatory rebels' directive. Rioting broke out in the camp following the Abuja Peace Agreement between the government and the largest opposition faction, the Sudan Liberation Movement (SLM) of Minni Arcua Minnawi, in May 2006. Though the SLM represents a smaller ethnic group (the Zaghawa), it has more armed power than does the Fur group of Abd Alwahid Nur, who rejected the agreement, calling it unfair to the Darfurian people because of Western parties' undue pressure (Sudanile, http://www.sudanile.com, May 2006). The rioting vividly demonstrated the power of the opposing parties, who quickly mobilized their groups to reject the agreement and to brand Western aid workers and their Sudanese allies as traitors, partial to the official government and its Janjawid proxy.

Apparently, the rioting began when a woman in the refugee camp shouted "Janjawid! Janjawid!" at the Sudanese translator, an AU employee accompanying Jan Egeland. The terrified scream led to this man's murder and the mutilation of his body. Demonstrators then threatened the visiting UN representative. Nic Robertson, the accompanying CNN senior reporter, videotaped the riot on his cell phone camera. His voice rising, he anxiously ordered his chauffeur, "Drive away, drive away!" to flee the anger of a "blood-thirsty mob" of refugees who turned a "friendly encounter" into a chaotic one in "one of the most dangerous corners of the globe" (CNN report on Darfur, May 8, 2006).

This is not an isolated incident in a war fueled by local and global inequalities, political interests, divided visions, and territorialized identities. A Sudanese newspaper reported that a similar incident had occurred in the same camp in 2004, when a group of women spread rumors that a Sudanese working for a Western NGO was Janjawid. The employee was killed and his sexual parts mutilated (*Alray Alaam*, newspaper in Arabic, May 24, 2006). Impartiality thus becomes a myth in a conflict zone where political players change positions according to their place on the scale of power.

As the Darfur conflict moves to the spotlight of Hollywood shows and series, actors like Don Cheadle and George Clooney and TV show hosts like Oprah Winfrey appear as important agents in mediating the crisis to the American public, "bringing the tragedy [right into] their living room" (*ER*, episode 260, season 12, Internet ad, March 2, 2006). The sketchy dramatic captions that introduced Darfur on media shows and dramas—"Painful to watch," "There is a Holocaust going on right now," "They need help"—worked powerfully to draw public attention and solicit donations and signatures for further public and state action. This "glamorous visibility" renders the tragedy a poignant foreign affair and legitimates the intervention of both state and public in the name of global citizenship and universal humanitarianism. Janjawid militia members invade villages, rape women, and burn villagers' copies of the Quran. The "bad Arab Muslims," they emerge as a recognizable identity associated with media discourses on Islam and America's war on terror. The *ER* episode represented Darfurian women in particular as "violated bodies" subjected to the masculine violence of "Arab aggressors" whose political tactic of rape is intended to wipe out Darfurian racial identity by forcing women to "reproduce Arab babies."[7] Images of Africa as a remote, chaotic place that can be rescued only through international intervention and humanitarian aid also have manifested in the binaries of civilized/barbaric, as Dr. Carter in the *ER* episode struggles to save a raped Darfurian woman from the atrocities of the Janjawid (see also Nicholas Kristof's 2005 video reportages on Darfur).

Whereas rape in Darfur has been widely covered in American media and professional reports—in line with Western feminist understandings of it as a crime of violence against individual women's personhood—Sudanese media are rather silent on the issue because of its local association with women's sexuality and the demasculinization of kinsmen. Contrary to the Western understanding of rape as a crime against individual women, many Darfurians and other Sudanese groups understand rape not as a private matter but rather as a political violation that signals the dehumanization of entire kin groups and populations.

I once raised the question of rape to a Darfurian scholar after his public lecture about the conflict, wondering why he had glossed over an issue so preoccupying Western media. He first paused, while the Sudanese man accompanying him looked down, indicating embarrassment. Then he said, "This is a sensitive issue, you know." Indeed, rape is a violation of women's human rights, an atrocity that signals their subordinate status and the objectification of their sexuality and womanhood. For this reason, it is included in many NGOs' policy agendas. Sometimes, however, it is approached without consideration of the cultural and social contexts within which African women's sexuality is discussed or negotiated. The United Nations Population Fund (UNPF), for instance, as part of its humanitarian efforts among Darfurian women, had required women to fill out certain forms in order to get counseling or medical attention. The clause proved such a major obstacle to treatment that the organization had to eliminate it.[8]

International reporting of rape atrocities in Darfur, as well, has focused more on exposing the identities and tactics of the perpetrators than on women's well-being. Janjawid atrocities receive wide reportage as "terror tactics," but rape crimes committed by AU and opposition soldiers are glossed over, framed as accusations, or contested by the parties themselves. On July 11, 2006, for instance, the Sudanese newspaper *Alray Alaam* posted a front-page article titled "Arcua faction demand a formal apology from the United Nations." The article stated that the UN mission had criticized the SLM for committing major atrocities of rape and murder against Darfurian civilians during its fights with nonsignatory factions. Though the UN denied any formal accusation against the SLM, it had used as evidence a complaint by one Darfurian refugee who witnessed the rape and killing of fifteen women by Minnawi soldiers. The accusations angered the opposition leader, who formally challenged the UN report as inaccurate and unjust against a liberation movement.

The African Union leadership has contested similar rape accusations. On February 2006, Sudanile (http://www.sudanile.com) published an article stating that British TV channel 4 reported a wide range of rape atrocities against women and girls by AU soldiers. Girls under eleven years of age from Qirida, a village in southern Darfur, said that they had been threatened by these soldiers and forced into sexual intercourse. The five-minute report also described how the soldiers, sent to protect the population, had used several pretexts to lure their victims and had impregnated many of them.

The Sudanese government has focused on the reports of rape by AU soldiers in terms of public health, accusing the soldiers of spreading AIDS among the population (Sudanile, March 2006, http://www.sudanile.com). AIDS-related accusations have not been associated with Janjawid atrocities, but only with the seven thousand AU soldiers who entered the country as foreign guards. The government's accusation, of course, supports not only the stance of denouncing intervention but also the attribution of AIDS to "foreigners," who violate both women's bodies and the national body politic.

While the political scene shifts to highlight escalating fights among the signatory and nonsignatory partners to the Abuja agreement, Minni Minnawi, who shook hands with both the Sudanese and American presidents, now stands accused of human rights violations: rape, murder, and other atrocities against his fellow Darfurian fighters. Reportage about the conflict in its two different stages (before and after the signing of the agreement) has fragmented the refugee into both agent and victim. Despite the "violent masculinization" of war atrocities against women, women themselves were depicted in media reports as perpetrators of violent acts, propelled by their own sexual trauma and objectification, and as political actors for their parties' cause. The reporting of the Darfur rape atrocities, however, distinguishes clearly between rape committed by "aggressors" and accusations of rape against "liberator-protectors," ignoring gendered inequalities and power differentials in the expanding global tendencies toward the violent masculinization of war and militarism.

As more recent reports implicate all parties in the Darfurian conflict in escalating war crimes and sexual assaults against women, perpetrators now are often referred to as "unidentified groups of armed men."[9] Shifting media reports raise a significant question: to what extent, then, has rape been used as a weapon of war and demasculinization and also as a weapon of criminalization? This is not to raise doubts about the atrocities of rape and murder committed by the warring parties in Darfur, but to highlight how a discourse on violence and terror has also used women's bodies as sites of conflicting national and international interests and to legitimate the call for military and humanitarian interventions (see also Meznaric 1994).

FAITHFUL CITIZENS: THE DARFUR RALLY AND THE CASE FOR INTERVENTION

The Save Darfur campaign has been championed particularly by a faith-based coalition whose objective of ending genocide in Darfur fits neatly with the various media representations of the conflict as a religious war, an ethnic cleansing orchestrated by Muslim Arabs against the black Muslim minority. Again, images of women and children, as icons of untainted innocence and helplessness, have dominated the campaign's circulated ads and brochures and the discourses of rally speakers who stand witness to the plight of Darfurian victims. An American "Save Darfur" pamphlet, distributed at the Darfur rally on the National Mall in May 2006, showed images of young Darfurian girls on its front cover and described the violent atrocities committed against Darfurian subjects: "Nearly three years since the violence began, the massacres continue, women are still routinely raped as a means of ethnic cleansings, and children still go hungry."[10] The Save Darfur group is a coalition of "over 100 'faith-based,' humanitarian and human rights organizations" with the goal to help end "the mass killing and ethnic cleansing carried out by the Arab-led Muslim Sudanese government against the ethnically black farmers living in the western region of Darfur" ("Save Darfur" pamphlet, 2006). Initiated by the American Jewish community and the Holocaust Museum, the rally served as a political space for the visible presence of various Jewish organizations, Christian evangelists, a few other religious groups, political leaders, and celebrities.

Walking through the crowd of ten-to-fifteen thousand participants, I was moved by the angry vows and declarations of "Never Again," "Not on Our Watch, Mr. Bush," "Stop Violence in Darfur," all against a big TV screen showing clips of the Darfur region and life in the refugee camps there. While I spoke to some people and overheard others' comments, I managed to map the ethnosociopolitical rallyscape: There were a few Sudanese here and there among the overwhelming majority of white participants. A little girl, her mother, and their greyhound puppy pushed through the crowd, and I stopped them to take a photo of the "Save

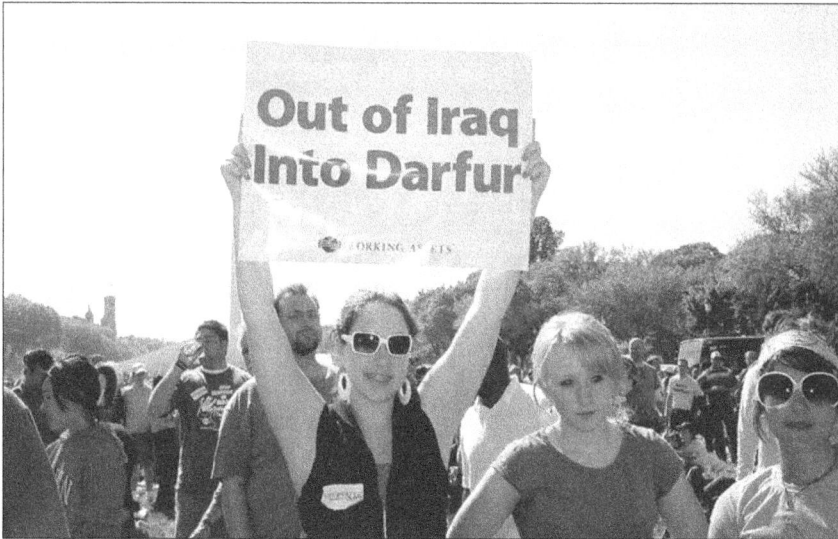

FIGURE 11.1

"Out of Iraq Into Darfur" at the National Mall, April 6, 2006. Photograph courtesy of the author.

Darfur" sticker on the puppy's back. A little boy asked his father, "How do I say 'Never again' in Hebrew, Dad?" I spotted a few black students and read their banners: "Denial is not another river in Africa" and "Stop the Violence in Darfur." A white youth stood in the crowd with a banner that showed images of emaciated African children; it read: "If I Lived in Darfur." And just behind me, a young white girl proudly chanted the words written on her banner: "Out of Iraq Into Darfur" (figure 11.1).

The rally, held on the day of a final deadline for the warring parties to sign a peace agreement, was a distinct cry for intervention in Darfur. Though the Sudanese government opposed the decision, its southern partner welcomed intervention on the grounds that the North–South agreement allowed the deployment of ten thousand UN troops in the south. Since the peace agreement was signed in 2005, southern Sudanese leaders have been actively conducting independent talks and negotiations with the Bush administration, which has led to the spread of many conspiracy theories, among many Sudanese intellectuals in exile, of an orchestrated attempt to divide the country. Such tensions were evident in the organization of the Darfur rally.

At the beginning of the rally, a demonstration of about one hundred southern Sudanese entered the Mall carrying "Save Darfur" banners,

FIGURE 11.2
Sudanese rallying for Darfur at the National Mall, April 6, 2006. Photograph courtesy of Elshafei Dafalla Mohamed.

chanting anti-Bashir slogans, and calling for a new Sudan (figure 11.2). Darfurians, who have active community organizations in the east coast area and beyond, were not much represented among the rally's speakers or participants. Their absence compelled some of the Sudanese with whom I spoke after the rally to believe that it was not only a push for intervention but also a political strategy that staged the "southern Sudanese" as a model "black Christian minority" in order to rule or divide the country. The underrepresentation of Darfurians in the rally might have other explanations, as an article in the *Washington Post* stated:

> Keeping the peace within the diverse Save Darfur Coalition has not been easy. Tensions have arisen, in particular, between evangelical Christians and immigrants from Darfur, whose population is almost entirely Muslim and deeply suspicious of missionary activity. Organizers rushed this week to invite two Darfurians to address the rally after Sudanese immigrants objected that the original list of speakers included eight Western Christians, seven Jews, four politicians and assorted celebrities—but no Muslims and no one from Darfur. [Cooperman 2006]

The *Washington Post* also maintained that some Darfurian activists had complained about the involvement of Sudan Sunrise, a missionary evangelical group, in the organization of the rally. Sudan Sunrise's website (http://www.sudansunrise.org) self-definition is as a "faith-based" organization initiated by Americans and Christian southern Sudanese in 2004 to bring "the Sudan mercy story" to the attention of the world while facilitating "the reconciliation and Christian mission in Sudan." A call for donation concludes: "Supporting Sudan Sunrise represents a golden opportunity for Americans of all faiths to 'walk their talk,' and to help a movement in Africa that could inspire a new way of overcoming animosities among nations and groups of people around the globe."

But the *Washington Post* reported that Sudan Sunrise eliminated a reference from its website appealing for money to help convert Darfurians in Chad, the justification being to bring the "kingdom of God to an area of Sudan where the light of Jesus rarely shines." Sudan Sunrise, like many other faith-based organizations, thus resorted to a discourse of mercy and compassion as the underlying logic of its humanitarian intervention, in order to appeal to its nonmembers and to de-emphasize its proselytizing mission. "Forgive us for killing you," one Darfurian refugee allegedly said. "We thought you were infidels, but we see that you are our brothers." The discourse of mercy and compassion that is assumed to transcend bounded political and religious identities was also manifest in the rhetoric many speakers used at the rally. They stressed that atrocities such as the Holocaust, Rwanda, Bosnia, and Darfur were genocidal crimes that negated the essence of humanity and necessitated the turn to moral authority.

A New York rabbi, one in a long line of religious activist speakers, began with a heartfelt story about his two-day visit to a Darfurian refugee camp in Chad. A nameless three-year-old Darfurian boy there took his hand and would not let go: "He is an African Muslim, and I am a rabbi from New York, but then and now, we are joined in faith and fate. As I left, his eyes cried out, 'Don't forget me.' I still feel his hand in mine." The rabbi pledged not to let down the Darfurian child or to condone a carnage that conjures his own historical minoritization as a Jewish, religious subject in America. This invocation of positionality through reference to the Nazi genocide worked, many there claimed, to unleash a spirit of faith, love, and compassion that erased geographical, racial, and religious differences, uniting demonstrators as equal members of the global family in a humane, moral universe. This rhetoric, evoking the We Are the World campaigns of the 1980s, employs kinship metaphors to expand the notion of the nuclear family and to embrace the globe through a religiously linked moral sensibility:

"We stand here today as members of the human family. We are people of conscience and action."

"We are the people of Darfur....If Darfur lives, our humanity lives....If Darfur dies, our humanity dies. This choice is moral and not political...so stand up, America, and show your compassion."

"Throughout history, the greatness of a nation has been defined not by the size of its army or the strength of its economy, but by the power of its compassion that moves the cause of humanity."

"We believe that the children of Darfur are our children, the women of Darfur are our mothers, sisters, and wives."

This familial bond of universal compassion is necessary not only to justify military and humanitarian intervention but also to protect the Sudan from becoming another terror-territory threatening global security and the modern values of democracy and freedom. To this end, an American army captain and AU adviser declared at the rally, "Today, everyone is Sudanese. I am Sudanese. *Ana Sudani* [in Arabic]." He described how Darfurians had applauded him because they thought that "Bush and his army had landed" in Darfur.

A few days after the rally and in response to Bin Laden's latest letter, which labeled international intervention in the Sudan as the colonization of another part of Dar al Islam (Islamic territory), President Bush declared that "America will stand up" to help Darfurians and alleviate their misery. He advised groups wanting to join the "help drive" to consult the USAID website. For the American president, intervention was necessary to deter Bin Laden from "encouraging fellow Muslim to kill fellow Muslim" and from hindering the work of humanitarian and international peace groups. Dispatching secretary of state Condoleeza Rice to negotiate a UN intervention, Bush encouraged Sudanese president Bashir, after congratulating him for signing the peace agreement, to ease visa and other restrictions imposed on aid workers. He also committed $2.5 million in food aid to Darfur, to be shipped via Port Sudan, passing through a region whose people, the Muslim Beja of the eastern Sudan, are dying of hunger and disease.

To warn Bin Laden and the Janjawid, President Bush used the case of a Darfurian woman named Zahra. Her village was burned by the Janjawid, who also murdered her husband. Zahra relayed their message that there was no mercy for her and "No God but them." In response, Bush emphasized, "A just God will prevail." Contemporary discourses of mercy and compassion, therefore, reveal the porosity of humanitarian ideology, its openness to both neoliberal and neoconservative logics, and make visible the binaries between competing religious ideologies: a "just" religious order will defeat an "intolerant one," not only in Darfur but in other Islamic territories.

After the rally on the Mall, reports, photos, and stories celebrating the solidarity and compassion of faith-based groups filled the pages of many American newspapers. Again, journalists framed their reports in terms of "Southern Sudanese," "Lost Boys," "Jewish teens," leaders, and celebrities (for example, Chmel 2006; Doolittle and Wagner 2006). They also celebrated a Jewish/black Muslim alliance, mediated through the overarching rhetoric of familial globality and compassion, stemming in this case from the "suffering of Jews during the Holocaust and from the religious tradition of social activism" that empathizes with comparable human suffering (Banerjee 2006b; Beckerman 2006). Another rabbi addressed the rally, proclaiming that in the Sudan there is "a pharaoh who is as cruel as no other pharaohs," a logic that legitimates a Jewish alliance with minority black Muslims and Christians against their Arab Muslim aggressors. This anchoring of solidarity and compassion in a notion of universal humanitarianism, however, elides the root causes of the Middle East conflicts, significant among them the current Iraq war and the Israeli–Palestinian conflict and the various ways in which the latter has shaped American policies in the Middle East over the past half century.

Some Sudanese activists were skeptical about the question of "neutral compassion" (see Berlant 2004; Malkki 1994; Ticktin 2006) that colored the rally speeches, but others offered a broader appreciation of the rally as a sociopolitical space that granted them visibility as marginalized citizens in America. For many of them, it represented an opportunity to voice their anger against the politics of the Sudanese government and its suppression of opponents in different parts of the country, including the North. The conflation of humanitarianism and compassion, with their underlying politics, however, was hard to avoid. An activist with whom I spoke after the rally commented on this predicament: "Oh, there is so much politics in there, but we are also angry at what is happening there and it has to stop. At least some Darfurians said what they think, and even the River Nile band sang for Darfur!" He giggled. The River Nile is a musical band of diasporic "hybrid Sudanese" musicians who, like many other immigrant artists, have struggled to gain visibility in the American art scene. Because I had followed the band's progress since its inception, it was indeed heartwarming to see the group members on stage singing "Darfur *baladna*": "Darfur is our land. Let's build it and raise its status, all [Sudanese] ethnicities."

Visiting some Sudanese websites the following day made it evident that the tensions embedded in rallying for Darfur have been rearticulated by many Sudanese participants to express their own personal and political visions. Many were keen to bring the Darfur conflict to the fore in line with the rally's humanitarian sentiments; others invoked histories of colonialism and intervention as they fought for a just resolution of the Darfurian conflict.

The tensions embedded in these different visions of the rally reveal the innate contradictions of humanitarian discourses that, despite their appeal to many, prevent us from attending to the histories of colonialism and post-colonial interventions. Many Sudanese, even those in exile, read intervention as "invasion," though many have also hoped for conflict resolution through negotiations and international pressures on the warring parties. What is unequivocal in many anti-interventionist statements, however, is a strong masculinist discourse about nationalism that envisions international troops as invaders of both *ard* and *'ard*—the country and its female honor —which should be protected by "national men," including the president (*Alray Alaam*, June 21, 2006). The hierarchical binaries of invader/masculine–invaded/feminine infuse nationalist and internationalist discourses as "patriarchal hegemonies" that converse through metaphors of nationhood, universal humanitarianism, and a familial globality that thrives on images of subordinate motherhood, childhood, and sisterhood (see also Alarcón, Kaplan, and Moallem 1999).

Toward the end of the Save Darfur rally, a member of the Berkeley College of Music introduced her musical group as witnesses to the atrocities against Darfurian women through their own narratives. After some Darfurian women "gave a gift" of their local songs, the Berkeley group reciprocated, singing back about global sisterhood:

> Sisters of the world,
>
> We are all connected
>
> by the love in our hearts
>
> Sister of the world,
>
> I hear your cries
>
> You are in our thoughts and dreams
>
> We will always be there for you

Though Darfurian women recognize hierarchical differences, one member of the musical group related, they seem to naturalize and celebrate this bond of global sisterhood in a romantic vision: "At the end [of the trip], one woman said to us, 'When we see Westerners coming, we feel so ashamed. We are dirty and poor, we have no shoes, our clothes are ripped. When we hear you singing to us, you have captured our emotion to the utmost, and we no longer feel ashamed. We feel you are our sisters.'"

As much as we need solidarity and compassion in these turbulent times of escalating intolerance and violence, this representation of compassion is another manifestation of a neoliberalized consciousness (di Leonardo, chapter 10, this volume) that elides the liberating potential of activism on the part of the dispossessed. Filling our TV screens and overloading our email, the calls promoting humanitarian efforts exhort us to donate funds or participate in "long walks" to end poverty and suffering.[11] Poverty, wars, and epidemics are viewed as unfortunate phenomena, but also as the responsibility of hard-working citizens who have succeeded and now should lend a generous hand to unfortunate fellow citizens and lift them out of misery and suffering. The "naturalization of injustice" (Brauman 2004) renders efforts to end disparities a matter of choice that only the privileged, the conscientiously compassionate, and the religiously faithful can afford. Instituting humanitarianism as the only strategy for eliminating poverty and suffering also reproduces a colonialist narrative of modernity and progress within which the privileged/West is compassionate and agentive and the "third world" is only helpless (see di Leonardo 1998; Said 1978, 1981, 1993).

Having worked with many NGOs during droughts and famines in the Sudan, I can relate to the dilemma of trying to save lives on the ground while working within malfunctioning institutions and organizations. My skepticism is not intended to dismiss NGOs or their neoliberal, well-meaning efforts to alleviate suffering, but to interrogate the forces that have instituted humanitarianism as part of a neoliberal political economy of "spatial governmentalities" (Foucault 1980; Gupta 1992; Gupta and Ferguson 2002) and "accumulation by dispossession" that further enriches the already wealthy and traps the poor in endless cycles of debt economies and embodied violence (Farmer and Bertrand 2000; Harvey 2003, 2005; Williams, chapter 4, this volume).

Modern humanitarian compassion, then, fails to escape the politics of religious fundamentalisms and territorialized identities. It also overlooks the increasing privatization of humanitarian relief, the state's failures, and the inequalities created by a global capitalism that grants certain classes of global citizens immunity from poverty, hunger, and border controls while putting many others at risk of war, displacement, starvation, disease, and death.

Notes

1. "Darfur Rebels Pledge to Allow Aid Delivery." IRIN (The United Nation Information Network), August 6, 2007. http://www.irinnews.org, accessed August 2007.

2. My analysis is limited to and by the US popular media reviewed in this article and to my observation of the Darfur rally and does not make reference to other progressive American media, because their analyses are not as mainstream and widely accepted. I have also consulted a few Sudanese and other web-media articles to give a broader context to the arguments presented.

3. The Irish singer Bob Geldof was the first, recording his hit song "Do They Know It's Christmas?" for his project Band Aid, through which he raised awareness about the Somali famine of 1984. His efforts inspired the American recording of the top hit song "We Are the World" and the organizing of USA for Africa in 1985.

4. Figures for aid workers in Darfur, Society for Threatened Peoples website, January 31, 2007, http://www.gfbv, accessed June 2007.

5. Such was the case of Emri and Kajbar dams in northern Sudan and of the Dar Alsalam residential area in Khartoum, where segments of the rural population and urban poor were forcibly removed and relocated to other areas.

6. *Janjawid* means "evil spirit [jinn] on horseback," an appropriated term given to militia men from Abbala (camel herder) ethnic groups, recruited by the government to fight its war against the rebels in the southern and western Sudan.

7. On the day of the rally, the *Washington Journal* radio program aired an interview with the southern Sudanese exile Simon Deng. According to Deng, "Darfurians were killed because they did not take the Arab culture, though they are Muslims." By raping women, therefore, "the Janjawid are forcing women to reproduce Arab babies" (*Washington Journal*, interview with Simon Deng, April 30, 2006).

8. "Gender-Based Violence Still Rampant in Darfur, Say Aid Agencies." IRIN, December 5, 2005. http://www.irinnews.org, accessed June 2007.

9. "Armed Fighters on the Streets of Gereida Town, South Darfur State." IRIN, December 20, 2006. http://www.irinnews.org, accessed September 2007.

10. The Darfur rally was one among several protests organized by religious activists in various US cities on April 30, 2006. Also, it roughly coincided with the Latino migrants' nationwide protest at the National Mall on May 1, 2006.

11. I refer here to a UN World Food Program (WFP) brochure titled "Fight Hunger, Walk the World," handed to me by an activist on the Mall during the Darfur rally. The walk represented an attempt to raise awareness and funds to support WFP's school-feeding program and "bring the suffering of [more than three hundred million] hungry children to the forefront of public attention."

References

Abdel-Ati, Hassan

1988   The Process of Famine: Causes and Consequences in Sudan. Development and Change 19: 267–300.

Abu-Lughod, Janet

1999   New York, Chicago, Los Angeles: America's Global Cities. Minneapolis: University of Minnesota Press.

Adam, Barry D.

2003   The Defense of Marriage Act and American Exceptionalism: The "Gay Marriage" Panic in the United States. Journal of the History of Sexuality 12(2):259–276.

Afflicted Powers

2004   The State, the Spectacle and September 11. New Left Review 27(May/June):5–21.

Agamben, Giorgio

2004   The State of Exception. Kevin Attell, trans. Chicago: University of Chicago Press.

Agarwal, Bina

1992   The Gender and Environment Debate. Feminist Studies 18(1):119–158.

Ahmed, Abdel Ghafar

1980   Planning and the Neglect of Pastoral Nomads in the Sudan. *In* Problems of Savannah Development. Gunar Haland, ed. Pp. 39–54. Occasional Papers in Social Anthropology 19. Norway: University of Bergen.

Alarcón, Norma, Caren Kaplan, and Minoo Moallem

1999   Introduction. *In* Between Woman and Nation: Nationalism, Transnational Feminism, and the State. Caren Kaplan, Norma Alarcón, and Minoo Moallem, eds. Pp. 1–19. Durham, NC, and London: Duke University Press.

REFERENCES

Alston, Dana, and Nicole Brown
1993   Global Threats to People of Color. *In* Confronting Environmental Racism: Voices from the Grassroots. Robert Bullard, ed. Pp. 179–194. Boston: South End Press.

Altheide, David L.
2002   Creating Fear: News and the Construction of Crisis. Hawthorne, NY: Aldine de Gruyter (Transaction).

American Banker
2004   In Brief: Ace Buys 39 Southern Stores. American Banker 169(138):7.

American Civil Liberties Union (ACLU)
2003   Freedom under Fire: Dissent in Post-9/11 America. http://www.aclu.org/safe free/resources/17281pub20031208.html, accessed September 2006.
2006   Enduring Abuse: Torture and Cruel Treatment by the United States at Home and Abroad. New York: American Civil Liberties Union. http://www.aclu.org/safefree/torture/25354pub20060427.html, accessed September 2006.

Anderson, Carol
2003   Eyes off the Prize: The United Nations and the African American Struggle for Human Rights, 1944–1955. New York: Cambridge University Press.

Anderson Forest, Stephanie
2004   Tom Joyner: P&G's Favorite Deejay. BusinessWeek Online, July 12.

Andrews-McKinney, Joyce
2005   Letter to the Editor. Lakefront Outlook, July 6.

Angell, Marcia
2004   The Truth about the Drug Companies: How They Deceive Us and What to Do about It. New York: Random House.

Anglin, Mary
1998   Dismantling the Master's House: Cancer Activists, Discourses of Prevention, and Environmental Justice. Identities 5(2):183–217.

Appadurai, Arjun
1996   Modernity at Large: Cultural Dimensions of Globalization. Minneapolis: University of Minnesota Press.
2002   Disjuncture and Difference in the Global Cultural Economy. *In* The Anthropology of Globalization. Jonathan Xavier Inda and Renato Rosaldo, eds. Pp. 46–64. New York: Blackwell.

Applebome, Peter
1996   Dixie Rising: How the South Is Shaping American Values, Politics, and Culture. New York: Harcourt, Brace & Co.

Arbitron
2005   Black Radio Today. http://www.arbitron.com/study/blackrt.asp, accessed October 2005.

Associated Press
2005   Signs May Have Contributed to Sex Offender's Suicide. April 22.

ATSDR (US Agency for Toxic Disease Registry)
1994   Health Consultation Final Release. March 3. Augusta Richmond County, Georgia: US Department of Health and Human Services.
1995   Petitioned Public Health Assessment Addendum. November 21. Augusta Richmond County, Georgia: US Department of Health and Human Services.

Augstums, Ieva
2005   Payday Lenders Hit by FDIC Ruling. Dallas Morning News, March 3: 1.

Austin, Regina
2004   Of Predatory Lending and the Democratization of Credit. American University Law Review 53(6):1217–1257.

Bajaj, Vikas
2006   US Trade Deficit Sets Record, with China and Oil the Causes. New York Times, February 11.
2007a   A Cross-Country Blame Game. New York Times, May 24.
2007b   More Trouble in Subprime Mortgages. New York Times, June 15: C1, C7.

Baker, Dean
2007   Ratio of Mortgage Debt to Housing Value Hits New Record. Center for Economic and Policy Research, June 7. http://www.cepr,net/index.php? option=com_, accessed June 2007.

Balibar, Etienne
1991   Is There a "Neo-Racism"? In Race, Nation, Class: Ambiguous Identities. Etienne Balibar and Immanuel Wallerstein, eds. Pp. 15–28. New York: Verso.

Banerjee, Neela
2005   Black Churches Struggle over Their Role in Politics. New York Times, March 6.
2006a   Black Churches' Attitudes toward Gay Parishioners Is Discussed at Conference. New York Times, January 21.
2006b   Muslims' Plight in Sudan Resonates with Jews in US. New York Times, April 30: 19.

Bass, Paul, and Douglas W. Rae
2006   Murder in the Model City: The Black Panthers, Yale, and the Redemption of a Killer. New York: Basic Books.

Bazar, Emily
2006   Suspected Shooter Found Sex Offenders' Homes on Website. USA Today, April 14. http://www.usatoday.com/news/nation/2006-04-16-maine-shootings_x.htm, accessed September 2006.

Beckerman, Gal
2006   US Jews Leading Darfur Rally Planning. The Jerusalem Post, April 27.

REFERENCES

Bederman, Gail
1995   Manliness and Civilization: A Cultural History of Gender and Race in the
        United States, 1880–1917. Chicago: University of Chicago Press.

Bennett, Larry
1989   Postwar Redevelopment in Chicago: The Declining Politics of Party and the
        Rise of the Neighborhood. *In* Unequal Partnerships: The Political Economy of
        Urban Redevelopment in Postwar America. Gregory D. Squires, ed. Pp.
        161–177. New Brunswick, NJ: Rutgers University Press.
1999   The Shifting Terrain of Neighborhood Politics. *In* Community Politics and
        Policy. Gwenn Moore and J. Allen Whitt, eds. Pp. 21–41. Stamford, CT: JAI
        Press.

Bennett, Larry, Janet Smith, and Patricia Wright
2006   Where Are Poor People to Live? Transforming Public Housing Communities.
        Armonk, NY: M. E. Sharpe, Inc.

Bergquist, Erick
2006   Payday Lenders at a Crossroads, Drawing Bidders. American Banker
        171(135):1.

Berlant, Lauren
1997   The Queen of America Goes to Washington City: Essays on Sex and
        Citizenship. Durham, NC: Duke University Press.
2004   Compassion: The Culture and Politics of an Emotion. New York: Routledge.

Berlowitz, Marvin J., and Nathan A. Long
2003   The Proliferation of JROTC: Education Reform or Militarization. *In*
        Education as Enforcement: The Militarization and Corporatization of Schools.
        Kenneth J. Saltman and David A. Gabbard, eds. Pp. 163–174. New York and
        London: Routledge.

Bernhardt, Annette, Laura Dresser, and Joel Rogers
2004   Taking the High Road in Milwaukee: The Wisconsin Regional Training
        Partnership. *In* Partnering for Change: Unions and Community Groups Build
        Coalitions for Economic Justice. David Reynolds, ed. Pp. 230–248. New York:
        M. E. Sharpe.

Best, Joel, and Gerald T. Horiuchi
1985   The Razor Blade in the Apple: The Social Construction of Urban Legends.
        Social Problems 32(5):488–499.

Betancur, John J., Teresa Cordova, and Maria de los Angeles Torres
1993   Economic Restructuring and the Process of Incorporation of Latinos into the
        Chicago Economy. *In* Latinos in a Changing US Economy. Rebecca Morales
        and Frank Bonilla, eds. Pp. 109–132. New York: Sage.

Bhagwati, Jagdish
2004   In Defense of Globalization. New York: Oxford University Press.

Billingsley, Andrew, and Jeanne M. Giovannoni
1972   Children of the Storm: Black Children and American Child Welfare. New York: Harcourt Brace Jovanovich.

Biondi, Martha
2003   To Stand and Fight: The Struggle for Civil Rights in Postwar New York City. Cambridge, MA: Harvard University Press.

Blanton, Kimberly
2007a   Overdue Mortgages Linked to Risky Loans. The Boston Globe, March 5. http://www.boston.com/business/personalfinance/articles/2007/03/05/overdue.mortgages_li, accessed June 2007.
2007b   Subprime Woes Hit Buyers. The Boston Globe, May 10. http://www.boston.com/business/personalfinance/articles/2007/05/10/subprime_woes_hit, accessed June 2007.
2007c   More Face Auctions of Homes. The Boston Globe, May 16. http://www.boston.com/business/globe/articles/2007/05/16/more_face_auction_of_homes, accessed June 2007.

Bloice, Carl
2007   The Mortgage Crisis and Its "Ugly Geographic Pattern." The Black Commentator. http://www.blackcommentator.com/224/224_left_margin_mortgage-crisis_pattern_bloice.html, accessed June 2007.

Bloom, Alexander, and Wini Breines
1995   "Takin' It to the Streets": A Sixties Reader. New York: Oxford University Press.

Bloom, Jack M.
1987   Class, Race and the Civil Rights Movement. Bloomington: Indiana University Press.

Bolton, Kerra L.
2006   Sex Offender Tracking Ramps Up: GPS Monitoring, Other New Efforts Start in January. Asheville Citizen-Times, September 14. http://www.citizen-times.com/apps/pbcs.dll/article?AID=/20060914/NEWS01/60913096/1009, accessed September 2006.

Boris, Eileen
1999   When Work Is Slavery. *In* Whose Welfare? Gwendolyn Mink, ed. Pp. 36–55. Ithaca, NY: Cornell University Press.

Boyd, Michelle R.
2000   Reconstructing Bronzeville: Racial Nostalgia and Neighborhood Redevelopment. Journal of Urban Affairs 22(2):107–122.
2005   The Downside of Racial Uplift: The Meaning of Gentrification in an African American Neighborhood. City & Society 17(2):265–288.
n.d.   Defensive Development: The Role of Racial Politics in Gentrification. Urban Affairs Review.

REFERENCES

Boyer, Paul, and Stephan Nissenbaum
1974   Salem Possessed: The Social Origins of Witchcraft. Cambridge, MA: Harvard University Press.

Braman, Donald
2004   Doing Time on the Outside: Incarceration and Family Life in Urban America. Ann Arbor: University of Michigan Press.

Brauman, Rony
2004   From Philanthropy to Humanitarianism: Remarks and an Interview. The South Atlantic Quarterly 103(2/3):398–417.

Braverman, Harry
1974   Labor and Monopoly Capital: The Degradation of Work in the Twentieth Century. New York: Monthly Review Press.

Brennan, Mary C.
1995   Turning Right in the Sixties: The Conservative Capture of the GOP. Chapel Hill: University of North Carolina Press.

Breyer, Stephen
2005   Active Liberty: Interpreting Our Democratic Constitution. New York: Knopf.

Brinkley, Alan
1994   The Problem of American Conservatism. American Historical Review 99(2):409–429.

Brooks, Dwight E., and George L. Daniels
2002   *The Tom Joyner Morning Show.* Activist Radio in an Age of Consolidation. Journal of Radio Studies 9(1):8–32.

Brooks-Gunn, Jeanne, Greg J. Duncan, Pamela Kato Klebanov, and Naomi Sealand
1993   Do Neighborhoods Influence Child and Adolescent Development? American Journal of Sociology 99(2):353–395.

Brown, Michael, Martin Carnoy, Elliott Currie, Troy Duster, David B. Oppenheimer, Marjorie M. Shultz, and David Wellman
2003   Whitewashing Race: The Myth of a Color-Blind Society. Berkeley: University of California Press.

Brown, Michael, and David Wellman
2005   Embedding the Color Line: The Accumulation of Racial Advantage and the Disaccumulation of Opportunity in Post-Civil Rights America. Du Bois Review 2(2):187–207.

Brunvald, Jan Harold
1989   Curses! Broiled Again! The Hottest Urban Legends Going. New York: Norton.

Bryant, Bunyan
1995   Pollution Prevention and Participatory Research as a Methodology for Environmental Justice. Virginia Environmental Law Journal 14(4):589–611.

Bullard, Robert

2000   Dumping in Dixie: Race, Class and Environmental Quality. 3rd edition.
        Boulder, CO: Westview Press.

Bullard, Robert, Paul Mohai, Robin Saha, and Beverly Wright

2007   Toxic Wastes and Race at Twenty, 1987–2007. Report prepared for the United
        Church of Christ Justice & Witness Ministries. Cleveland, OH: United Church
        of Christ.

Burke, Edmund

1990   A Philosophical Enquiry into the Origin of Our Ideas of the Sublime and
[1756] Beautiful. Introduction and note on text by Adam Phillips. Oxford: Oxford
        University Press.

Burroughs, Todd Steven

2001   Drums in the Global Village: Toward an Ideological History of Black Media.
        Ph.D. dissertation, University of Maryland, College Park.

Callahan, Thomas

2007   Make Mortgage Lending More Responsible. The Boston Globe, March 27.
        http://www.boston.com/news/globe/editorial_opinion/oped/articles/
        2007/03/27/make_mort, accessed June 2007.

Cancian, Maria, Robert Haveman, Daniel Meyer, and Barbara Wolfe

2002   Before and after TANF: The Economic Well-Being of Women Leaving Welfare.
        Institute for Research on Poverty Discussion Paper no. 1244-02. Madison:
        University of Wisconsin.

Cardyn, Lisa

2002   Sexualized Racism/Gendered Violence: Outraging the Body Politic in the
        Reconstruction South. Michigan Law Review 100(4):675–867.

Carey, David

2005   JLL Partners to Buy Specialty Finance Firm. The Deal, July 25: 1.
        http://www.jllpartners.com/news/2005/0724.php, accessed June 2007.

Cassel, Elaine

2004   The War on Civil Liberties: How Bush and Ashcroft Have Dismantled the Bill
        of Rights. Chicago: Lawrence Hill Books.

Cassell-Low, Brian

2003   ACE Cash Express Reaches Deals with 2 States on Payday Loans. Wall Street
        Journal, January 3: C7.

Center for Responsible Lending

2007   Nine Signs of a Predatory Payday Loan. http://www.responsiblelending.
        org/issues/payday/ninesigns.html, accessed June 2007.

Center for Urban Economic Development

1986   Greater Grand Boulevard Economic Development Study. University of Illinois
        at Chicago.

REFERENCES

CFRC (Children and Family Research Center)
2006   CFRC Fact Book. http://xinia.social.uiuc.edu/outcomes/factbook/fb_index. html, accessed August 2006.

Chan, Sewell
2006   An Outcry Rises as Debt Collectors Play Rough. New York Times, July 5: A1, A17.

Chase, John, and Joah Noel
2005   State Sets Limits on Payday Loans. Chicago Tribune, June 10.

Checker, Melissa
2005a   Environmental Justice Pushed Backwards by Bush Administration. Anthropology News 46(6).
2005b   Polluted Promises: Environmental Racism and the Search for Justice in a Southern Town. New York: New York University Press.
2007   "But I Know It's True": Environmental Risk Assessment, Justice and Anthropology. Human Organization 66(2):112–124.

Chen, David
2004   US Set to Alter Rules for Banks Lending to Poor. New York Times, October 20: A1, C14.

Chen, Michelle
2006   As Predatory Lending Adapts to Weak Regulations, the Poor Pay. The New Standard, July 20.

Chicago Fact Book Consortium
1995   Local Community Fact Book, Chicago Metropolitan Area, 1990. Chicago: Office of Publication Services, University of Illinois at Chicago.

Chicago Historical Society
n.d.   Bronzeville: The Past and the Promise.

Chicago Housing Authority
2005   The Plan for Transformation.

Chicago Urban League, Latino Institute, and Northern Illinois University
1994   The Changing Economic Standing of Minorities and Women in the Chicago Metropolitan Area, 1970–1990. Final Report. Chicago: Chicago Urban League.
1995a   When the Job Doesn't Pay: Contingent Workers in the Chicago Metropolitan Area. The Working Poor Project, March. Chicago: Chicago Urban League.
1995b   Jobs That Pay: Are Enough Jobs Available in Metropolitan Chicago? The Working Poor Project, November. Chicago: Chicago Urban League.

Child Welfare League of America
2000   Children of Color in the Child Welfare System, Race/Ethnicity Foster Care Rates. http://ndas.cwla.org/research_info/minority_child/, accessed August 2006.

Children and Family Research Center. *See* **CFRC**

Chisti, Muzaffer A., Doris Meissner, Demetrios G. Papademetriou, Jay Peterzell, Michael J. Wishnie, and Stephen W. Yale-Loehr

2003   America's Challenge: Domestic Security, Civil Liberties, and National Unity after September 11. Washington DC: Migration Policy Institute.

Chmel, Holli

2006   Thousands Rally in Support of American Aid to Darfur. New York Times, May 1: A16.

Clear, Todd R., Dina Rose, Elin Waring, and Kristen Scully

2003   Coercive Mobility and Crime: A Preliminary Examination of Concentrated Incarceration and Social Disorganization. Justice Quarterly 20(1):33–64.

Clifford, Clark

1991   Counsel to the President. New York: Random House.

CNN

2001   "Bring It Down" Was about a Car, Students' Lawyer Says. http://archives.cnn.com/2002/US/09/15/fla.terror.students, accessed September 2006.

2004   CNN.com election results: American Votes 2004. http://www.cnn.com/ELEC-TION/2004/pages/results/states/US/P/00/epolls.0.html accessed May 2006.

Cobb, James

1982   The Selling of the South: The Southern Crusade for Industrial Development, 1936–1980. Baton Rouge: Louisiana State University Press.

1984   Industrialization and Southern Society, 1877–1984. Lexington: University of Kentucky Press.

Cohen, Adam

2004   The Courts: The Supreme Struggle. New York Times, January 18.

Cohen, Stanley

2002   Folk Devils and Moral Panics. Thirtieth-anniversary edition. New York:
[1972]   Routledge.

Cole, Luke, and Sheila R. Foster

2001   From the Ground Up: Environmental Racism and the Rise of the Environmental Justice Movement. New York: New York University Press.

Collins, Jane

2003   Threads: Gender, Labor and Power in the Global Apparel Industry. Chicago: University of Chicago Press.

n.d.   The Opposite of Fordism: Wal-Mart Hijacks a New Regime of Accumulation. *In* What's Wrong with America? Catherine Bestemann and Hugh Gusterson, eds. Berkeley: University of California Press.

Conan, Neal

2005   "Talk of the Nation," with guest Tom Joyner. NPR (National Public Radio), September 17.

Conquergood, Dwight
1992   Life in Big Red. *In* Structuring Diversity. Louise Lamphere, ed. Pp. 95–144. Chicago: University of Chicago Press.

Cooperman, Alan
2006   Groups Plan Rally on Mall to Protest Darfur Violence: Bush Administration Is Urged to Intervene in Sudan. The Washington Post, April 27: A21.

Corcoran, Mary, Sandra K. Danziger, Ariel Kalil, and Kristin Seefeldt
2000   How Welfare Reform Is Affecting Women's Work. Annual Review of Sociology 26:241–269.

Cordova, Teresa
1991   Community Intervention Efforts to Oppose Gentrification. *In* Challenging Uneven Development: An Urban Agenda for the 1990s. Philip W. Nyden and Wim Wiewel, eds. Pp. 25–48. New Brunswick, NJ: Rugters University Press.

Courtney, Mark E.
1998   The Costs of Child Protection in the Context of Welfare Reform. The Future of Children 8(1):88–103.

Courtney, Mark E., Richard P. Barth, Jill D. Berrick, Devon Brooks, Barbara Needell, and Linda Park
1998   Race and Child Welfare Services: Past Research and Future Directions. Child Welfare 75(2):99–137.

Cowie, Jefferson
1999   Capital Moves: RCA's 70-Year Quest for Cheap Labor. New York: New Press.

COWS (Center on Wisconsin Strategy)
2000   Kenosha, Racine and Walworth Counties: An Economic, Social, Environmental and Political Snapshot. Regional Briefing Paper Series. Madison, WI. www.cows.org and www.sustainingwisconsin.org, accessed January 2006.

2002   Milwaukee, Ozaukee, Washington and Waukesha Counties: An Economic, Social, Environmental and Political Snapshot. Regional Briefing Paper Series. Madison, WI. www.cows.org and www.sustainingwisconsin.org, accessed January 2006.

2004   Working Hard and Falling Short: Wisconsin's Working Families and the Pursuit of Economic Security. Madison, WI.

Curtis, Bryan
2005   Tom Joyner: The Voice of Hurricane Katrina. Slate, September 21. http://slate.msn.com/id/2126688/, accessed December 2005.

Dahl, Robert
1961   Who Governs? New Haven, CT: Yale University Press.

Daniel, Pete
1985   Breaking the Land: The Transformation of Cotton, Tobacco, and Rice Cultures since 1880. Urbana: University of Illinois Press.

Dark, Alx
1998   Public Sphere Politics and Community Conflict over the Environment and

Native Land Rights in Clayoquot Sound, British Columbia. Ph.D. dissertation, New York University.

Darlin, Damon
2006   The Credit Game Is Getting a Second Scorekeeper. New York Times, July 8: B6.

Dash, Eric, and Stephen Labaton
2006   Mortgage Giant Is Expected to Pay $400 Million in Settlement. New York Times, May 23.

Davey, Monica
2006   Iowa's Residency Rules Drive Sex Offenders Underground. New York Times, March 15: A1.

Davis, Angela
2003   Are Prisons Obsolete? New York: Seven Stories Press.

Davis, Kristin
2006   Graduated Interest. The Washington Post, June 18: F1, F5.

Davis, Mike
2006   Who Is Killing New Orleans? The Nation, April 10. http://www.thenation.com/doc/20060410/davis.

Davis, Stephania
1996   Bronzeville's Golden Past Relies on City for Rebirth. Chicago Tribune, May 29.

De Waal, Alex
1989   Famine That Kills: Darfur, Sudan, 1984–1985. Oxford Studies in African Affairs. Oxford: Clarendon Press.
1997   Famine Crimes: Politics and the Disaster Relief Industry in Africa. Bloomington: Indiana University Press.

Deng, Francis
1995   War of Visions for the Nation. *In* Sudan: State and Society in Crisis. John Voll, ed. Pp. 24–43. Bloomington: Indiana University Press.

Deng, Francis, and Larry Minear
1992   The Challenges of Famine Relief: Emergency Operations in the Sudan. Washington DC: The Brookings Institution.

DeParle, Jason
2004   American Dream: Three Women, Ten Kids, and a Nation's Drive to End Welfare. New York: Viking.

Derman, William, and Anne Ferguson
2004   Whose Water? Political Ecology of Water Reform in Zimbabwe. *In* Political Ecology across Spaces, Scales, and Social Groups. Susan Paulson and Lisa Gezon, eds. Pp. 61–75. New Brunswick, NJ: Rutgers University Press.

di Leonardo, Micaela
1998   Exotics at Home: Anthropologies, Others, American Modernity. Chicago: University of Chicago Press.

2004   Human Cultural Diversity. Paper presented at "Race and Human Variation: Setting an Agenda for Future Research and Education," Alexandria, VA, September 12–14.

n.d.   Whose Homeland? The New Imperialism, Neoliberalism, and the American Public Sphere. *In* Rethinking America: The Imperial Homeland in the 21st Century. Jeff Maskovksy and Ida Susser, eds. Kent, WA: Paradigm Press.

Diffee, Christopher
2005   Sex in the City: The White Slavery Scare and Social Governance in the Progressive Era. American Quarterly 57(2):411–437.

Docena, Herbert
2003   Iraq Reconstruction's Bottom Line. Asia Times online, December 25. http://atimes.com.

Domhoff, William
1978   Who Really Rules? New Haven and Community Power Reexamined. Santa Monica, CA: Goodyear Publishing Company.

Doolittle, Amy, and Arlo Wagner
2006   Rally Decries Darfur Killings: Celebrities and Religious Leaders Urge an End to "A Genocide." The Washington Times, May 1: 1–A18.

Dorsey, Michael
2002   Environmental Justice for All—Even Tuvalu! Special to Outreach, a daily publication from the Stakeholder Forum at the Fourth Preparatory Meeting of the World Summit on Sustainable Development. Bali, Indonesia, June 7. http://www.ifg.org/analysis/un/wssd/mdorsey.htm, accessed August 2007.

Douglas Development Corporation
1979   Douglas Development and Planning Study: Creating Better Neighborhoods. Chicago. Photocopy.

Douglas, Mary
1992   Risk and Blame: Essays in Cultural Theory. New York: Routledge.

Douglas, Mary, and Aaron Wildavsky
1982   Risk and Culture: An Essay on the Selection of Technological and Environmental Dangers. Berkeley: University of California Press.

Douglas, Susan J.
2004   Listening In: Radio and the American Imagination. Minneapolis: University of Minnesota Press.

Dove, Michael
2001   Interdisciplinary Borrowing in Environmental Anthropology and the Critique of Modern Science. *In* New Directions in Anthropology and Environment: Intersections. Carole Crumley, A. Elizabeth Van Deventer, and Joseph J. Fletcher, eds. Pp. 90–112. Lanham, MD: Alta Mira.

Downey, Kristin
2007   Foreclosure Wave Bears Down on Immigrants. The Washington Post, March 26: A1, A8.

Drake, St. Clair, and Horace R. Cayton

1993   Black Metropolis: A Study of Negro Life in a Northern City. Chicago:
[1945]   University of Chicago Press.

Dresser, Laura, and Joel Rogers

2004   The State of Working Wisconsin. Madison, WI: Center on Wisconsin Strategy
          (COWS).

Dubey, Madhu

2003   Signs and Cities: Black Literary Postmodernism. Chicago: University of Chicago
          Press.

Dudziak, Mary

2000   Cold War Civil Rights: Race and the Image of American Democracy. Princeton,
          NJ: Princeton University Press.

Dyer, Joel

2000   The Perpetual Prisoner Machine: How America Profits from Crime. Boulder,
          CO: Westview.

Eckholm, Erik

2006   Black and Hispanic Home Buyers Pay Higher Interest on Mortgages, Study
          Finds. New York Times, June 1: A22.

Edelman, Lee

2004   No Future: Queer Theory and the Death Drive. Durham, NC: Duke University
          Press.

Edelstein, Michael

2003   Contaminated Communities: Coping with Residential Toxic Exposure. Boulder,
          CO: Westview Press.

Egerton, John

1974   The Americanization of Dixie, The Southernization of America. New York:
          Harpers Magazine Press.

Ehrenreich, Barbara

1997   When Governments Get Mean: Confessions of a Recovering Statist. The
          Nation, November 17: 11.

Eichenwald, Kurt

2005a   The Customers: Where the Credit Card Trail Leads. New York Times,
          December 19. http://www.nytimes.com/2005/12/19/business/19kidswebpred
          ators.html?ex=1160193600&en=7d58af2edb3d1534&ei=5070, accessed October
          2006.

2005b   Through His Webcam, a Boy Joins a Sordid Online World. New York Times,
          December 19: A1.

2006   Virginia Man Gets 150-Year Term in Child Pornography Case. New York Times,
          July 16: A17.

Eisinger, Peter

1998   City Politics in an Era of Federal Devolution. Urban Affairs Review
          33(3):308–325.

REFERENCES

Electronic Payments International

2005   ACE Buys Popular Chain, as Loan Regulation Bites. Electronic Payments International Newsletter EPI 220: October 17, http://www.electronicpayment international.com, accessed November 16, 2007.

Elsner, Alan

2004   Gates of Injustice: The Crisis in America's Prisons. New York: Prentice Hall.

Enloe, Cynthia

2000   Maneuvers: The International Politics of Militarizing Women's Lives. Berkeley: University of California Press.

Ernst, Keith, Kathleen Keest, Li Wei, and Ellen Schloemer

2006   Losing Ground: Foreclosures in the Subprime Market and Their Cost to Homeowners. Washington DC: Center for Responsible Lending.

Escobar, Arturo

1988   Power and Visibility: Development and the Invention and Management of the Third World. Cultural Anthropology 3(4):428–443.

Escobar, Arturo, and Susan Paulson

2004   The Emergence of Collective Ethnic Identities and Alternative Political Ecologies in the Colombian Pacific Rainforest. *In* Political Ecology across Spaces, Scales, and Social Groups. Susan Paulson and Lisa Gezon, eds. Pp. 257–278. New Brunswick, NJ: Rutgers University Press.

Fadlalla, Amal Hassan

2005   Modest Women, Deceptive Jinn: Identity, Alterity, and Disease in Eastern Sudan. Identities 12(2):143–174.

2007   Embodying Honor: Fertility, Foreignness and Regeneration in Eastern Sudan. Madison: University of Wisconsin Press.

Fagan, Jeffrey, Valerie West, and Jan Holland

2003   Reciprocal Effects of Crime and Incarceration in New York City Neighborhoods. Fordham Urban Law Journal 30:1551–1602.

Fair Disclosure Wire

2006   ACE Cash Express, Inc., Introduces the CSO Loan Product in Texas and Provides a Tax Season Update—Final. February 21: 1–5.

Farmer, Paul, and Didi Bertrand

2000   Hypocrisies of Development and the Health of the Haitian Poor. *In* Dying for Growth: Global Inequality and the Health of the Poor. Jim Yong Kim, Joyce V. Millen, Alec Irwin, and John Gershman, eds. Pp. 65–91. Monroe, ME: Common Courage Press.

Federal Bureau of Investigation (FBI)

2001   Uniform Crime Reports: Hate Crime Statistics. http://www.fbi.gov/ucr/ucr.htm, accessed September 2006.

Ferguson, Niall

2006   Reasons to Worry. New York Times Magazine, June 11: 46–50.

Ferman, Barbara
1996   Challenging the Growth Machine: Neighborhood Politics in Chicago and Pittsburgh. Lawrence: University Press of Kansas.

Fine, Janice
2006   Worker Centers: Organizing Communities at the Edge of the Dream. Ithaca, NY: Industrial and Labor Relations Press.

Finnegan, William
1990   Out There. The New Yorker, September 10:17.

Fisher, Luchina
2003   Year Ends with Wider-Than-Ever Wage Gap. womansnews, December 30.

Fisher, Robert
1994   Community Organizing in the Conservative '80s and Beyond. Social Policy 25(1):11–21.

Fitchen, Janet
1988   Anthropology and Environmental Problems in the US: The Case of Groundwater Contamination. Practicing Anthropology 10(3–4):5, 18.

Flint, Julie
2006   The Arabs Are Victims Too. The Washington Post, November 19: B01.

Flint, Julie, and Alex De Waal
2005   Darfur: A Short History of a Long War. London: Zed Books.

Flores-González, Nilda
2002   School Kids/Street Kids: Identity Development in Latino Students. New York: Teachers College Press.

Foner, Eric
1998   The Story of American Freedom. New York: W. W. Norton.

Foner, Eric, ed.
1971   Nat Turner. Englewood Cliffs, NJ: Prentice-Hall.

Foucault, Michel
1980   Power/Knowledge: Selected Interviews and Other Writings, 1972–1977. Colin Gordon, ed. New York: Pantheon.

Frank, Thomas
2004   What's the Matter with Kansas? How Conservatives Won the Heart of America. New York: Henry Holt and Co.

Fraser, Nancy, and Linda Gordon
1994   A Genealogy of Dependency: Tracing a Keyword of the US Welfare State. Signs 19(2):309–336.

Frazer, Sir James George
2005   The Golden Bough: A Study in Magic and Religion, IX, Part Six: The
[1920] Scapegoat. New York: Elibron Classics (Macmillan and Company).

REFERENCES

Freedman, Estelle B.
1987   "Uncontrolled Desires": The Response to the Sexual Psychopath, 1920–1960. The Journal of American History 74(1):83–106.

Friedman, Thomas L.
2005   The World Is Flat: A Brief History of the Globalized World in the Twenty-First Century. London: Allen Lane.

Fuller, Joseph
2007   The Shifting Financial Winds. The Boston Globe, February 23. http://www.boston.com/news/globe/editorial_opinion/oped/articles/2007/02/23/theshiftin, accessed February 2007.

Fuquay, Jim
2006   Ace Cash Express to Be Bought Out. Knight Ridder Tribune Business News, Washington, June 8: 1.

Garland, David
2001   The Culture of Control: Crime and Social Order in Contemporary Society. Chicago: University of Chicago Press.

Gaus, Mischa
2006   Hey Millenials, Debt Becomes You. In These Times, May 17.

Gaylord, Chris
2006   For Graduates, Student Loans Turn into an Albatross. The Christian Science Monitor, May 17.

Gertner, Jon
2006   Forgive Our Student Debts. New York Times Magazine, June 11: 60–68.

Gill, Lesley, and Camilo Romero
2006   The Underside of Coke. Anthropology News 47(6):46.

Gills, Douglas C.
2001   Unequal and Uneven: Critical Aspects of Community–University Partnerships. *In* Collaborative Research: University and Community Partnerships. Myrtis Sullivan and Marilyn Willis, eds. Pp. 27–47. Washington DC: American Public Health Association.

Gilmore, Glenda
1996   Gender and Jim Crow: Women and the Politics of White Supremacy in North Carolina, 1896–1920. Chapel Hill: University of North Carolina Press.

Girard, René
1986   The Scapegoat. Yvonne Freccero, trans. Baltimore, MD: Johns Hopkins
[1982]   University Press.

Gitlin, Todd
2002   Media Unlimited: How the Torrent of Images and Sounds Overwhelms Our Lives. New York: Henry Holt.

Glassner, Barry
1999   The Culture of Fear: Why Americans Are Afraid of the Wrong Things. New York: Basic.

Gledhill, John

2005   Neoliberalism. *In* Companion to an Anthropology of Politics. David Nugent
            and Joan Vincent, eds. Pp. 332–348. New York: Blackwell.

Glenn, Evelyn Nakano

2002   Unequal Freedom: How Race and Gender Shaped American Citizenship and
            Labor. Cambridge, MA: Harvard University Press.

Goerge, Robert M., and Lee J. Bong

2001   The Entry of Children from the Welfare System into Foster Care: Differences
            by Race. Urbana-Champaign: Children and Family Research Center, School of
            Social Work, University of Illinois.

Goldberg, Robert Alan

1995   Barry Goldwater. New Haven, CT: Yale University Press.

Goldschmidt, Henry

2004   Food Fights: Contesting "Cultural Diversity" in Crown Heights. *In* Local
            Actions: Cultural Activism, Power and Public Life in America. Melissa Checker
            and Maggie Fishman, eds. Pp. 159–183. New York: Columbia University Press.

Goode, Erich, and Nachman Ben-Yehuda

1994   Moral Panics: The Social Construction of Deviance. New York: Blackwell.

Goode, Judith, and Jeff Maskovsky

2001   The New Poverty Studies: The Ethnography of Power, Politics and
            Impoverished People in the United States. New York: New York University
            Press.

Goodenough, Abby

2005   After 2 Cases in Florida, Crackdown on Molesters. New York Times, April 30:
            A26.

Gordon, Colin

2003   Dead on Arrival: The Politics of Health Care in Twentieth-Century America.
            Princeton, NJ: Princeton University Press.

Gordon, Linda

1988   What Does Welfare Regulate? Social Research 55(4):609–630.

1999   The Great Arizona Orphan Abduction. Cambridge, MA: Harvard University
            Press.

Governor's Task Force

1996   Governor's Task Force on the Long-Term Health Care Needs for Southern
            Wood Piedmont Residents, Augusta, Georgia.

Gramsci, Antonio

1971   Selections from the Prison Notebooks. Quintin Hoare and Geoffrey Nowell
            Smith, eds. and trans. New York: International.

Grazian, David

2003   Blue Chicago: The Search for Authenticity in Urban Blues Clubs. Chicago:
            University of Chicago Press.

Greenhouse, Steven, and David Leonhardt
2006   Real Wages Fail to Match Rise in Productivity: Political Fallout Is Seen. New
        York Times, August 28.

Gregory, Steven
1994   We've Been Down This Road Already. *In* Race. Steven Gregory and Roger
        Sanjek, eds. Pp. 18–40. New Brunswick, NJ: Rutgers University Press.
1998   Black Corona: Race and the Politics of Place in an Urban Community.
        Princeton, NJ: Princeton University Press.

Griffith, Robert
1987   The Politics of Fear: Joseph R. McCarthy and the Senate. Amherst: University
[1970] of Massachusetts Press.

Gross, Samuel R., Kristin Jacoby, Daniel J. Matheson, Nicholas Montgomery, and Sujata Patil
2005   Exonerations in the United States, 1989 through 2003. Journal of Criminal
        Law and Criminology 95(2):523–560.

Grossman, James
1989   Land of Hope: Chicago, Black Southerners, and the Great Migration. Chicago:
        University of Chicago Press.

Gupta, Akhil
1992   The Song of the Nonaligned World: Transnational Identities and the
        Reinscription of Space in Late Capitalism. Cultural Anthropology 7(1):63–79.

Gupta, Akhil, and James Ferguson
1997   Culture, Power, Place: Ethnography at the End of an Era. *In* Culture, Power,
        Place: Explorations in Critical Anthropology. Akhil Gupta and James
        Ferguson, eds. Pp. 1–33. Durham, NC: Duke University Press.
2002   Spatializing States: Toward an Ethnography of Neoliberal Governmentality.
        American Ethnologist 29(4):981–1002.

Gwaltney, John Langston
1993   Drylongso: A Self-Portrait of Black America. New York: The New Press.

Hacker, Andrew
2006   The Rich and Everyone Else. The New York Review of Books 53(9):16–19.

Hadley, Earl
2006   The Raid on Student Aid. Tom Paine.common sense, April 14. http://www.
        tompaine.com/articles/2006/04/14/the_raid_on_student_aid.php, accessed
        April 2007.

Hakim, Danny
2004   Defendant Is Released in Detroit Terror Case. New York Times, October 13:
        A16.

Hall, Jacquelyn Dowd
2005   The Long Civil Rights Movement and the Political Uses of the Past. Journal of
        American History 91(4):1233–1263.

Hall, Peter, and David Soskice

2001   Varieties of Capitalism: The Institutional Foundations of Comparative
        Advantage. Oxford: Oxford University Press.

Hall, Stuart, Chas Critcher, Tony Jefferson, John Clark, and Brian Roberts

1978   Policing the Crisis: Mugging, the State, and Law and Order. New York: Holmes
        and Meier.

Harrigan, Anthony

1958   The South *Is* Different. National Review, March 8: 225–227.

Harris-Lacewell, Melissa Victoria

2004   Barbershops, Bibles, and BET: Everyday Talk and Black Political Thought.
        Princeton, NJ: Princeton University Press.

Harrison, Faye

1995a   "Give Me That Old-Time Religion": The Genealogy and Cultural Politics of an
        Afro-Christian Celebration in Halifax County, North Carolina. *In* Religion in
        the Contemporary US South: Diversity, Community, Identity. D. Kendall White
        Jr. and Daryl White, eds. Pp. 34–45. Athens: University of Georgia Press.

1995b   The Persistent Power of "Race" in the Cultural and Political Economy of
        Racism. Annual Review of Anthropology 24:47–74.

Hartocollis, Anemona

2005   Sex Offenders Held Illegally, Judge Rules. New York Times, November 16: B1.

Hartung, William D.

2003   The New Imperialism. The Nation, February 17. http://www.thenation.com/
        doc/20030217/hartung, accessed September 2003.

Harvey, David

1989   The Condition of Postmodernity: An Enquiry into the Origins of Cultural
        Change. Cambridge, MA: Blackwell.

2003   The New Imperialism. New York and Oxford: Oxford University Press.

2005   A Brief History of Neoliberalism. New York and Oxford: Oxford University
        Press.

Henderson, Nell

2007   An ATM That's out of Money. The Washington Post, May 31: D1, D3.

Henriques, Diana

2005   Creditors Press Troops despite Relief Act. New York Times, March 28: A1, A10.

Henwood, Doug

2004   Income Down, Poverty Up. Left Business Observer 112 (December):4–5.

2007   Blackstone's Bell. The Nation, July 16: 6; July 23: 8.

Herman, Edward, and Noam Chomsky

1988   Manufacturing Consent: The Political Economy of the Mass Media. New York:
        Pantheon.

Hewell, Hal

1989   Samples Collected at Park. Augusta Herald, June 24: 1A, 8A.

REFERENCES

Hill, Amelia
2004   "Stranger Danger" Drive Harms Kids. The Observer (UK), May 23.

Hirsch, Arnold R.
1983   Making the Second Ghetto: Race and Housing in Chicago, 1940–1960. New York and Cambridge: Cambridge University Press.

Hirsch, Arnold, and Raymond Mohl
1993   Urban Policy in Twentieth-Century America. New Brunswick, NJ: Rutgers University Press.

Hirschman, Albert O.
1991   The Rhetoric of Reaction: Perversity, Futility, Jeopardy. Cambridge, MA: Harvard University Press.

Hochschild, Jennifer
1996   Facing Up to the American Dream: Race, Class and the Soul of the Nation. Princeton, NJ: Princeton University Press.

Hoover's
2007   Ace Cash Express. http://www.hoovers.com, accessed August 2007.

Hubbard, Ruth, and Elijah Wald
1993   Exploding the Gene Myth: How Genetic Information Is Produced and Manipulated by Scientists, Physicians, Employers, Insurance Companies, Educators, and Law Enforcers. Boston: Beacon Press.

Huggler, Justin
2004   Axis of Execution: American Justice Ranked alongside World's Most Repressive Regimes. The Independent, independent.co.uk, April 7.

Huth, Elizabeth
1991a   Dow Wants Dismissal. Augusta Herald, July 16: 1A, 7A.
1991b   Guidelines Shed Light on Wood-Plant Soil Tests. Augusta Herald, July 20: 1A, 7A.

Hwang, Suein
2004   Asset Acceptance, a New Type of Collector, Hits Paydirt Suing for Modest Sums. Wall Street Journal, October 25: A1.

Hyatt, Susan
2006   Community Collaboration, Accountability and Civic Participation on Indianapolis' Eastside. Paper presented at the meetings of the Society for the Anthropology of North America, New York, April 30.

Ignatieff, Michael
2003   American Empire (Get Used to It). New York Times Magazine, January 5: cover piece.

Imam, Ayesha
1994   SAP Is Really Sapping Us, Squeezing the South. New Internationalist 257:12–13. http://www.newint.org, accessed August 2007.

Ince, John

2006   Crumbling under Debt. AlterNet, April 8.

Inda, Jonathan Xavier, and Renato Rosaldo, eds.

2002   The Anthropology of Globalization. New York: Blackwell.

Irvine, Janice M.

2004   Talk about Sex: The Battles over Sex Education in the United States. 2nd edition, with a new preface. Berkeley: University of California Press.

Israel, Brian

1995   An Environmental Justice Critique of Risk Assessment. New York University Environmental Law Journal 3(2):469–522.

Jackson, John, Jr.

2001   Harlemworld: Doing Race and Class in Contemporary Black America. Chicago: University of Chicago Press.

Jameson, Frederick

1991   Postmodernism, or the Cultural Logic of Late Capitalism. Durham, NC: Duke University Press.

Jenkins, Philip

1998   Moral Panic: Changing Concepts of the Child Molester in Modern America. New Haven, CT: Yale University Press.

2006   Decade of Nightmares: The End of the Sixties and the Making of Eighties America. Oxford: Oxford University Press.

Jennings, James

2005   Social Capital, Race and Inner City Neighborhoods. Paper delivered at the annual meeting of the National Conference of Black Political Scientists, March 25, Washington DC.

Johnson, Chalmers

2001   "Blowback." The Nation, October 15. Web archive, http://www.thenation.com/doc/20011015/johnson.

2004   Blowback: The Costs and Consequences of American Empire. New York: Henry
[2000]   Holt and Company.

Johnson, David K.

2003   The Lavender Scare: The Cold War Persecution of Gays and Lesbians in the Federal Government. Chicago: University of Chicago Press.

Joyner, Tom

1995   Clearing the Air: The Making of a Radio Personality. Self-published.

Kahn, Si, and Elizabeth Minnich

2005   The Fox in the Henhouse: How Privatization Threatens Democracy. San Francisco: Berrett-Koehler.

Kamenetz, Anya

2006   Generation Debt. New York: Riverhead Books.

REFERENCES

Katz, A.

2000   Mommy Nearest. City Limits, http://citylimits.org/content/articles/ articleView.cfm?articlenumber=337, accessed August 2006.

Kaye, Kerwin

2003   Male Prostitution in the Twentieth Century: Pseudohomosexuals, Hoodlum Homosexuals, and Exploited Teens. Journal of Homosexuality 46(1/2):1–77.

Kessler-Harris, Alice

1991   A Woman's Wage: Historical Meanings and Social Consequences. Lexington: University of Kentucky Press.

2001   In Pursuit of Equity: Women, Men and the Quest for Economic Citizenship in 20th-Century America. New York: Oxford.

Kiley, David

2005   Imus Audience Slips in New York, but He Still Packs a Punch. Businessweekonline, April 26. http://businessweek.com, accessed May 2005.

Kilman, Carrie

2005   Food Redlining: A Hidden Cause for Hunger. Tolerance.org, accessed August 2007.

Kincaid, Harold

1990   Assessing Functional Explanations in the Social Sciences. PSA: Proceedings of the Annual Meeting of the Philosophy of Science Association 1990(1):341–354.

Kincaid, James R.

1998   Erotic Innocence: The Culture of Child Molesting. Durham, NC: Duke University Press.

Kingston, Jennifer

2004   Free Credit Reports Coming, with Pitches. New York Times, November 30: C1, C4.

Kiser, Jim

2006   N. Carolina, Georgia Offer Model on Payday Lenders. Arizona Daily Star, March 8.

Klein, Jennifer

2003   For All These Rights: Business, Labor, and the Shaping of America's Public-Private Welfare State. Princeton, NJ: Princeton University Press.

Kleinman, Arthur, and Joan Kleinman

1997   The Appeal of Experience, The Dismay of Images: Cultural Appropriations of Suffering in Our Times. In Social Suffering. Arthur Kleinman, Veena Das, and Margaret Lock, eds. Pp. 1–25. Berkeley: University of California Press.

Kleppner, Paul

1985   Chicago Divided: The Making of a Black Mayor. DeKalb: Northern Illinois University Press.

Kligman, Gail, and Stephanie Limoncelli

2005   Tracking Women after Socialism: To, Through and From Eastern Europe. Social Politics 12(1):118–140.

Koch, Wendy

2006   States Get Tougher with Sex Offenders. USA Today, May 25. http://www.usato
        day.com/news/nation/2006-05-23-sex-offenders_x.htm, accessed September
        2006.

Kolko, Gabriel

1963   The Triumph of Conservatism: A Reinterpretation of American History,
        1900–1916. New York: Free Press.

Koprowsky, Gene J.

2006   Loan Spam Leads an Inbox Influx. The Washington Post, July 10: F1, F8.

Korstad, Robert Rodgers

2003   Civil Rights Unionism: Tobacco Workers and the Struggle for Democracy in the
        Mid-Twentieth-Century South. Chapel Hill: University of North Carolina Press.

Kracauer, Siegfried

2004   From Caligari to Hitler: A Psychology of the German Film. Introduction by
[1947] Leonardo Quaresima, ed. Princeton, NJ: Princeton University Press.

Kriebel, David, J. Tickner, P. Epstein, J. Lemons, R. Levins, E. L. Loechler, M. Quinn, R. Rudel, T. Schettler, and M. Stoto

2001   The Precautionary Principle in Environmental Science. Environmental Health
        Perspectives 109(9):871–876.

Kristof, Nicholas

2005   The Century's First Genocide. Video, New York Times Multimedia.

Krugman, Paul

2002   For Richer: How the Permissive Capitalism of the Boom Destroyed American
        Equality. New York Times, October 20.

2006   Debt and Denial. New York Times, February 13.

Kruse, Kevin M.

2005   White Flight: Atlanta and the Making of Modern Conservatism. Princeton, NJ:
        Princeton University Press.

Kunkle, Fredrick

2006   Caught in a Neighborhood Web: Innocent Man Mistaken for Registered
        Offender. The Washington Post, May 13: A1.

Kuttner, Robert

2005   True West: At the Democratic Party's Western States Caucus in Montana,
        Evidence Abounds of a Region "Red on the Outside, Blue on the Inside." The
        American Prospect 16(7):13–14.

2007   Hedging Disaster. The Boston Globe, April 28. http://www.boston.com/news/
        globe/editorial_opinion/oped/articles/2007/04/28, accessed April 2007.

Kwiatowski, Karen

2004   The New Pentagon Papers. Salon.com, March 10.

Ladd-Taylor, Molly

1985   Women Workers and the Yale Strike. Feminist Studies 11(3):465–489.

Lancaster, Roger N.
2003   The Trouble with Nature: Sex in Science and Popular Culture. Berkeley: University of California Press.

Lane, Wendy G., David M. Rubin, Ragin Monteith, and Cindy W. Christian
2002   Racial Differences in the Evaluation of Pediatric Fractures for Physical Abuse. Journal of the American Medical Association 288(13):1603–1609.

Lassiter, Matthew D.
2006   The Silent Majority: Suburban Politics in the Sunbelt South. Princeton, NJ: Princeton University Press.

Latino Institute
1994   A Profile of Nine Latino Groups in Chicago. Chicago: Latino Institute.
1995   Facts on Chicago's Puerto Rican Population. Chicago: Latino Institute.

Lears, Jackson
2006   The American Way of Debt. New York Times Magazine, June 11: 13–17.

Lee, Duk-Hee, In-Kyu Lee, Kyungeun Song, Michael Steffes, William Toscano, Beth A. Baker, and David R. Jacobs Jr.
2006   A Strong Dose-Response Relation between Serum Concentrations of Persistent Organic Pollutants and Diabetes. Diabetes Care 29:1638–1644.

Leonhardt, David
2005   US Poverty Rate Was Up Last Year. New York Times, August 31.

Levine, Judith
2003   Harmful to Minors: The Perils of Protecting Children from Sex. Foreword by
[2002]   Dr. Jocelyn M. Elders. Afterword by the author. New York: Thundermouth Press.

Levine, Marc V.
2003a   "Stealth Depression": Joblessness in the City of Milwaukee since 1990. University of Wisconsin Milwaukee, Center for Economic Development, Report, August 25. http://www.ced.uwm.edu, accessed January 2006.
2003b   The Two Milwaukees: Separate and Unequal. Presentation for the Milwaukee County Task Force on Segregation and Race Relations, April 30.
2004   After the Boom: Joblessness in Milwaukee since 2000. University of Wisconsin Milwaukee, Center for Economic Development, Report, April 5. http://www.ced.uwm.edu, accessed January 2006.

Lewin, Tamar
2001   Sikh Owner of Gas Station Is Fatally Shot in Rampage. New York Times, September 17: B16.

Lichtenstein, Alex
1996   Twice the Work of Free Labor: The Political Economy of Convict Labor in the New South. New York: Verso.

Lichtenstein, Nelson
2003   State of the Union: A Century of American Labor. Princeton, NJ: Princeton University Press.

Lind, Michael

2005   Conservative Elites and the Counterrevolution against the New Deal. *In* Ruling America: A History of Wealth and Power in a Democracy. Steve Fraser and Gary Gerstle, eds. Pp. 250–285. Cambridge, MA: Harvard University Press.

Lindsey, Duncan

1994   The Welfare of Children. New York: Oxford University Press.

Lipman, Pauline

2003   Cracking Down: Chicago School Policy and the Regulation of Black and Latino Youth. *In* Education as Enforcement: The Militarization and Corporatization of Schools. Kenneth J. Saltman and David A. Gabbard, eds. Pp. 31–101. New York and London: Routledge.

Lipman, Pauline, and Nathan Haines

2005   From Education Accountability to Privatization and African American Disenfranchisement—The Case of Chicago Public Schools. Unpublished paper.

Lipsitz, George

1995   The Possessive Investment in Whiteness: Racialized Social Democracy and the "White" Problem in American Studies. American Quarterly 47(3):369–387.

2006   The Possessive Investment in Whiteness: How White People Profit from Identity Politics. 2nd edition. Philadelphia: Temple University Press.

Liptak, Adam

2004   Study Suspects Thousands of False Convictions. New York Times, April 19.

Lister, Ruth

1997   Citizenship: Feminist Perspectives. New York: New York University Press.

Logan, John R., and Harvey L. Molotch

1987   Urban Fortunes: The Political Economy of Place. Berkeley: University of California Press.

Long, Jerome

1996   The Urban Campus: Realizing the Promise. Catalyst (Spring).

López, Nancy

2003   Hopeful Girls, Troubled Boys: Race and Gender Disparity in Urban Education. New York: Routledge.

Lott, Eric

1993   Love and Theft: Blackface Minstrelsy and the American Working Class. New York: Oxford University Press.

Lott, Trent

1984   A Partisan Conversation with Trent Lott. Richard T. Hines, interviewer. Southern Partisan 4(4):44–45.

Low, Setha

2003   Behind the Gates: Life, Security, and the Pursuit of Happiness in Fortress America. New York: Routledge.

Lowe, Lisa
1996   Immigrant Acts: On Asian American Cultural Politics. Durham, NC: Duke University Press.

Lucas, Harold
1997   Historic Summary of Black Metropolis Bronzeville and Its Significance. South Street Journal, February 28–March 13.

Luebbert, Gregory M.
1991   Liberalism, Fascism, or Social Democracy: Social Classes and the Political Origins of Regimes in Interwar Europe. New York: Oxford University Press.

Lutz, Catherine
2001   Homefront: A Military City and the American 20th Century. Boston: Beacon Press.

Lutz, Catherine, and Lesley Bartlett
1995   Making Soldiers in the Public Schools. Philadelphia: American Friends Service Committee.
1998   Disciplining Social Difference: Some Cultural Politics of Military Training in Public High Schools. The Urban Review 30(2):119–136.

Lutz, Catherine, and Jane Collins
1993   Reading National Geographic. Chicago: University of Chicago Press.

Lynd, Staughton, and Alice Lynd
2000   The New Rank and File. Ithaca, NY: Industrial and Labor Relations Press.

MacLean, Nancy
2000   From the Benighted South to the Sun Belt: The South in the Twentieth Century. *In* Making Sense of the Twentieth Century: Perspectives on Modern America. Harvard Sitkoff, ed. Pp. 216–217. New York: Oxford University Press.
2006   Freedom Is Not Enough: The Opening of the American Workplace. Cambridge, MA: Harvard University Press and the Russell Sage Foundation.

Malkki, Liisa
1996   Speechless Emissaries: Refugees, Humanitarianism, and Dehistoricization. Cultural Anthropology 11(3):377–404.
1994   Citizens of Humanity: Internationalism and the Imagined Community of Nations. Diaspora 3(1):41–68.

Mamdani, Mahmood
2004   Good Muslim, Bad Muslim: America, the Cold War, and the Roots of Terror. New York: Pantheon.
2007   The Politics of Naming: Genocide, Civil War, Insurgency. London Review of Books 29(5). http://www.lrb.co.uk, accessed August 2007.

Manley, Theodoric, Jr., Avery Buffa, and Caleb Dube
2006   The Revanchist City: Downtown Chicago and the Rhetoric of Redevelopment in Bronzeville. Unpublished manuscript.

Mansnerus, Laura

2003   Unfinished Sentences: Keeping Prisoners as Patients; Questions Rise over Imprisoning Sex Offenders past Their Terms. New York Times, November 17: A1.

Mariscal, George

2004   No Where to Go: Latino Youth and the Poverty Draft. Public Affairs (November). http://www.politicalaffairs.net/article/articleview/295/1/36, accessed August 17, 2007.

Markusen, Ann R.

1991   The Rise of the Gunbelt: The Military Remapping of Industrial America. New York: Oxford University Press.

Marshall, T. H.

1950   Citizenship and Social Class. New York: Cambridge University Press.

Massey, Douglas, and Nancy A. Denton

1993   American Apartheid: Segregation and the Making of the Underclass. Cambridge, MA: Harvard University Press.

Mayer, Jane

2005   Outsourcing Torture: The Secret History of America's "Extraordinary Rendition" Program. The New Yorker, February 14.

McAlister, Melanie

2001   Epic Encounters: Culture, Media, and US Interests in the Middle East, 1945–2000. Berkeley: University of California Press.

McChesney, Robert W.

2004   The Problem of the Media: US Communication Politics in the 21st Century. New York: Monthly Review Press.

McClain, Linda C.

2006   The Place of Families: Fostering Capacity, Equality, and Responsibility. Cambridge, MA: Harvard University Press.

McGeehan, Patrick

2004   The Plastic Trap: Mountains of Interest Add to Pain of Credit Cards. New York Times, November 21.

McGirr, Lisa

2001   Suburban Warriors: The Origins of the New American Right. Princeton, NJ: Princeton University Press.

McLaren, Peter

1994   Multiculturalism and the Postmodern Critique: Toward a Pedagogy of Resistance and Transformation. In Between Borders: Pedagogy and the Politics of Cultural Studies. Henry Giroux and Peter McLaren, eds. Pp. 192–224. New York: Routledge.

McLaughlin, Kathleen

2006   Chinese Villages, Poisoned by Toxins, Battle for Justice. The Christian Science Monitor, June 23: 1–3.

Mettler, Suzanne
1998   Dividing Citizens: Gender and Federalism in New Deal Public Policy. Ithaca, NY: Cornell University Press.

Meznaric, Silva
1994   Gender as an Ethno-Marker: Rape, War, and Identity Politics in the Former Yugoslavia. *In* Identity Politics and Women: Cultural Reassertions and Feminisms in International Perspective. Valentine Moghadam, ed. Pp. 76–98. Boulder, CO: Westview Press.

Micklethwait, John, and Adrian Wooldridge
2004   The Right Nation: Conservative Power in America. New York: Penguin.

Mid-South Planning and Development Commission (Mid-South)
1993   Mid-South Strategic Development Plan: Restoring Bronzeville. Chicago.

Mink, Gwendolyn
2001   Violating Women: Rights Abuses in the Welfare Police State. Annals of the American Academy of Political and Social Science 577(1):79–93.

Moeller, Susan D.
1999   Compassion Fatigue: How the Media Sell Disease, Famine, War, and Death. New York: Routledge.

Mohl, Bruce
2007   Fees Can Put You over Your Head in Overdraft Charges. The Boston Globe, March 11. http://www.boston.com/business/globe/articles/2007/03/11/fees_can_put_you_over, accessed August 2007.

Moloney, Brian
2005   Radio Equalizer: Annual Talk Host Rankings Revealed. May 24. http://radioe qualizer.blogspot.com/2005/05/annual-talk-host-rankings-revealed.html, accessed December 2005.

Montague, Peter
2003   Environmental Justice Requires Precautionary Action. Testimony before the California Environmental Protection Agency Advisory Committee on Environmental Justice.

Montejano, David
1987   Anglos and Mexicans in the Making of Texas, 1836–1986. Austin: University of Texas Press.

Moore, Kesha S.
2002   Creating the Black American Dream: Race, Class and Community Development. Ph.D. dissertation, University of Pennsylvania.
2005   What's Class Got to Do with It? Community Development and Racial Identity. Journal of Urban Affairs 27(4):437–451.

Moreton, Bethany E.
2006   "It Came from Bentonville": The Agrarian Origins of Wal-Mart Culture. *In* Wal-

Mart: The Face of Twenty-First-Century Capitalism. Nelson Lichtenstein, ed. Pp. 57–82. New York: New Press.

Morgenson, Gretchen, and Vikas Bajaj
2007   Rising Rates Start to Squeeze Consumers and Companies. New York Times, June 15: A1, C2.

Muhammad, James G.
2006   "The Good and the Bad of Segregation." N'Digo, February 9–15: 6–7, 16.

Murphy, Paul V.
2001   The Rebuke of History: The Southern Agrarians and American Conservative Thought. Chapel Hill: University of North Carolina Press.

Nathan, Debbie, and Michael Snedeker
1995   Satan's Silence: Ritual Abuse and the Making of a Modern American Witch Hunt. New York: Basic Books.

National Clearinghouse on Child Abuse and Neglect Information
n.d.   Child Abuse and Neglect Fatalities: Statistics and Interventions. Washington DC: US Department of Health and Human Services. http://nccanch.afc.hhs. gov.pubs/factsheets/fatality.cfm, accessed September 2006.

National Employment Law Project. *See* NELP

National MCH (Maternal and Child Health) Center for Child Death Review
n.d.   United States Child Mortality, 2002. http://www.childdeathreview.org/national childmortalitydata.htm, accessed September 2006.

NELP (National Employment Law Project)
2002   Welfare and Low-Wage Workforce: Workfare and Work Requirements: Employment Rights of Workfare Participants and Displaced Workers, March. http://www.nelp. org/wlwp/requirements/rights/workfarerights0302.cfm, accessed January 2006.

New York Times
2006   Chicago Orders "Big Box" Stores to Raise Wage. New York Times, July 27: A1.

News and Noteworthy: Articles Concerning Sex Offender Issues
2006   Charts Library. http://www.geocities.com/voicism/index-charts.html, accessed September 2006.

NISMART (National Incidence Studies of Missing, Abducted, Runaway, and Thrownaway Children)
2002a   Highlights from the NISMART Bulletins. Washington DC: US Department of Justice.
2002b   National Estimates of Missing Children: An Overview. Washington DC: US Department of Justice.
2002c   Nonfamily Abducted Children: National Estimates and Characteristics. Washington DC: US Department of Justice.
2004   National Estimates of Missing Children: Selected Trends, 1988–1999. Washington DC: US Department of Justice.

Northeastern Illinois Planning Commission
2002   Census 2000 General Profiles for the 77 Chicago Community Areas from
        Summary File 1. http://www.nipc.org/test/Y2K_SF1_prof_CA.pdf, accessed
        August 2007.

Novotny, Patrick
1998   Popular Epidemiology and the Struggle for Community Health in the
        Environmental Justice Movement. *In* The Struggle for Ecological Democracy:
        Environmental Justice Movements in the United States. Daniel Faber, ed.
        Pp. 137–158. New York: Guilford.

Oberdeck, Kathryn
1991   Labor's Vicar and the Variety Show: Popular Religion, Popular Theater, and
        Cultural Class Conflict in Turn-of-the-Century America. Ph.D. dissertation, Yale
        University.

O'Brien, Jay
1985   Sowing the Seeds of Famine: The Political Economy of Food Deficits in Sudan.
        Review of African Political Economy 33:23–101.

Offe, Claus
2006   Reflections on America: Tocqueville, Weber and Adorno in the United States.
        Patrick Camiller, trans. Cambridge, UK: Polity.

Office of Justice Programs
n.d.   Frequently Asked Questions on AMBER Alert. Washington DC: US
        Department of Justice. http://www.amberalert.gov/faqs.html, accessed
        September 2006.

Ohi, Kevin
2000   Molestation 101: Child Abuse, Homophobia, and the Boys of St. Vincent.
        GLQ: A Journal of Lesbian and Gay Studies 6(2):195–248.

Okome, Mojúbàolú
1997   Sapped Democracy: The Political Economy of the Structural Adjustment
        Program and the Democratic Transition in Nigeria, 1983–1993. Baltimore,
        MD: University Press of America.

Oliver, Pamela
2001   Summary of Findings on Racial Disparities in Criminal Justice in Wisconsin.
        Prepared for Community Justice Action Coalition Conference, November 2,
        Madison.

Oliver, Pamela, and James Yocum
2002   Racial Disparities in Criminal Justice: Madison and Dane County in Context.
        Institute for Research on Poverty, Discussion Paper no. 1257-02. Madison:
        University of Wisconsin.

Omi, Michael, and Howard Winant
1986   Racial Formation in the United States. New York: Routledge.

Ordower, Garrett
2007   The Loan Shark Lobby. The Nation, April 9: 5–6.

Paletta, Damian

2007   Curbs on Military Payday Loans Cover Narrow List of Products. Wall Street Journal, April 10: 7.

Paley, Amit

2007   US Student Loan Office Gets New Rules and a New Chief. The Washington Post, June 2: A5.

Parenti, Christian

1999   Lockdown America: Police and Prisons in the Age of Crisis. London: Verso.

"Pariah"

2006   Scapegoats and Shunning: Sexual Fascism in Progressive America. Counterpunch, weekend edition, March 4/5. http://www.counterpunch.org/pariah03042006.html, accessed March 2006.

Parreñas, Rhacel

2001   Servants of Globalization: Women, Migration, and Domestic Work. Stanford, CA: Stanford University Press.

Peck, Jamie

2001   Workfare States. New York: Guilford Press.

Pelton, Leroy H.

1993   Has Permanency Planning Been Successful? No. *In* Controversial Issues in Child Welfare. Eileen Gambrill and Theodore J. Stein, eds. Pp. 268–271. Needham Heights, MA: Allyn & Bacon.

Perez, Alfred, Kasia O'Neil, and Sarah Gesiriech

2003   Demographics of Children in Foster Care. http://pewfostercare.org/research/docs/Demographics0903.pdf, accessed August 2006.

Pérez, Gina

2002   The Other "Real World": Gentrification and the Social Construction of Place in Chicago. Special issue, Urban Legends: Race, Class, and the Politics of Mythical Revitalizations. Urban Anthropology 31(1):37–68.

2004   The Near Northwest Side Story: Migration, Displacement and Puerto Rican Families. Berkeley: University of California Press.

2006   How a Scholarship Girl Becomes a Soldier: The Militarization of Latina/o Youth in Chicago Public Schools. Identities 13(1):53–72.

Perin, Constance

1977   Everything in Its Place: Social Order and Land Use in America. Princeton, NJ: Princeton University Press.

Perlstein, Rick

2001   Before the Storm: Barry Goldwater and the Unmaking of the American Consensus. New York: Hill and Wang.

Peterson, Christopher

2007   Cleaning Up a Consumer Lending Mess. The Boston Globe, March 3. http://www.boston.com/news/globe/editorial_opinion/oped/articles/2007/03/03/cleaning, accessed August 2007.

REFERENCES

Phillips, Kevin

1969   The Emerging Republican Majority. New York: Arlington House.

Philpott, Thomas

1991   The Slum and the Ghetto. Immigrants, Blacks, and Reformers in Chicago, 1880–1930. Belmont, CA: Wadsworth Publishing Co.

Piven, Frances Fox

1999   Welfare and Work. *In* Whose Welfare? Gwendolyn Mink, ed. Pp. 83–99. Ithaca, NY: Cornell University Press.

Piven, Frances Fox, and Richard Cloward

1971   Regulating the Poor: The Functions of Public Welfare. New York: Vintage.

1993   Regulating the Poor: The Functions of Public Welfare. New York: Vintage.
[1971]

Polanyi, Karl

2001   The Great Transformation. Boston: Beacon Press.
[1944]

Polletta, Francesca

1998   "It Was like a Fever…": Narrative and Identity in Social Protest. Social Problems 45(3):137–159.

Pollin, Robert

2003   Contours of Descent. New York: Verso.

Powledge, Fred

1970   Model City: A Test of American Liberalism: One Town's Efforts to Rebuild Itself. New York: Simon and Schuster.

Price, Susannah

2006   "Scant Help" for Tsunami Victims. BBC News, February 1. http://news.bbc.co.uk/2/hi/asia-pacific/4671884.stm.

Prince, Sabiyha Robin

2002   Changing Places: Race, Class and Belonging in the "New" Harlem. Urban Anthropology 31(1):5–35.

2004   Constructing Belonging: Class, Race and Harlem's Professional Workers. New York: Routledge.

Putnam, Robert

1995   Bowling Alone: America's Declining Social Capital. Journal of Democracy 6(1):65–78.

Quadagno, Jill

1994   The Color of Welfare: How Racism Undermined the War on Poverty. New York: Oxford University Press.

Rae, Nicol C.

1989   The Decline and Fall of the Liberal Republicans. New York: Oxford University Press.

Raghunathan, Anuradha

2003   Ace Cash Express Secures New Credit. Knight Ridder Tribune Business News, The Dallas Morning News, April 3: 1.

Rall, Ted

2007   Ban the Banks: Corrupt Student Loan Biz Can't Be Reformed. http://www.uexpress.com/tedrall/UExpress.com, accessed June 2007.

Ramos-Zayas, Ana Yolanda

2004   Delinquent Citizenship, National Performances: Racialization, Surveillance, and the Politics of "Worthiness" in Puerto Rican Chicago. Latino Studies 2(1):26–44.

Ranney, David

2003   Global Decisions, Local Collisions: Urban Life in the New World Order. Philadelphia: Temple University Press.

Ranney, David C., and William Cecil

1993   Transnational Investment and Job Loss in Chicago: Impacts on Women, African-Americans and Latinos. Chicago: Center for Urban Economic Development, University of Illinois at Chicago.

Rast, Joel

1999   Remaking Chicago: The Political Origins of Urban Industrial Change. DeKalb: Northern Illinois University Press.

Reed, Adolph, Jr.

1996   Romancing Jim Crow: Black Nostalgia for a Segregated Past. The Village Voice, April 16.

2005   The 2004 Election in Perspective: The Myth of "Cultural Divide" and the Triumph of Neoliberal Ideology. American Quarterly 57(1):1–15.

Reed, Merl E.

1991   Seedtime for the Modern Civil Rights Movement: The President's Committee on Fair Employment Practice, 1941–1946. Baton Rouge: Louisiana State University Press.

Rezendes, Michael, Beth Healy, Francie Latou, and Walter V. Robinson

2006   Debtors' Hell. Four-part series. The Boston Globe, July 28, July 29, August 1, and August 2. http://www.boston.com/news/special/spotlight_debt/part3/page1.html, accessed August 2006.

Ribuffo, Leo P.

1994   Why Is There So Much Conservatism in the United States, and Why Do So Few Historians Know Anything about It? American Historical Review 99(2):438–449.

Rierden, Andi

1991   Armed Youths Turn New Haven into a Battleground. New Haven Register, May 26.

Roberts, Dorothy

1996   Welfare and the Problem of Black Citizenship. Yale Law Journal 105:1563–1597.

REFERENCES

1999   Welfare's Ban on Poor Motherhood. *In* Whose Welfare? Gwendolyn Mink, ed.
        Pp. 152–170. Ithaca, NY: Cornell University Press.
2001   Kinship Care and the Price of State Support for Children. Chicago-Kent Law
        Review 76(3):1619–1642.
2002   Shattered Bonds: The Color of Child Welfare. New York: Basic Books/Civitas.
2004a   The Social and Moral Cost of Mass Incarceration in African American
        Communities. Stanford Law Review 56(5):1271–1305.
2004b   Welfare Reform and Economic Freedom: Low-Income Mothers' Decisions
        about Work at Home and in the Market. Santa Clara Law Review
        2003–2004(44):1029–1063.
2006   High Rates of Child Welfare Agency Involvement in African-American
        Neighborhoods: The Impact on Community and Civic Life. Northwestern
        University Institute for Policy Research. Working Paper. Evanston, IL:
        Northwestern University.

Robertson, Stephen
2001   Separating the Men from the Boys: Masculinity, Psychosexual Development,
        and Sex Crime in the United States, 1930s–1960s. Journal of the History of
        Medicine and Allied Sciences 56(1):3–35.

Robin, Corey
2004   Fear: The Political History of an Idea. Oxford: Oxford University Press.

Robinson, Dean
2001   Black Nationalism in American Politics and Thought. Cambridge: Cambridge
        University Press.

Robles, Andrea, Fred Doolittle, and Susan Gooden
2003   Community Service Jobs in Wisconsin Works: The Milwaukee County
        Experience. MDRC (Manpower Development Research Corporation), June.
        New York: MDRC.

Rogal, Brian
2006   Bankruptcy Law in Shambles. In These Times, June 5.

Ross, Andrew, ed.
1997   No Sweat: Fashion, Free Trade, and the Rights of Garment Workers. New York:
        Verso.

Ruben, Matthew
2001   Suburbanization and Urban Poverty under Neoliberalism. *In* The New Poverty
        Studies: The Ethnography of Power, Politics, and Impoverished People in the
        United States. Judith Goode and Jeff Maskovsky, eds. Pp. 435–479. New York:
        New York University Press.

Rubin, Gayle
1984   Thinking Sex: Notes for a Radical Theory of the Politics of Sexuality. *In*
        Pleasure and Danger: Exploring Female Sexuality. Carole S. Vance, ed.
        Pp. 267–319. New York: Routledge and Kegan Paul.

Sabatini, Patricia
2006   Days May Be Numbered for State's Payday Lenders. Pittsburgh Post-Gazette, March 26: 1.

Said, Edward
1978   Orientalism. New York: Vintage Books.
1981   Covering Islam: How the Media and the Experts Determine How We See the Rest of the World. New York: Pantheon Books.
1993   Culture and Imperialism. New York: Alfred A. Knopf.

Sakinga, Ahmad
1996   Slaves into Workers: Emancipation and Labor in Colonial Sudan. Austin: University of Texas Press.

Sale, Kirkpatrick
1975   Power Shift: The Rise of the Southern Rim and Its Challenge to the Eastern Establishment. New York: Random House.

Saltman, Kenneth J.
2003   Introduction. *In* Education as Enforcement: The Militarization and Corporatization of Schools. Kenneth J. Saltman and David A. Gabbard, eds. Pp. 1–23. New York and London: Routledge.

Sampson, Robert
2001   How Do Communities Undergird or Undermine Human Development? Relevant Contexts and Social Mechanisms. *In* Does It Take a Village? Community Effects on Children, Adolescents, and Families. Alan Booth and Ann C. Crouter, eds. Pp. 3–30. Mahwah, NJ: Lawrence Ehrlbaum Associates, Inc.
2002   Transcending Tradition: New Directions in Community Research, Chicago Style. Criminology 40(2):213–230.

Sampson, Robert, Jeffrey Morenoff, and Thomas Gannon-Rowley
2002   Assessing "Neighborhood Effects": Social Processes and New Directions in Research. Annual Review of Sociology 28(1):443–478.

Sassen, Saskia
1998   Globalization and Its Discontents: Essays on the New Mobility of People and Money. New York: The New Press.
2001   The Global City: New York, London, Tokyo. Princeton, NJ: Princeton University Press.

Schein, Louisa
1997   The Consumption of Color and the Politics of White Skin in Post-Mao China. *In* The Gender/Sexuality Reader: Culture, History, Political Economy. Roger Lancaster and Micaela di Leonardo, eds. Pp. 473–486. New York: Routledge.

Schema, Diana Jean
2007   With Few Limits and High Rates, Private Loans Deepen Student-Debt Crisis. New York Times, June 10: 22.

Schettler, Ted, Katherine Barrett, and Carolyn Raffensperger
2002   The Precautionary Principle: Protecting Public Health and the Environment. *In* Life Support: The Environment and Human Health. Michael McCally, ed. Pp. 239–256. Cambridge, MA: MIT Press.

Schoepf, Brooke, Claude Schoepf, and Joyce Millen
2000   Theoretical Therapies, Remote Remedies: SAPs and the Political Ecology of Poverty and Health in Africa. *In* Dying for Growth: Global Inequality and the Health of the Poor. Jim Yong Kim, Joyce V. Millen, Alec Irwin, and John Gershman, eds. Pp. 91–127. Monroe, ME: Common Courage Press.

Schulman, Bruce J.
1991   From Cotton Belt to Sunbelt: Federal Policy, Economic Development, and the Transformation of the South. New York: Oxford University Press.
1994   Lyndon B. Johnson and American Liberalism. Boston: Bedford Books of St. Martin's Press.

Seelye, Katherine Q.
2004   Moral Values Cited as a Defining Issue of the Election. New York Times, November 4.

Sekhri, Rajiv
1997   Company Cashes In on Payday Loan Boom. Cincinnati Business Courier, May 5: 7. http://cincinnati.bizjournals.com/cincinnati.stories/1997/05/05/story6.html, accessed June 2007.

Self, Robert O.
2003   American Babylon: Race and the Struggle for Postwar Oakland. Princeton, NJ: Princeton University Press.

Sen, Amartya
1981   Poverty and Famines: An Essay on Entitlement and Deprivation. Oxford: Clarendon Press.

Sender, Henny
2006   Debt Buyers versus the Indebted: Showdown between Hedge Funds and Private Equity May Be Inevitable. Wall Street Journal, October 17: C1.

Shankar, Shalini
2004   Fobby or Tight?: "Multicultural Day" and Other Struggles in Two Silicon Valley High Schools. *In* Local Actions: Cultural Activism, Power and Public Life in America. Melissa Checker and Maggie Fishman, eds. Pp.184–288. New York: Columbia University Press.

Shapiro, Bruce
1997   Victims and Vengeance: Why the Victims' Rights Amendment Is a Bad Idea. The Nation 264(5):11–17.

Shapiro, Isaac, and Joel Friedman
2006   New CBO Data Indicate Growth in Long-Term Income Inequality Continues. Center on Budget and Policy Priorities, January 2. http://www.cbpp.org/1-29-06tax.htm, accessed March 2006.

Shaver, Sheila
1989   Gender, Class and the Welfare State: The Case of Income Security in Australia. Feminist Review 32(Summer):90–110.

Sherry, Michael
2005   Dead or Alive: American Vengeance Goes Global. Special issue, "Force and Diplomacy," Review of International Studies 31(December):246–263.

Sherwell, Philip
2007   American Dream Sours as Housing Market Collapses. Denver Sunday Telegraph, July 5. http://www,telegraph,co/uk/core.html, accessed June 2007.

Shevory, Thomas
2004   Notorious HIV: The Media Spectacle of Nushawn Williams. Minneapolis: University of Minnesota Press.

Shipak, Mitzi
2007   Listening to Environmental Justice Communities: A Model for Government Agencies Identifying Environmental Health Problems and Solutions. Paper presented at the State of Environmental Justice in America 2007 Summit, Washington DC, March 29–31.

Shklar, Judith
1991   American Citizenship: The Quest for Inclusion. Cambridge, MA: Harvard University Press.

Siegel, Lee
2006   Thank You for Sharing: The Strange Genius of Oprah. The New Republic, June 5–12: 19.

Singletary, Michelle
2005   Overdraft Fees Can Overwhelm. The Washington Post, June 26: F1, F6.

Sitkoff, Harvard
1978   A New Deal for Blacks: The Emergence of Civil Rights as a National Issue. New York: Oxford University Press.

Sluss, Michael
2006   Panel Seeks Evidence Castration Is Effective: A Lawmaker Proposes Offering Convicted Sex Offenders Castration and Conditional Release. Roanoke Times, September 13. http://www.roanoke.com/politics/wb/wb/xp-82452, accessed September 2006.

Smale, Pauline
2004   Credit Scores: Development, Use, and Policy Issues. Washington DC: Library of Congress, Congressional Research Service.

Smith, Anna Marie
2007   Welfare Reform and Sexual Regulation. New York: Cambridge University Press.

Smith, Neil
1996   The New Urban Frontier: Gentrification and the Revanchist City. New York: Routledge.

Smith, Paul

2004   Why "We" Lovehate "You." Social Science Research Council web forum: Contemporary Conflicts. http://conconflicts.ssrc.org/USA/smith/, accessed September 2006.

2007   Primitive America. Minneapolis: University of Minnesota Press.

Smith, Rogers

2003   Stories of Peoplehood: The Politics and Morals of Political Membership. Cambridge: Cambridge University Press.

Smith, Vern

1998   "Fly Jock" Rides High. Newsweek 131(8):55.

Sociology Research Methods Students, Kim Davies, Robert Johnston, Ernestine Thompson, Robin Bengtson, Sarah Firman, Albert Jimenez, Karen Jones, and Regina Murray

1998   The 1998 Hyde Park Neighborhood Survey Report. Department of Sociology, Augusta State University, Augusta, GA.

Solinger, Rickie

1999   Dependency and Choice: The Two Faces of Eve. *In* Whose Welfare? Gwendolyn Mink, ed. Pp. 7–35. Ithaca, NY: Cornell University Press.

Somers, Margaret, and Fred Block

2005   From Poverty to Perversity: Ideas, Markets and Institutions over 200 Years of Welfare Debate. American Sociological Review 70(April):260–286.

Spear, Allan H.

1967   Black Chicago: The Making of a Negro Ghetto, 1890–1920. Chicago: University of Chicago Press.

Squires, Gregory, Larry Bennett, Katherine McCourt, and Phillip Nyden

1987   Chicago: Race, Class and Urban Decline. Philadelphia: Temple University Press.

Stacey, Judith

1997   The Neo-Family Values Campaign. *In* The Gender/Sexuality Reader. Roger Lancaster and Micaela di Leonardo, eds. Pp. 453–470. New York: Routledge.

Stack, Carol

1996   Call to Home: African Americans Reclaim the Rural South. New York: Basic Books.

Stansell, Christine

1987   City of Women. Urbana: University of Illinois Press.

STATS

2002   Phony Numbers on Child Abduction. Washington DC: Statistical Assessment Service. http://www.stats.org/stories/2002/phony_aug01_02.htm, accessed September 2006.

Steinberg, Stephen

1995   Turning Back: The Retreat from Racial Justice in American Thought and Policy. Boston: Beacon Press.

Stepan, Alfred

1985   State Power and Civil Society in the Southern Cone of Latin America. *In* Bringing the State Back. Peter B. Evans, Dietrich Rueschemeyer, and Theda Skocpol, eds. Cambridge: Cambridge University Press.

Stevens, Michelle

1982   Douglas Area Comes Back to Life. Chicago Sun-Times, April 30.

Stone, Clarence, and Heywood Sanders

1987   Reexamining a Classic Case of Development Politics: New Haven, Connecticut. *In* The Politics of Urban Development. Clarence Stone and Heywood Sanders, eds. Pp. 159–181. Lawrence: University of Kansas Press.

Stovall, David, and Janet Smith

2005   Selling Homes and Schools: Towards a New Politics of Containment. Unpublished manuscript.

Strom, Stephanie, and Lydia Polgreen

2007   Darfur Advocacy Group Undergoes a Shake-Up. New York Times, June 2, http://www.nytimes.com.

Sugrue, Thomas J.

1996   The Origins of the Urban Crisis: Race and Inequality in Postwar Detroit. Princeton, NJ: Princeton University Press.

Sullivan, Patricia

1996   Days of Hope: Race and Democracy in the New Deal Era. Chapel Hill: University of North Carolina Press.

Sunstein, Cass R.

2005   Radicals in Robes: Why Extreme Right-Wing Courts Are Wrong for America. New York: Basic Books.

Takaki, Ronald, ed.

2002   Debating Diversity: Clashing Perspectives on Race and Ethnicity in America. New York: Oxford University Press.

Taylor, Monique

2002   Harlem: Between Heaven and Hell. Minneapolis: University of Minnesota Press.

Teixiera, Rex, and Joel Rogers

2001   America's Forgotten Majority: Why the White Working Class Still Matters. New York: Basic.

Terris, Harry

2007   New Payday Deal, Few See Pace Slowing. American Banker 172(55):1.

Tesh, Sylvia Noble

2000   Uncertain Hazards: Environmental Activists and Scientific Proof. Ithaca, NY: Cornell University Press.

REFERENCES

Testa, Mark, and Frank Furstenberg

2002   The Social Ecology of Child Endangerment. *In* A Century of Juvenile Justice. Margaret Rosenheim, Franklin E. Zimring, David S. Tanenhaus, and Berbardine Dohrn, eds. Pp. 237–263. Chicago: University of Chicago Press.

Themba, Makani

2001   Black Entertainment Television's "Lifestyle" Choice. The Nation, May 14. http://thenation.com/doc.mhtml?I=20010514&s=themba, accessed November 2005.

Ticktin, Miriam

2006   Where Ethics and Politics Meet: The Violence of Humanitarianism in France. American Ethnologist 33(1):33–49.

Tilly, Christopher

1997   Glass Ceilings and Bottomless Pits: Women's Work, Women's Poverty. Boston: South End Press.

Trumbull, Mark

2006   Inflation's Rising Toll on Consumers. The Christian Science Monitor, May 18.

Turner, Terrence

1993   Anthropology and Multiculturalism: What Is Anthropology That Multiculturalists Should Be Mindful of It? Cultural Anthropology 8(4):411–429.

Uchitelle, Louis

2004   Women Are Gaining Ground on the Wage Front. New York Times, December 31.

2006   Inflation Rising, Markets Tumble. New York Times, May 18.

United Nations Development Program

1999   Human Development Report. New York: Oxford University Press.

Urbina, Ian

2006   With Parents Absent, Trying to Keep Child Care in the Family. New York Times, July 23: 13.

US Agency for Toxic Disease Registry. *See* ATSDR

US Department of Health and Human Services. *See* US DHHS

US Department of Justice

2003   Recidivism of Sex Offenders Released from Prison in 1994. Washington DC: Bureau of Justice Statistics. http://www.ojp.usdoj.gov/bjs/abstract/rsorp94.htm, accessed October 2006.

US Department of Labor

2005   Labor Protections and Welfare Reform. Office of Assistant Secretary for Policy, May 3. www.dol.gov/asp/w2w/welfare.htm, accessed January 2006.

US DHHS (US Department of Health and Human Services)

1997   National Study of Protective, Preventive, and Reunification Services Delivered to Children and Their Families. Washington DC: US Government Printing Office.

2005a   Fatalities: Child Maltreatment 2004. http://www.childwelfare.gov/can/fatali ties.cfm, accessed September 2006.

2005b   National Survey of Child and Adolescent Well-Being, 1997–2005. http://www.acf.hhs.gov/programs/opre/abuse_neglect/nscaw/index.html, accessed August 2007.

2005c   Perpetrators: Child Maltreatment 2004. http://www.childwelfare.gov/can/ perpetrators/, accessed September 2006.

2006   The AFCARS Report, Preliminary FY 2005 Estimates as of September 2006 (13). http://www.acf.hhs.gov/programs/cb/stats_research/afcars/ report13.htm, accessed August 2007.

US EPA (US Environmental Protection Agency)

2003   Framework for Cumulative Risk Assessment, Risk Assessment Forum, US Environmental Protection Agency, Washington DC.

Vance, Carole

1997   Negotiating Sex and Gender in the Attorney General's Commission on Pornography. *In* The Gender Sexuality Reader: Culture, History, Political Economy. Roger N. Lancaster and Micaela di Leonardo, eds. Pp. 440–452. New York: Routledge.

Venkatesh, Sudhir Alladi

2006   Off the Books. Cambridge, MA: Harvard University Press.

Walkowitz, Judith R.

1992   City of Dreadful Delight: Narratives of Sexual Danger in Late-Victorian London. Women in Culture and Society Series. Chicago: University of Chicago Press.

Wallace, A. F. C.

1956   Revitalization Movements. American Anthropologist 58(2):264–281.

Warren, Dorian T.

2005   Think Locally, Act Locally: A Strategy for Organizing Wal-Mart. New Labor Forum 14:8–15.

Warren, Elizabeth

2007   Testimony of Professor Elizabeth Warren. United States Senate, Committee on the Judiciary, February 10.

Warren, Elizabeth, and Amelia Warren Tyagi

2003   The Two-Income Trap. New York: Basic Books.

Washington, James Melvin, ed.

1986   A Testament of Hope: The Essential Writings of Martin Luther King, Jr. New York: Harper & Row.

Washington Post

2006a   Md. Legislature Overrides Veto on "Wal-Mart Bill." The Washington Post, January 13: A01.

2006b   "Wal-Mart Law" in Maryland Rejected by Court. The Washington Post, July 20: A01.

REFERENCES

Weaver, Richard M.
1959   The Regime of the South. National Review, March 14: 587–589.

Weeks, Jeffrey
1981   Sex, Politics, and Society: The Regulation of Sexuality since 1800. London: Longman.

Weinstein, James
1968   The Corporate Ideal in the Liberal State, 1900–1918. Boston: Beacon Press.

Weisbrot, Mark
2006   Fed Treading on Thin Ice as US Housing Bubble Weakens. Center for Economic and Policy Research. http://www.cepr.net.columns/weisbrot/2006_6_30.htm, accessed June 2006.

Weissman, Robert
2003   Grotesque Inequality: Corporate Globalization and the Global Gap between Rich and Poor. Multinational Monitor 24(7&8).

Went, Robert
2000   Globalization: Neoliberal Challenge, Radical Responses. London: Pluto Press.

Wessel, David
2003   Racial Discrimination Still at Work. Wall Street Journal, September 4.

West, Patrick C., J. Mark Fly, Frances Larkin, and Robert W. Marans
1992   Minority Anglers and Toxic Fish Consumptions: Evidence from a Statewide Survey in Michigan. *In* Race and the Incidence of Environmental Hazards: A Time for Discourse. Bunyan Bryant and Paul Mohai, eds. Pp. 100–113. Boulder, CO: Westview Press.

White, Chris
2006   Support Your Local Banker. New York Times, June 1: A25.

White, Renee T.
1999   Putting Risk in Perspective: Black Teenage Lives in the Era of AIDS. Lanham, MD: Rowman and Littlefield.

White, Richard
1991   It's Your Misfortune and None of My Own: A New History of the American West. London: University of Oklahoma Press.

Whittaker, John D.
1986   Evaluation of Acceptable Risk. Journal of the Operational Research Society 37(6):541–547.

Wigley, Daniel, and Kristin Shrader-Frechette
1996   Environmental Racism and Biased Methods of Risk Assessment. Risk: Health, Safety and Environment 7(Winter):55–88.

Williams, Brett
1998   Babies and Banks: "The Reproductive Underclass" and the Raced, Gendered Masking of Debt. *In* Race. Steven Gregory and Roger Sanjek, eds. Pp. 348–365. New Brunswick, NJ: Rutgers University Press.

1999   The Great Family Fraud of Postwar America. *In* Without Justice for All: The
         New Liberalism and Our Retreat from Racial Equality. Adolph Reed Jr., ed. Pp.
         65–89. Boulder, CO: Westview Press.
2001   What's Debt Got to Do with It? *In* The New Poverty Studies: The Ethnography
         of Politics, Policy, and Impoverished People in the US. Judith Goode and Jeff
         Maskovsky, eds. Pp. 79–102. New York: NYU Press.
2004   Debt for Sale. Philadelphia: University of Pennsylvania Press.

Williams, Gilbert A.
1998   Legendary Pioneers of Black Radio. Westport, CT: Praeger.

Williams, Joan
2001   Unbending Gender. New York: Oxford University Press.

Williams, Kristian
2003   The Demand for Order and the Birth of Modern Policing. Monthly Review
         55(7):1–9.

Williams, Melvin D.
1974   Community in a Black Pentecostal Church: An Anthropological Study.
         Pittsburgh: University of Pittsburgh.

Wills, Garry
1999   A Necessary Evil: A History of American Mistrust of Government. New York:
         Simon & Schuster.

Wilson, William Julius
1987   The Truly Disadvantaged. Chicago: University of Chicago Press.

Winfrey, Oprah
2005   Oprah's Child Predator Watch List. Website, http://www2.oprah.com/
         presents/2005/predator/predator_main.jhtml, accessed September 2006.

Wirth, Gregg
2007   Mending SOX...out of Existence. Left Business Observer 115(May 31):3, 7.

Wisconsin Department of Workforce Development (DWD)
1999a   Division of Economic Support. Wisconsin Works Manual, Release 98-03.
1999b   Wisconsin Works Overview. http://www.dwd.state.wi.us/dws/w2/wisworks.htm,
         accessed August 2005.
2004   Wisconsin Works (W-2) Sanctions Study.

Wisconsin Legislative Audit Bureau
2005   An Evaluation: Wisconsin Works (W-2) Program. Report 05-6. Madison:
         Wisconsin Legislative Audit Bureau.

Wolff, Rick
2005   Personal Debts and US Capitalism. MRZine (Monthly Review), October 15.
         http://mrzine.monthlyreview.org/wolff170207.html, accessed August 2007.
2006   The Fallout from Falling US Wages. MRZine (Monthly Review), June 12.
         http://mrzine.monthlyreview.org/wolff120606.html, accessed June 2006.

2007   The Decline of Public Higher Education. MRZine (Monthly Review), February 17. http://mrzine.monthlyreview.org/wolff170207.html, accessed August 2007.

Woodruff, Bob

2005   Sex Offender Registry Said Flawed, Inconsistent: Thousands of Offenders Slip through Cracks, Experts Say. ABC's World News Tonight, March 21. http://abc news.go.com/WNT/story?id=601536&page=1, accessed October 2006.

Woods, Jeff

2004   Black Struggle, Red Scare: Segregation and Anti-Communism in the South, 1948–1968. Baton Rouge: Louisiana State University Press.

Woodward, C. Vann

2002   The Strange Career of Jim Crow. Afterword by William S. McFeely. Oxford:
[1955] Oxford University Press.

World Resources Institute

1999   Population and Human Well-Being: Economic Growth and Human Development. http://www.wri.org/wr-98-99/econgrow.htm#poverty, accessed March 2006.

Wright, Gavin

1986   Old South, New South: The Southern Economy since the Civil War. New York: Basic Books.

Wright, Paul, and Tara Herivel, eds.

2003   Prison Nation: The Warehousing of America's Poor. New York: Routledge.

Wuthnow, Robert

1990   The Restructuring of American Religion. Princeton, NJ: Princeton University Press.

1998   After Heaven: Spirituality in America since the 1950s. Berkeley: University of California Press.

Wypijewski, JoAnn

2004   Priest Abuse and Recovered Memory: The Passion of Paul Shanley. Legal Affairs (September/October). http://www.legalaffairs.org/issues/September-October-2004/feature_wypijewski_sepoct04.msp, accessed September 2006.

X, Malcolm, and George Breitman

1966   Malcolm X Speaks: Selected Speeches and Statements. New York: Grove Press.

Zeidenberg, Matthew

2004   Moving Outward: The Shifting Landscape of Poverty in Milwaukee. Report, Center on Wisconsin Strategy, August.

Zukin, Sharon

1995   The Cultures of Cities. Cambridge, MA: Blackwell.

Zweig, Michael

2000   The Working Class Majority: America's Best Kept Secret. Ithaca, NY: ILR Press.

Index

School for Advanced Research Advanced Seminar Series

PUBLISHED BY SAR PRESS

AMERICAN ARRIVALS: ANTHROPOLOGY
ENGAGES THE NEW IMMIGRATION
Nancy Foner, ed.

VIOLENCE
Neil L. Whitehead, ed.

LAW & EMPIRE IN THE PACIFIC:
FIJI AND HAWAI'I
Sally Engle Merry & Donald Brenneis, eds.

ANTHROPOLOGY IN THE MARGINS
OF THE STATE
Veena Das & Deborah Poole, eds.

PLURALIZING ETHNOGRAPHY: COMPARISON
AND REPRESENTATION IN MAYA CULTURES,
HISTORIES, AND IDENTITIES
John M. Watanabe & Edward F. Fischer, eds.

THE ARCHAEOLOGY OF COLONIAL
ENCOUNTERS: COMPARATIVE PERSPECTIVES
Gil J. Stein, ed.

COMMUNITY BUILDING IN THE TWENTY-
FIRST CENTURY
Stanley E. Hyland, ed.

AFRO-ATLANTIC DIALOGUES:
ANTHROPOLOGY IN THE DIASPORA
Kevin A. Yelvington, ed.

COPÁN: THE HISTORY OF AN ANCIENT MAYA
KINGDOM
E. Wyllys Andrews & William L. Fash, eds.

GLOBALIZATION, WATER, & HEALTH:
RESOURCE MANAGEMENT IN TIMES OF
SCARCITY
Linda Whiteford & Scott Whiteford, eds.

A CATALYST FOR IDEAS: ANTHROPOLOGICAL
ARCHAEOLOGY AND THE LEGACY OF
DOUGLAS W. SCHWARTZ
Vernon L. Scarborough, ed.

THE ARCHAEOLOGY OF CHACO CANYON: AN
ELEVENTH-CENTURY PUEBLO REGIONAL
CENTER
Stephen H. Lekson, ed.

THE SEDUCTIONS OF COMMUNITY:
EMANCIPATIONS, OPPRESSIONS, QUANDARIES
Gerald W. Creed, ed.

THE EVOLUTION OF HUMAN LIFE HISTORY
Kristen Hawkes & Richard R. Paine, eds.

IMPERIAL FORMATIONS
*Ann Laura Stoler, Carole McGranahan,
& Peter C. Perdue, eds.*

THE GENDER OF GLOBALIZATION: WOMEN
NAVIGATING CULTURAL AND ECONOMIC
MARGINALITIES
*Nandini Gunewardena &
Ann Kingsolver, eds.*

OPENING ARCHAEOLOGY: REPATRIATION'S
IMPACT ON CONTEMPORARY RESEARCH AND
PRACTICE
Thomas W. Killion, ed.

THE ANASAZI IN A CHANGING ENVIRONMENT
George J. Gumerman, ed.

REGIONAL PERSPECTIVES ON THE OLMEC
Robert J. Sharer & David C. Grove, eds.

THE CHEMISTRY OF PREHISTORIC HUMAN
BONE
T. Douglas Price, ed.

THE EMERGENCE OF MODERN HUMANS:
BIOCULTURAL ADAPTATIONS IN THE LATER
PLEISTOCENE
Erik Trinkaus, ed.

THE ANTHROPOLOGY OF WAR
Jonathan Haas, ed.

THE EVOLUTION OF POLITICAL SYSTEMS
Steadman Upham, ed.

CLASSIC MAYA POLITICAL HISTORY:
HIEROGLYPHIC AND ARCHAEOLOGICAL
EVIDENCE
T. Patrick Culbert, ed.

TURKO-PERSIA IN HISTORICAL PERSPECTIVE
Robert L. Canfield, ed.

CHIEFDOMS: POWER, ECONOMY, AND
IDEOLOGY
Timothy Earle, ed.

RECONSTRUCTING PREHISTORIC PUEBLO
SOCIETIES
William A. Longacre, ed.

PUBLISHED BY UNIVERSITY OF CALIFORNIA PRESS

WRITING CULTURE: THE POETICS
AND POLITICS OF ETHNOGRAPHY
James Clifford &
George E. Marcus, eds.

PUBLISHED BY UNIVERSITY OF ARIZONA PRESS

THE COLLAPSE OF ANCIENT STATES AND
CIVILIZATIONS
Norman Yoffee &
George L. Cowgill, eds.

PUBLISHED BY UNIVERSITY OF NEW MEXICO PRESS

NEW PERSPECTIVES ON THE PUEBLOS
Alfonso Ortiz, ed.

STRUCTURE AND PROCESS IN LATIN AMERICA
Arnold Strickon &
Sidney M. Greenfield, eds.

THE CLASSIC MAYA COLLAPSE
T. Patrick Culbert, ed.

METHODS AND THEORIES OF
ANTHROPOLOGICAL GENETICS
M. H. Crawford & P. L. Workman, eds.

SIXTEENTH-CENTURY MEXICO:
THE WORK OF SAHAGUN
Munro S. Edmonson, ed.

ANCIENT CIVILIZATION AND TRADE
Jeremy A. Sabloff &
C. C. Lamberg-Karlovsky, eds.

PHOTOGRAPHY IN ARCHAEOLOGICAL
RESEARCH
Elmer Harp, Jr., ed.

MEANING IN ANTHROPOLOGY
Keith H. Basso & Henry A. Selby, eds.

THE VALLEY OF MEXICO: STUDIES IN
PRE-HISPANIC ECOLOGY AND SOCIETY
Eric R. Wolf, ed.

DEMOGRAPHIC ANTHROPOLOGY:
QUANTITATIVE APPROACHES
Ezra B. W. Zubrow, ed.

THE ORIGINS OF MAYA CIVILIZATION
Richard E. W. Adams, ed.

EXPLANATION OF PREHISTORIC CHANGE
James N. Hill, ed.

EXPLORATIONS IN ETHNOARCHAEOLOGY
Richard A. Gould, ed.

ENTREPRENEURS IN CULTURAL CONTEXT
Sidney M. Greenfield, Arnold Strickon,
& Robert T. Aubey, eds.

THE DYING COMMUNITY
Art Gallaher, Jr. & Harlan Padfield, eds.

SOUTHWESTERN INDIAN RITUAL DRAMA
Charlotte J. Frisbie, ed.

LOWLAND MAYA SETTLEMENT PATTERNS
Wendy Ashmore, ed.

SIMULATIONS IN ARCHAEOLOGY
Jeremy A. Sabloff, ed.

CHAN CHAN: ANDEAN DESERT CITY
Michael E. Moseley & Kent C. Day, eds.

SHIPWRECK ANTHROPOLOGY
Richard A. Gould, ed.

ELITES: ETHNOGRAPHIC ISSUES
George E. Marcus, ed.

THE ARCHAEOLOGY OF LOWER CENTRAL
AMERICA
Frederick W. Lange &
Doris Z. Stone, eds.

LATE LOWLAND MAYA CIVILIZATION:
CLASSIC TO POSTCLASSIC
Jeremy A. Sabloff &
E. Wyllys Andrews V, eds.

Participants in the School for Advanced Research advanced seminar "The New Landscapes of Inequality," Santa Fe, New Mexico, March 12–16, 2006. From left to right: Nancy MacLean, Michelle Boyd, Gina Pérez, Melissa Checker, Brett Williams, Jane Collins, Dorothy Roberts, Roger Lancaster, Amal Hassan Fadlalla, Micaela di Leonardo.

www.ingramcontent.com/pod-product-compliance
Lightning Source LLC
Chambersburg PA
CBHW032344280326

41935CB00008B/451